IF CHINS C

IF CHINS COULD KILL

CONFESSIONS OF A B MOVIE ACTOR

AN AUTOBIOGRAPHY BY
BRUCE CAMPBELL

ART DIRECTION AND GRAPHIC DESIGN BY
CRAIG "KIF" SANBORN

AN LA WEEKLY BOOK FOR
THOMAS DUNNE BOOKS/ST. MARTIN'S PRESS
NEW YORK

THOMAS DUNNE BOOKS.
An imprint of St. Martin's Press.

www.stmartins.com

ISBN 0-312-24264-6

CONTENTS

CONTENTS

FOREWORD

BY IVAN AND SAM RAIMI

EDITOR'S NOTE by Barry Neville

As an editor at St. Martin's Press, it is my responsibility to hire the author, edit the text and arrange for the book's introduction as based on the author's wishes. Mr. Campbell requested that brothers Ivan and Sam Raimi write the introduction for *If Chins Could Kill*.

In September of 1999 I telephoned Mr. Ivan Raimi and conveyed Mr. Campbell's request. At first, he seemed rather impressed that such a large publishing house was handling Mr. Campbell's book and happily agreed.

Within the hour, I received a call from his "literary agent," who refused to give his name, but claimed he was negotiating on behalf of the brothers. Strangely, the caller ID feature on my telephone revealed the telephone number of this "agent" to be the same as that of Mr. Ivan Raimi. I will allow the reader to draw his or her own conclusions.

This "agent" said that the fee was three thousand dollars. He asked whether it would be possible for St. Martin's Press to cut the check today? I informed the "agent" that customarily there is no fee paid for introductions. Usually an autobiography's introduction is written as a gesture of friendship toward the author. The agent claimed that the three thousand dollars was the "discounted friendship fee."

After some discussion, St. Martin's Press issued a cashier's check in the amount of $280 made out, as requested, to Ivan Raimi. The check was cashed the same day.

Two weeks had passed and where was my introduction? I telephoned Ivan Raimi, who claimed there must have been a misunderstanding. Apparently, his "agent" had told him that the $280 check was just the "starter fee" and should be treated as such. He mentioned that if I wanted to meet him, "somewhere nice, for say, lunch and drinks," that could be arranged.

Instead, I thought it best that he and his brother, Sam, come down to my office to discuss the introduction. He said he was far too busy to be bothered with that. I suggested that if his time was at a premium, I could tape-record the meeting, capturing the Raimi brothers' thoughts about Mr. Campbell, and have a ghostwriter put the introduction together. In this way, I assured him, no real effort would be required from him or his brother. This aroused his interest. He agreed, upon the condition that the subject of fees not be discussed in front of his brother, Sam, as he had distaste for all matters of business.

On October 22, 1999, Ivan Raimi entered my office and what follows is a transcription of that meeting:

Barry: Hello, Mr. Raimi. Welcome to St. Martin's Press. I'm Barry Neville, Bruce's editor. We spoke on the phone.

Ivan Raimi: Hi. Yeah. This place is really nice. Speaking of which, you got a damn good-looking secretary out there. I mean when I dropped those papers and she had to bend down and—

Barry: Yes. Thank you. As mentioned, I've got the tape running . . .

Ivan Raimi: I mean that's the kind of woman . . . I'd drink her bath water—

Barry: —We're tape-recording . . .

Ivan Raimi: Sure, play anything you want. Listen, Sam's coming up in a second . . . so we should get this fee thing out of the way.

Barry: Fee? As in . . . "additional fee"?

Ivan Raimi: Fee. As in "fee structure." It's an ugly word, but I think we need to get it out of the way before Sam comes back. Or he'll walk.

Barry: But we paid the fee. The two hundred and eighty—

Ivan Raimi: Barry, you paid the starter fee. Good. Good for you. But now let's talk completion. You still owe us some kind of completion fee. And please, do it quick, before Sam gets here.

EDITOR'S NOTE****

At that point I paid Ivan Raimi an additional $120 from my personal cash. Shortly thereafter, Sam Raimi entered the room.

Sam Raimi: The headlights weren't on.

Ivan Raimi: Really? Hey. This is that guy I was telling you about.

Barry: Hi, I'm Barry Neville, pleased to meet you. Bruce is very excited to have you aboard.

Sam Raimi: Bruce. Bruce. Bruce this. Bruce that.

Barry: We think our readers will really respond to this book. Kind of an insider's—

Sam Raimi: You want to know what I think, Barry? I think, your readers are tired of the same old drivel pushed on them, time after time. Tired of being force fed purée by half-artists. Your readers have teeth. For God's sake, let 'em chew.

Barry: What do you mean?

Sam Raimi: I mean let's tell a different story. The story of an ordinary man—

Ivan Raimi: An extraordinary man!

Sam Raimi: Either way. But the forces of mediocrity are against him. I'm talking the story of a guy who fights his way up *from* the B movies!

Barry: Who?

Sam Raimi: Not Who. The question is . . . "why?"!

Ivan Raimi: I like it. It's good! Barry, let's do it!

Barry: Well, it's really interesting . . . but the task at hand is the introduction to *If Chins Could Kill*.

Sam Raimi: I see. And who, may I ask, is going to read this book? His illiterate fans? Barry, people get the wrong idea sometimes. See, Bruce is like a puppet. *My* puppet. I pull a string, he smiles. I pull another, and he runs through the woods and hits his head against the tree. And that's it. So tell me, Barry, whose story is more interesting? The puppet or the puppet master?

Barry: Well, we think that Bruce has developed quite a big following over the years. We believe this book has its own niche.

Sam Raimi: Uh-huh. Well, if there's such a big following, how come yer only paying my brother and I a hundred bucks to write the intro?

Barry: Guys, maybe this project isn't your cup of—

Ivan Raimi: Please, Barry, this is a *great* project, one that Sam and I both believe in and want to make special for you. Now, we agree to do the touch-up on Bruce's book, but don't expect—

Barry: "Touch-up"?

Ivan Raimi: What we in the film world call a "polish"—but don't expect us to work for nothing, even if Bruce is our close friend—'cause that's like slappin' Bruce in the face.

Barry: But—

Sam Raimi: So what's this book about anyway?

Barry: Didn't you read it?

Ivan Raimi: Sure he read it. We both read it. It's got its own niche.

Barry: Gentlemen . . . the book does not need a polish. It needs an introduction. What I'd like to do now is to leave you alone, so that you might ruminate on your memories of Bruce. How you met, how you work together . . . I'll come back with a writer who will give some form to it, and put it in the context of a proper introduction.

Ivan Raimi: Why don't you send up some drinks and sandwiches. Something nice. And we'll start the creative process right away, Barry.

EDITOR'S NOTE****

At that point, I left the room. What follows has been transcribed from the tape recording made in my office:

Sam Raimi: This is horse shit.

Ivan Raimi: Tell you something else, I smell a screw job.

<u>Sam Raimi:</u> This guy'll pay.

<u>Ivan Raimi:</u> Right. Like those guys at United Artists paid? Did you ever get your money outta them?

<u>Sam Raimi:</u> Are you absolutely sure they never paid? 'Cause when I called, they said they sent the check to you.

<u>Ivan Raimi:</u> Somehow, I'm not surprised. I'll tell you what we do. This time we screw them before they screw us.

<u>Sam Raimi:</u> High five!

<u>Ivan Raimi:</u> High five!

<u>Sam Raimi:</u> Check this out. . . .

<u>Ivan Raimi:</u> Look what I got.

EDITOR'S NOTE****

The remainder of the tape had no more voices, merely the sounds of drawers opening and closing. When I returned to my office, the Raimi brothers were gone. A gold pen and an antique silver clock were missing from my desk. In addition, my cellular phone was missing. I had it disconnected the next day, but when the phone bill arrived, I noticed that more than a dozen calls had been made to a series of 1-900 numbers that day.

I leave the reader to draw his or her own conclusions. But having had the privilege of getting to know Mr. Campbell through the preparation of this book, I beg the reader not to judge his character by the quality of his friends.

—Barry Neville, Editor, St. Martin's Press

INTRODUCTION

Genealogies appearing in book form usually begin with a great statesman, a renowned warrior, an illustrious divine, poet, author or reformer, and are so blended with fabulous detail as scarce to leave room for the supposition that the founder of the family ever had a father. Not so in this case, for the worthy progenitor of our race, first to cross the Atlantic Ocean, with whom, for lack of earlier information, our genealogy must begin, was a man of lowly origin and humble occupation . . .

— Great-grandfather Hugh Campbell in 1906

So, another actor writes a book about their glamorous, whirlwind life. Personally, as an ex-Detroiter, that crap bores me to tears. I've always been more interested in the working stiffs of Hollywood, ninety-nine percent of whom are overlooked in those phony "tell-all" books. For every Bruce Willis and Steven Spielberg, there are a hundred no-name slobs scraping out a living in this shockingly difficult profession.

Therefore, this is not a memoir about what I said to so-and-so at the Beverly Hills Hotel. It's also *not* about an actor's "meteoric" rise, or "tragic" fall. Rather, this book is dedicated to the players on the second string, the "B" people, if you will, and I cheerfully include myself in that lot.

I was the first member of my immediate family to make a living in the arts. I can't say that I was the first Campbell to be published, because George John Douglass Campbell, eighth Duke of Argyll, kicked out a half dozen books in the late 1800s—my personal favorite being *The History and Antiquities of Iona.*

Great-great-great-grandfather Peter Campbell was a shepherd in Killin, Perthshire, Scotland. Tiring of that (and who could blame him?), Peter and his wife, Catherine, set sail to America in March of 1798 and eventually took up the farming life in Caledonia, upstate New York. The family became "official" in 1810, when Peter was awarded his Certificate of Citizenship.

According to family records, this man was "spare in frame, somewhat stooped, long features, solemn but pleasant countenance, with piercing black eyes and wavy black hair." An extremely pious fellow, he was a teetotaler and "endeavored by precept and example to cause others to abstain from their baneful use."

Grandfather Campbell.

He wasn't exactly Mr. Excitement, but ol' Pete got the Clan Campbell up and going in the States.

Four generations later, my grandfather ventured westward to attend the University of Michigan as a pre-med student. World War I interrupted his studies, and Donald MacKenzie Campbell found himself serving a tour of duty in France. His father, Hugh, was a pacifist and objected to his involvement, so Donald enlisted in the ambulance corps, reasoning that he could "save lives instead of taking them." Ironically, the horrors of war outraged him so much, he transferred to the artillery division without telling his father.

After the war, which he refused to discuss, Donald changed majors and graduated from college with a degree in history—the first in his family to do so.

Right out of college, Donald landed his first and only job as a sales engineer for Alcoa Aluminum in Detroit. Forty-four years later, he retired. His marriage to childhood sweetheart Dorothy lasted almost as long—forty-three years.

The Campbells, up until 1928, had been a serious, hardworking lot, but with the birth of Charles Newton Campbell, everything changed. Charlie didn't want to be another "Man in the Grey Flannel Suit"—he had dreams in the late forties of becoming a painter, so when he attended the University of Michigan, it was to study art and history.

Upon graduating, his parents persuaded him to find a "real" job—this came in the form of a billboard inspector for the Campbell/Ewald (no relation) advertising agency in downtown Detroit.

At least in advertising, Charlie thought to himself, *I can still be creative.*

Yes, my father was creative—very creative. His territory of inspection was everything east of the Rockies, and Charlie could, in the days predating cell phones and fax machines, get anywhere via Chicago—where he knew a cute girl.

After two years of this, Charlie moved up to the "creative" world of media buying. By all accounts he excelled—so much so, he caught the eye of an attractive secretary across the hall named Joanne.

Joanne Louise Pickens was different than the other women Dad met at the ad agency. As a practicing Christian Scientist, she was a far cry from the hard-drinking crowd Dad hung with.

Good Time Charlie & Hard-charging Joanne.

"The other women were a hell of a lot of fun," Dad recalled, "but I couldn't see myself marrying one of them."

Joanne was also unique in another way for a woman in the mid-fifties—she was a single mom with a three-year-old son named Mike. Charlie didn't seem to mind, and a year later they married and moved into a house in the suburbs.

That's where I come in. . . .

IF CHINS COULD KILL

THE PROVING GROUNDS 1

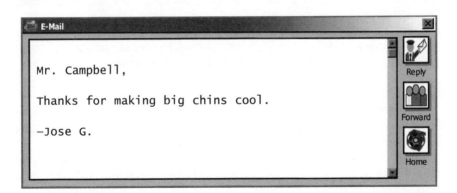

Mr. Campbell,

Thanks for making big chins cool.

—Jose G.

There is an L-shaped scar on the left side of my chin. People always ask me how I got it and I've told them everything from "One dark night in Bombay," to "A scuffle with bad, bad, Leroy Brown . . ."

In actuality, it came about because I was a fearless kid. I played outside a great deal of the time, in any weather and in suburban Detroit, Michigan, that's saying something. In this age where laser surgery rushes to correct every imperfection, I'm not going to touch that scar—it reminds me of too much fun.

Bilbo Baggins would have felt right at home in my neighborhood—it was a magical place. *The Braes of Bloomfield* was created by commuters hoping to get away from the faded glory of the Motor City, and the results were impressive. As a kid exploring the woods between these upper-middle-class homes, the city might as well have been a million miles away.

Unlike the embarrassing names attributed to subdivisions today—like "Pine Meadows," where there are neither pine trees nor meadows—if a

The old homestead.

street in my neighborhood was called Old Orchard, it was because there used to be an orchard on that very spot. Rogue trees in many of the yards still produced apples.

With street names like Braemoor, Idlewyle, and Darramoor, you'd think you were in rural Scotland. Most of the traditional ranch-style homes weren't all that big, but they had land around them. The best part of all is that there were virtually no fences—this was long before the "planned" communities of today, with guard gates, motion-sensitive lighting, and Neighborhood Watches.

Our neighborhood had an epic feel to it, and this broad range provoked a sense of unlimited possibility. As a result, the three Campbell boys (Mike, Don and Bruce) were "free range" and could explore at will.

I am the youngest of the three. Don is a year older. He and I wound up spending more time together than with Mike, six years our senior, but there were plenty of industrious summers spent as a threesome.

SIBLING RIVALS

Don and I were often mistaken as twins, although I still wonder why— his reddish brown hair and hazel eyes were a great contrast to my dark brown hair and muddy brown eyes.

As is normal for siblings, we competed for everything—particularly Mom's attention. That became obvious to me one school morning as I leaned down to buckle up my rain boots at the top of the stairs. Don saw this as the perfect opportunity to eliminate me from his world, so he planted a foot against my butt and shoved. I tumbled forward, sure of my fate, but Mom jabbed a finger into my belt loop and held me aloft just long enough to grab the railing.

This incident, no doubt, contributed to an altercation in our front yard years later. After provoking Don for some unknown reason, he chased me across our front lawn in a rage. Somewhere along my escape route, I managed to snag a screwdriver. As Don swung his fist, I raised the Phillips head and it promptly became impaled in his wrist.

"You stabbed me!" Don screamed, incredulous.

"I did not. You swung at me and I defended myself."

Aside from the occasional near-death experiences, Don and I actually got along well. As we aged and grew, our "roughhousing" became not only discouraged but feared. Epic wrestling matches encompassed the entire house and resulted in broken furniture. The fact that we were both on the junior high wrestling team only made things worse for my mother.

"What's the problem, Mom? We're practicing . . ."

In the late sixties, war films like *Kelly's Heroes*, *The Devil's Brigade* and *The Dirty Dozen* seemed to be everywhere. Our favorite TV show, *Combat*, only encouraged this preoccupation with war, and Vic Morrow soon became my

Mike, Don and Bruce: The nefarious Campbell Brothers.

first favorite actor. He was the embodiment of laid-back cool and I loved how his cigarettes bounced on the edge of his mouth when he talked.

Years later, I worked with Michael Caffey, who had directed several *Combat* episodes. Instead of asking him for motivation, all I cared to know was who could kick whose ass—Vic Morrow or his commanding officer, Rick Jason? Don, on the other hand, was partial to the character Kirby because he had the coolest gun—a Browning automatic rifle.

Don took all this make-believe stuff a little too seriously. The difference between us was fundamental: I'd watch *Combat* and think, *Gee, it would be fun to be an actor like that guy.* Don would watch the same scene and think, *Gee, it would be fun to be that guy.* He went on to join the army reserves and got to play the ultimate "war game" in Kuwait during Desert Storm.

Don and I passed many hours with G.I. Joes. We had the basic ones— the Russian, the Cadet, the Japanese guy, the German—who didn't? They were cool, but unless you were Billy Jazinski, the spoiled rich kid down the street, there was a limit to how many you owned.

Fighting with "Joes" meant that our military engagements were restricted to "skirmishes." That wasn't enough for the post–World War II, pre-Vietnam kids that we were—Don and I wanted to stage *full-scale invasions!*

The only way to do this was with those little green army men. Down at the brand-new Toys "R" Us, a bag of what seemed like hundreds only cost a couple bucks.

Somehow, it didn't seem right reenacting D day in our living room. Too may soldiers fell behind the sofa, so the great outdoors became the place to rumble.

The backyard, however, was a no-go. Our basset hound, Nuisance, reigned supreme back there. The dangers of fighting in her territory were twofold: running the risk of having entire platoons chewed to death or, even worse, mounting a frontal assault through scattered piles of "dog dirt."

Before...

...and after.

Our front lawn wasn't much better. There were too many trees and tall grass, so battles weren't practical. We'd lose a dozen of them with each "engagement" and Dad sliced any MIAs to ribbons mowing the lawn each Saturday. Of course, that wasn't all bad, because we could round up their shredded carcasses and use them as "casualties." Even at that tender age, we knew war was heck.

Our driveway proved to be a better staging area for campaigns. Because it was dirt, you had a good color contrast and we never lost a single green man. The driveway was also elevated above the lawn on fieldstone. This was ideal, because a defending army (usually Don's) could hole up in hundreds of nooks and it might take an entire weekend to flush them out.

A garden hose added the element of water. With it, an army could be flooded out into the open, where they could easily be massacred. The defending army in this case (usually me) had a certain amount of time to build up damlike fortifications until the evil attacker turned the hose on, unleashing torrents of water. The battles usually were declared over when either the water broke through the defender's dam, or Mom came back from the grocery store.

Eventually, the thrill of these games wore off, so Don and I resorted to more drastic measures: burning the little green men into puddles of goo. In the late sixties, before Ralph Nader halted all the fun in the world, the plastic used in those army guys *must* have been toxic—they made the coolest *zzziiiiip, zzziiiiip, zzziiiiip* noise with each burning drip. This game evolved into "lava tossing," where you flung the napalmlike substance at your opponent (or brother), as it dripped from the melting man.

Mom stopped us before Nader did, though, because one day a big flaming blob of plastic sizzled its way into my finger. I am reminded of this, happily, every time I type.

Born in 1952, my oldest brother Mike was a child of the Cold War. His favorite TV show, hands down, was *Man From U.N.C.L.E.,* so everything he was interested in revolved around espionage. To protect sensitive information—sent mostly from himself to himself—he spent hours creating elaborate codes and writing them into tiny paper books. There was the *Code of the Pointing Sticks,* the *Words-for-Numbers Code,* and who could forget the *O.O.R.A. Code* (Off and On Reversible Alpha Code).

When not saving the world from evil invaders, Mike was making stuff. Never one for those goofy shop class projects, Mike went right to the real deal—like a memory device, an electric "stop" light over his doorway, and a metal locator.

It made sense that Mike went into computers because his mind worked like one. He made lists of everything: untrustworthy people (Don and I were often on it), his weekly income from 1959 through 1967 (in cents), and secret hand-to-hand combat routines. To this day, I still rely on "Routine number 6" (to "run headlong into them and tackle them") whenever I'm confronted by an enemy.

RULES OF ENGAGEMENT

Mike's use of extensive lists came in handy when it came time to determine the "rules" of our childhood. In a household of three boys who were always tormenting each other, a system of rules and fines was drafted and strictly adhered to. Many contained wording that would make a contract lawyer proud and all fines were "payable on demand."

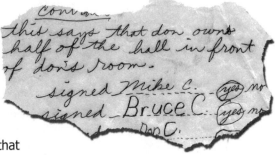

Contracts like this one added to our Draconian lifestyle.

It became our own brand of justice that addressed issues important to us all. A rule stating that *Don owns half of the hall in front of Don's room* was a key property right. The rule *If Don or Bruce leaves or throws belongings in my room, they are mine unless they want to pay 20¢* seemed a bit harsh, but I'm sure it was just Mike's way of saying "leave me the hell alone."

Simple crimes, like *borrowing stuff without permission, calling names* or *socking someone* only cost the perpetrator 5¢. More obscure offenses, like *hanging around doorway, fooling with light switches,* or Mike's legislative masterpiece, *squealing when I want to look at something Don or Bruce has,* shot up to 10¢.

Some rules were obviously the result of either a pet peeve, or a very specific incident. There would otherwise be no explanation for the 20¢ fine of *taking something from me while I was looking at it,* or the 40¢ whopper for *damaging rocket controls.* In our draconian world, you could even be fined for suspicion.

Some rules, however, did make sense. In the tight quarters of a garage fort, it was simply a matter of decency to place a ban on *"dirtey boots or shous"* (spelling unaltered) and *"letting gassers."*

Of course, all of these rules did absolutely nothing to stop the sibling abuse. Mike once laid out detailed plans to raid Don's *left-hand drawer* in his half of the room (that he and I shared) that included an overhead diagram, complete with escape routes and a comprehensive list of excuses to use if he got caught. For some reason, even though Don did "*hit, disobey, lie, steal stuff, and destroy,*" I don't think my mom would have let Mike off the hook.

Because these "raids" happened so often, we each devised ways to protect our "secret stuff." Mike hid things in every possible nook and cranny—I know, because I went through them all. Don often moved his precious things around, or hid them in "secret books." With a sharp razor blade, usually from Dad's shaver, he hollowed out numerous hard-cover masterpieces from the living room. It wasn't hard to spot which ones were bogus—*War and Peace* isn't usually paired with *The Cat in the Hat* on a ten-year-old's shelf.

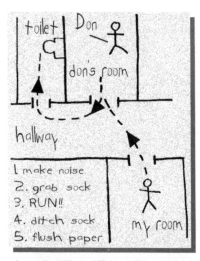

I was the "King of Thieves" long before Hercules and Xena came around.

Because invading each other's room was such a big deal, I had to do it as often as possible. One day, a plan to bother Don worked flawlessly. I raced into his room, made all kinds of noise and stole a white gym sock. Don was close on my heels as I ran away down the hall and ducked into the bathroom. As he entered the doorway, he saw me flush what he *thought* was his sock down the toilet.

"What did you do that for?! I'll kill you!"

In reality, I had ditched Don's real sock as I entered the bathroom and flushed a strip of white toilet paper (preplaced) into the septic tank. In the end, our fines evened out, because Don promptly gave me a thrashing—roughly equal to my 30¢ worth of transgressions. I wouldn't have been surprised if Don invented a fine for *pretending to flush socks down the toilet.*

Even the bathroom wasn't a reliable sanctuary. There was a lock on the door, sure, but it could easily be opened with a credit card. To combat this, a drawer by the door could be pulled out to block the way. This worked until Mike drilled a hole through the wall of our linen closet and rigged a coat hanger to the drawer itself.

I mocked Don through the door one day, protected by the door lock, only to look down and see the drawer magically slide back in all by itself.

"You were saying?" Don said, as he pushed the door open and began beating the grunt out of me.

INDUSTRIAL-STRENGTH FUN

Mike took charge of building a playhouse in our backyard. The end product wasn't some cute cardboard house with a couple of windows—it was a three-quarter-scale *tank.*

His plan was to make a mobile war machine that could presumably attack things and/or people. Taking into account all materials needed to build the tank, including plywood, two-by-fours, steering wheel, gun barrel, catapult, rubber slings, mirrors, fan belts and a pulley system, Mike estimated that the total weight would be 387½ pounds with occupants. I'll bet he wasn't far off. The only scheme that never came to bear was mounting the damn thing on Dad's riding lawn mower.

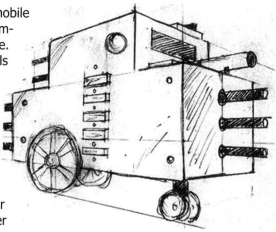

Mike's vision: A 387½ pound juggernaut.

To defend against attacking neighbors, we armed ourselves with cracker balls, rolls of caps, sparklers, balloons, squirt guns, sling shot rifles, rubber band shooters and the dreaded Ivory Liquid detergent bottles—the Super Soaker of their day. We used to beg Mom to buy the Ivory brand bottles because they had the best nozzles and could blast water the farthest. Mike was the best at this, because his hands were stronger. With a good squeeze, he could drench Don or me from twenty feet away. Over time, we learned to rinse the bottles out well—a soapy shot in the eye could ruin your whole afternoon.

The experience of building the tank only fueled other summer projects—like the tunnel. To protect ourselves from parental meddling, we always referred to it by the backward code name of "Lennut."

The first challenge was to choose a good dig site. To insure privacy, we picked a spot in the adjacent woods, but we had to be careful because tunneling too close to a large tree meant hassling with roots. Once we had the site, we excavated a horizontal trench and reinforced the sides with two-by-fours. This was then covered with plywood, six inches of dirt and plenty of camouflage. Now, we could begin digging the main shaft, which went straight down, until we hit water. To communicate with the outside world, a garden hose was lowered through a hole in the roof.

Play time in the "Lennut" was anything but—it was backbreaking work. After school, on weekends and even during vacations, we'd dig with hand trowels, chop and burn off roots, reinforce the walls, then dig some more. To provide a better working environment, Mike came up with an ingenious method of providing candlelight in a series of carved alcoves and even manufactured glow-in-the-dark candles from phosphorescent crayons.

Eventually, Don squealed about the use of candles, which was forbidden, and Dad gave the order to fill it in. We obeyed, but soon thereafter, Mike built a doghouse, supposedly for our basset hound, but it was ultimately just a front for a hidden tunnel entrance and we started the process all over again.

Most kids came home at lunch with grass stains. Mike, Don and I were a little more "earthy" than that, but it dawned on us that we could apply our extensive landscape knowledge to a project that wouldn't collapse, wouldn't get our knees muddy and didn't fill up with water every ten days—a golf course!

The Campbell/Ebbing Miniature Golf Course was next door, in neighbor Mike Ebbing's backyard. This club turned out to be very exclusive, mainly since few people actually played it, and our rule book (as you might expect) was more restrictive than the PGA's. People who brought in forged certificates or coupons, for example, were to be "escorted off the grounds," a measure that also applied to people with "malicious intentions," whatever that meant. No other "vendors" could sell their goods on or near the course unless a vast majority of the profit (between eighty and ninety-nine percent) went directly to the organizers—we didn't even give cut rates for people who brought their own clubs or balls.

Even with rampant overmanaging, we *did* make money—37¢ one day, $1.72 another. Personally, I lost interest in this venture when Don caught me in the bridge of my nose with a wicked backswing.

Soon, brother Mike was old enough to be more interested in girls and cars, so Don and I had to tackle any new construction projects by ourselves. Michigan is all about trees, so we decided to build the "mother of all tree forts" in the Tylers' backyard.

The proving grounds for adulthood.

Our growing neighborhood provided all the building materials we would ever need. At any one time, there would be half a dozen homes under construction within walking distance. Don and I would sneak out at night, under the guise of going to Scott Tyler's house, and haul rolls of tar paper, wood scraps and nails through the woods back to our "house."

The completed palace was impressive. There was a main level, comprised of a rumpus room, with several "guest" rooms off to each side. The second story was a smaller, single room and above it was a crow's nest. Don was the only one who ventured up there because it was just too high. Built over an entire summer, this wasn't a fort—it was a *fortress,* with a shingled roof, wall-to-wall carpeting and power, thanks to a buried extension cord to the Tylers' house.

This refuge also served as a proving ground for adulthood.

Here, commerce took on a whole new meaning. Judy, a close neighbor, was an adventurous lass. She was happy to dole out a "squeeze" at 10¢ a pop. Let's be clear—a "squeeze" meant wrapping a clammy hand around her breast and holding on until she brushed it away. My day in the sun came when I saw a dollar hanging out of Judy's back pocket. Being an opportunist, I snatched it and bought ten of the most protracted squeezes you could imagine.

My buddy Bruce Clark was a man of the world. He had, for a short time, co-starred in an English TV show, *The Double Deckers,* so he was the coolest guy to hang around with. His garage fort was a great place to talk about some of the cute girls he met while "on location." Though I had no experiences to relate, the fact that we even *talked* about them was huge and seemed to consume days on end.

Bruce was convinced that girls liked performers, so we put together a dance routine to The Monkees "Last Train to Clarksville" and presented it to Ms. Butcher's third-grade class. It got a big response from the girls all right—in the form of *laughter.*

I threw out my Beatle Boots as soon as I got home.

GROUND CONTROL TO MAJOR MIKE . . .

Mike was Chairman of Research and Development for OOMPH—the Organization to Observe and Manufacture Phenomena of the Heavens. The translation of this mumbo-jumbo was that he liked to build UFOs and send them skyward. Don and I were his willing apprentices.

A staple of the time was the Estes Rocket. They had to be assembled from a kit that included the rocket, balsa wood fins, rocket engine and the parachute. All we had to supply was a dry cell battery to ignite the engine.

These fancy rockets were exciting to watch, but the expense was prohibitive, especially when you considered the short amount of time they were actually airborne, so we opted instead to build home-grown UFOs. These came in the form of a dry cleaning bag, held open at the mouth by a cross of balsa wood struts. Simple birthday candles, glued to the struts, provided the heat needed to fill up the bag and keep it

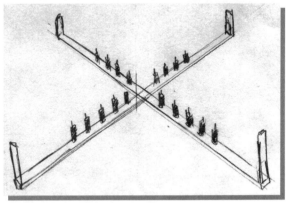

Balsa wood and birthday candles: The skeleton of the "UFO."

aloft. Once we got the hang of it, a successfully launched craft would rise up slowly above the treetops, then hang for an eternity until a cross wind caught it and took it away to goodness-knows-where.

Bright Yellow UFO Sighted Over Twp.

By BETH HOWARD
Staff Writer

"I don't claim to know what I saw the night of April 19," begins the account of the most recent possible UFO sighting reported to The Birmingham Journal.

For the first time in the weeks that such reports

"The object was luminous yellow and did not twinkle or pulsate. It appeared to be the size of a low-flying helicopter and was more or less cigar shape.

"There seemed to be a dark separation around the middle."

Not believing her eyes at the second sighting, she pull her car into a

Birmingham was none the wiser.

The *Birmingham Eccentric* newspaper ran a series of reports on strange, low-flying UFOs and it caused quite a stir. Cars pulled off the road to gawk at the mystifying crafts and mothers clutched their awestruck children. We thought this was hilarious, of course, and proceeded to launch dozens of "ships."

Typically, Don and I used our newfound knowledge of trajectory for evil purposes. Instead of UFOs reaching for the stars, we opted for bottle rockets that reached Mrs. Pastor's house. Mrs. Pastor enjoyed her spirits and had falsely accused Don and I of many infractions, so it only seemed right to extract our own brand of revenge.

Bottle rockets are volatile things—you can't aim them very well from a traditional bottle, so we manufactured bottle rocket "launchers" of our own. These were essentially wooden "guns" with U-hooks along the "barrel" to keep the rocket in place, and they improved accuracy to almost eighty percent.

One night, Don and I let a volley of bottle rockets go toward Mrs. Pastor's house. It had the desired effect, because she immediately flung open her side door.

"Goddamit! You kids knock it—" *BLAM!*

Before she could finish her sentence, a rocket exploded on the screen door in front of her. Knowing that she would call the police, Don and I hauled ass home. Mom and Dad were gone, so we tried to look as innocent as possible and turned on the TV. Within fifteen minutes, a large flashlight pounded on our door.

Don tossed the German helmet he was wearing under the couch and I answered the door.

<u>Cop:</u> Evening . . .

<u>Bruce:</u> Hello, officer. Everything okay?

<u>Cop:</u> Mrs. Pastor says you guys were shooting explosives at her house.

<u>Bruce:</u> Oh, come on—we were only shooting fireworks off in our front yard.

The cop squinted at me.

<u>Cop:</u> Really?

<u>Bruce:</u> Yeah. I mean, she was kinda drunk, right?

<u>Cop:</u> Yeah, she was.

I shrugged at the officer, as if to say "enough said," and he was on his way.

THE WOODS

Our house was surrounded by woods on two sides. Behind us, a buffer zone of trees shielded our view of other neighbors, and just outside my bedroom window was our beloved forest. There was nothing more pleasing than to wake up and look out upon my own exclusive playground.

Don's "biology lab."

The woods had all the childhood necessities—a Love Log, where every kid carved "I love so-and-so," great climbing trees and even a dead dog. The dog expired deep in the woods one spring and we watched it decay over the next three months. Don became overly fascinated with this biology experiment.

"Look, it's all bloated," he said. "I'm gonna poke it with my stick."

"No, don't!" I begged him. "C'mon, it stinks, let's get out of here . . ."

With that, Don thrust his stick into the side of the dog's bloated belly and it poked through his skin as easily as a wet paper towel.

"Aw, sick!" I screamed, trying not to puke.

"Cool," Don pointed out, "look at the maggots coming out of the hole!"

Mosquitoes were one of the few downsides of the Michigan outdoors. From May to September, you were sure to be attacked. Don decided to fight back with a vengeance. One summer, he kept track of every mosquito he killed and in a three-month period, he personally "terminated" 394 of them.

I wasn't so interested in killing mosquitoes as I was in inflicting cruel and unusual punishment. I didn't take out nearly as many as Don, but the ones that landed on me often regretted it. I found that you could trap an unsuspecting mosquito if you were willing to let it drill into your arm first. Then, as the little bugger sucks his heart out, you pinch the skin on either side of his stinger. Apply a little pressure, and he would be force-fed until his translucent belly filled up with blood and burst.

To keep our blessed woods free from development, Don and I would rip up any FOR SALE sign in the vicinity and toss it into a stream. It worked for a while, but we couldn't stop the real estate ads in the paper. One fateful day, the lot next to our house was sold.

The bad news was obvious, but the good news was that the Forbes family had two girls. Still, they were interlopers and had to be punished. As Mrs. Forbes was unloading groceries from her car one day, the youngest daughter was skipping about on their driveway. She looked so happy, playing in *my* woods. I looked at the Winchester BB gun in my hands and slowly cocked it. There were still trees between our houses, but if I timed my shot just right, I could nail her through a small opening. I also had to account for declining trajectory over such a distance, so I raised the barrel of my gun about ten feet above her head and squeezed off a shot.

"Owwww!"

Mrs. Forbes almost dropped her groceries as she whirled about.

"What is it, honey?"

"Something came through the woods and bit my leg!"

Mrs. Forbes looked up toward our house, but she saw nothing. I had long since retreated to our tunnel.

Even with the odd house being built here and there, our neighborhood was still pretty feral. Dogs were free to roam without leashes and, in many cases, without tags. Unfortunately, my rabbit George paid the price. He was usually good at holding his own outside his cage. Twice, he led Shadow, the Francises' German shepherd toward the deck in our backyard, only to slip underneath at the last minute. Each time, the unsuspecting dog would bash his head on the lip of the deck. Mike claims that Shadow was actually knocked unconscious one time and laid there, with its legs in the air, for about fifteen minutes.

George and I during happier times.

George's end came when I forgot to close the garage door one night. His cage wasn't enough to protect him from Molly, the Feldmans' hunting dog. It didn't take a DNA test to match the dog's fur with the tufts caught around the hole in the chicken wire. Don was so enraged, he marched down the street and chucked stones at the evil dog.

To make up for the loss of George we got another rabbit, an albino named Weaser. After I got through with him, he *wished* a dog had eaten him. Unwittingly, during his otherwise happy years with us, I slammed his head in the garage door and ran over him with my bike.

The only downside to a neighborhood without many homes was that Halloween was too much work for not enough return. The big haul could be found across the paved road of Walnut Lake, in the nirvana known as Kirkwood—a new subdivision where every third house was the same design. Hedgewood Street was long, straight, and always the best bet. Don and I would take pillowcases up and down each side and our bags would be half full in about twenty minutes.

For some reason I was fascinated by a wig my Mom had, so I went trick-or-treating as a girl two years in a row. This was fine until I cut between houses and got felt up by some guy with poor eyesight.

After stocking up in Kirkwood, we'd come back home for a local party. The Boraskis would open up their garage and neighbors would gorge themselves on fresh doughnuts and cider. A road island in front of their house made a great place for a bonfire and cos-tume contest. Grant Brady always won because, like Mike, he had a flair for engineering. His "electric"

Kirkwood: Trick-or-treating locale of choice.

turtle knocked them dead one year. Thankfully, the following year, some creative guy came as the Upside Down Man and snatched the title away.

THINGS THAT GO BUMP IN THE NIGHT

I'm grateful for my old neighborhood's tolerant view of adolescence—without it, I wouldn't have been able to engage in the tomfoolery I did.

There was something about those dark, warm summer nights that induced Don and I to roam the neighborhood like wild dogs. Many evenings, we'd pitch a tent in the backyard and be long gone by the time darkness fell.

What do adolescent boys do at night? Do they play hide-and-seek? Flashlight tag? Sometimes, sure, but that stuff gets boring after puberty kicks in. Don and I decided to cut to the chase and look into the windows of unsuspecting women—at every possible opportunity.

"Copping a perv" was harder than you might think. Even though our neighborhood had no streetlights, and crickets provided a fantastic blanket of noise, it took great discipline to sneak up to a girl's open window and actually get close enough to see anything worth the effort. The sound of crunching leaves is unmistakable, and if a girl's window was right next to the woods, as was often the case, we'd be screwed. Second-story windows also sucked, but Don and I excelled at climbing trees.

If it's any consolation to the shocked reader, our success rate was very low. After countless outings, I can recall only one time when we hit the jackpot. It was an extended, topless view of Carla, more woman than girl, and I will state, for the record, that it was worth every other failed attempt.

We took every advantage the cover of darkness provided. On our way to toss water balloons at cars, Steve Davis, Scott Tyler and I would make a swing past old man Morris's rhubarb patch to load up on the sour stuff. It wasn't that we really liked raw rhubarb, because it was too sour to eat, but it became a good dare. Mr. Morris by no means deserved to be a victim of such theft, but his property was our access to Maple Road—the water balloon staging area.

There was an art to knowing when to release your water balloon at a passing car. Early on, we discovered that no matter how good your timing was, most balloons bounced off their intended targets. In order to get the full effect, you had to bite a microscopic hole near the knot of the balloon. This tiny weakness caused the balloon to unzip instantly upon impact.

One night, my plan worked a little too well. As a truck passed, I let my bloated balloon go, but saw no effect whatsoever. Then, down the street, we heard the unmistakable sound of air brakes. We ran for cover and witnessed the angry trucker walking up the road, soaked from head to toe. Apparently, the water balloon had gone through an open window of his truck and hit him point-blank.

FEMALES OF THE OPPOSITE SEX

Stud-muffin.

My family used to vacation on Lake Michigan several weeks out of every summer and walks along the beach were not uncommon. One day, while rooting through the water for a decent Petoskey stone, I caught the silhouette of a girl at the top of the sand dunes above the beach. As I squinted into the July sun, I saw an image that remains indelible today—a girl with dark hair, wearing a dress that flowed seductively in the warm breeze.

Although I couldn't see her face, I sensed that she was looking directly at me. Entranced, I held her gaze for an indefinite length of time, until her parents met her at the edge of the dune and led her out of my sight. As she walked away, in slow-motion, the girl watched me the entire time. Whether this was true or not, my memory has logged it as indisputable fact.

When I was ten, I attended Camp Leelanau in the same part of Northern Michigan. It was an all-boy camp, but near the end of my three-week stay, we were bussed to the sister, "girl" camp for a day of "integration." I can only recall the terror of exiting the bus and seeing a line of cute girls across the road to greet us. My impressionable mind simply shut down and I don't remember any further events of the day.

Women had that effect on me.

The same applied to Joanna Spain. During third-grade Field Day, I admired how fast she could run. I was not "excited" in the typical sense—I didn't know enough about sexuality. Rather, I was just impressed in a *different* way than how, say, Mike Ditz won the Hop, Skip and Jump contest. I didn't win anything, but it didn't matter—I got to watch Joanna run.

I don't know what it is about the primal need for boys to impress girls, but every time I tried it, something disastrous happened.

Trying to impress the Brady twins, in particular, was a challenge. They weren't identical, but each had an irresistible quality. Karen, a redhead, was quiet, polite and a 9+ by any standard. Her blonde sister, Ann, was outgoing and flirtatious, but she was pushing a 10, so she was also harder prey. The only consolation was that Ann tortured my brother Don exponentially. To this day (are you reading Don?) the mere mention of her name sends this Desert Storm veteran into a foxhole, trembling in fear.

Watch out girls!

To me, it really didn't matter which one I dazzled first.

The Brady yard had several huge weeping willow trees. With long, droopy branches, they were a joy to climb. My plan, while Karen watched from below, was to leap from one branch to another, not unlike that guy in a loincloth. I may have even yodeled as I reached out for the targeted branch, but it was all over before it began. The branch I grabbed had been dead for years and broke off clean. The momentum swung my legs in front of me and I ended up in a muddy bog, flat on my back—branch still in hand. The air had been completely knocked from my lungs and all I could do was lay there and gasp.

"Oh, my God, Bruce—are you all right?" Karen asked, with genuine concern.

"Oh yeah, =cough= it was all =cough= part of my =cough= plan . . ."

Overwhelmed with humility, I jumped on my Huffy bike, and sped away as fast as I could.

One fall day, my mother brought my brothers and me to visit her friend. It seemed only natural that her three boys would enjoy interacting with the woman's three daughters.

Things started innocently enough—the kids all huddled in their basement while the moms drank tea and chatted in the kitchen. Music was playing, so we all proceeded to dance, or whatever it was young kids do when they heard music. I wound up running in circles around one of the cute daughters. Soon, we were heading in opposite directions and a collision seemed preordained. Seconds later, we bashed heads and dropped to the floor. The girl screamed and ran off to tell her mom while I hid behind the couch. Their mother didn't seem overly concerned, but the other, older daughters had blood in their eyes.

Mike, Don and I were chased out to the front yard. Mike had longer limbs, so he hauled ass down the street and climbed a tree. Don and I were left with no choice other than to lock ourselves inside Mom's '57 Chevy.

After catching our breath, we discovered a bag of Spanish peanuts in the glove compartment and proceeded to gorge ourselves. The girls, hungry from chasing us, begged for a few peanuts, so Don and I cracked the windows enough to pour some out. Instead of swallowing them, the girls chewed them into a paste and smeared the putrid mess across every window. Within seconds, my gag reflex kicked in.

"Don . . . Don—I'm gonna barf . . ."

"Oh, no you're not," he warned. "You barf and I'll pound you."

Smoldering Intensity.

Faced with an unpleasant choice, I clamped a hand over my mouth and held the vomit in check. I don't know how long I stayed like that, but the girls eventually went away and I was able to retch in the street.

I have never eaten Spanish peanuts since.

For some perverted reason, the fad of making yourself faint caught on at my elementary school. To pull it off, you'd inhale deeply several times, then hold your breath as someone gave you a bear hug from behind—within seconds, you'd be out cold. This was about the dumbest thing I'd ever done, but the girls seemed to get a giggle out of it, so I did it too many times for my own good.

I stopped the practice after I performed it in front of a group of kids out on the playground one day. I had figured out a way to faint by myself, but it required someone to catch you when you passed out. On this occasion, my loyal "friends" all thought it would be funny to step out of the way as I collapsed and let me land flat on my face. I woke up, all alone, feeling like someone had hit me over the head with a two-by-four. I went home early that day.

A "slam book" passed around in fifth grade gave me a true sense of how "women" perceived me. This spiral binder, with anonymous opinions about each student in class, proved to be a fascinating look into prepubescent social structure. Comments about me from girls (the hint was brightly colored ink and circles instead of dots over every "i") ranged from "really funny," to "looks like a witch." I must say, the experience left me even more confused. I know roughly the same about women today.

Only months before, Lennice Boraski had trampled my heart during a dramatic break-up at recess. Nothing was more devastating than to watch her smudge the message, *I love Bruce Campbell,* on her notebook into an illegible blot.

Several years later, Lennice and I repaired our friendship to the extent that it ultimately led to my first kiss. This concept is riddled with clichés, but it had a profound effect on me. Until the day when I sat with Lennice and a few other wanton kids playing Truth or Dare in the woods, I had never felt the raw intensity that intimacy promotes. Somewhere along the game, I lost a "dare," and it led to a challenge to kiss Lennice before the day was out.

The Meadowlake monkey bars: Scene of Lennice's crime.

The actual kiss didn't come until we walked back through the woods toward Lennice's house. We both realized that smooching in the open would be out of the question, so we found a quiet patch of woods to perform the deed.

It's amazing what the mind remembers about such incidents. To me, the kiss was rushed, awkward and unfulfilling. I'm sure Lennice shares the same complaint. Even so, it was exhilarating. This wasn't a good-night peck on Mom's rosy cheek—our kiss was a voyage into uncharted adolescent territory.

My neighborhood was a great source of fraternization with the opposite sex. Kathy Koska lived right next door to Lennice. Her Brother Kevin and I played softball often and Kathy would drop by some days to actually play. That was fine by me. She was extremely athletic and looked older than she was. I assumed she was off-limits because she hung out with Stud Boy Jim Linklater down the street. I surmised that because one day, Kevin and I unwittingly flushed the couple, red-faced, out of a field.

Much to my delight, as I walked home with her after a softball game in Boraski's pasture, she asked me if I knew her phone number. I did, of course, because of numerous calls to Kevin, and I reeled off the digits in rapid succession, ending in 1-3-6-9.

"How did you know that?" she marveled.

"Well, they're all odd numbers, see, in ascending order . . ."

Mr. Smoothie, that was me.

Kathy was very impressed and asked me to call her some time. It must have been months later when I finally mustered the courage, and our chat came on the heels of a casual call to her brother Kevin.

"Bruce, let me ask you something," she said, sounding amazingly sexy. Of course, I didn't know the meaning of the word at the time, but her tone really made my short hairs stand at attention.

"Shoot," I countered, failing to sound older and wiser than I was.

17

"If I asked you to kiss me some time . . . *would you*?"

After a long, long pause I blurted, *"Of course . . . you just say when."*

I wish I could report that Kevin flushed Kathy and I out of that same field soon thereafter, but it was not meant to be. I never called Kathy again simply because I blanched at the mere mention of her name. What would I do if I found myself alone with this older *woman*? What *could* I do? What if she attacked me? No doubt, if she had even so much as laid a hand on me, I would have wet myself (or worse) and fainted on the spot (already a skill I excelled at).

The downside of having only brothers was that there were no girls to provide crucial counseling. Mike was always busy putting Bond-O on his collection of rusted '57 Chevys and Don didn't know any more than I did.

When junior high rolled around and we merged into a larger school known as West Maple, I became surrounded by what seemed to be an ocean of beautiful women in halter-tops, bell-bottoms and Earth Shoes.

My locker was directly between Joan and Heather Campbell. Joan I knew—she was swell, but Heather was a whole new ballgame. She was a redhead with a great sense of humor and a body that would distract any postpubescent male on the planet.

I tried in vain to woo her.

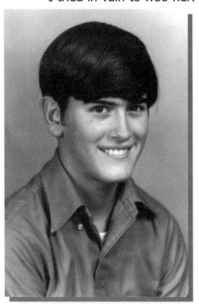

Mr. Smoothie.

"But Heather," I pleaded, "if we got married, you wouldn't even have to change your last name."

Heather had other plans. I'm sure she now is happily married to some lucky sap in a Detroit suburb and has fourteen kids.

Kathy Beard's locker wasn't far away either. For some as yet unexplained reason this tall, bronzed goddess and I found each other in an arranged relationship.

"You like each other," we were informed.

Our "dates" were set up by mutual friends: "You should go out with each other."

"Buy her stuff," came the next directive. The next thing I knew, I was buying Kathy the lamest pair of earrings ever sold and spending the longest hour of my life at her house. Don't get me wrong, Kathy was a knockout. The problem with this pairing was that there was nothing organic about it. Within a month, news of our dissolved relationship came through third parties as well.

"Sorry Bruce, she doesn't like you anymore."

I met Kathy at her locker and all I could manage to blurt out, in utter bewilderment, was, "I guess we should break up."

"Yeah, I guess so," was her equally confused reply.

I BEHELD THE FUTURE, AND THE FUTURE WAS PLAY   2

Childhood was coming to a halt and I didn't like it one bit.

The prospects were depressing: Adulthood meant that I'd have to stop having fun and do something I didn't really want to do for the rest of my life—which was apparently a considerable chunk of time.

I was convinced that there was a way out—a way to avoid becoming an unhappy adult—and I searched unconsciously for a profession that could perpetuate the concept of the endless summer.

St. Dunstan's provided the answer.

Back in 1887, George Booth, an iron magnate, married Ellen Scripps, daughter of *The Detroit News* owner—an event that was as much of a merger as it was a marriage. In 1904, they moved to the rolling farmlands of suburban Detroit and created a 174-acre estate, back when the word still had meaning.

Between 1922 and 1942, as their empire faded, George and Ellen donated much of their surrounding land to an educational academy which, in turn, gave birth to St. Dunstan's Guild of Cranbrook—or simply, St. D's.

This amateur theater guild put on a half dozen plays a year. Most of them were mounted in the indoor pavilion, but each summer

St. Dunstan's.

19

a showy musical was presented in the outdoor theater. Built in 1932 as a replica of a Greek theater, this amazing facility boasted circular, arena-type seating, towering pine trees and reflecting pools.

There, in the summer of 1966, I watched my dad Charlie perform in the musical, *The Pajama Game.* As an eight-year-old, there was something special about sipping hot chocolate atop cushions in this dreamy location while my dad goofed around on stage.

Until that night, I had no idea that the old man did that "actor" stuff. My dad always struck me as a relatively serious, "normal" guy, so what was up with the makeup and the funny clothes? The same guy who tucked me in at night was singing and dancing with a woman that wasn't my mom and he was having *fun.*

Right at that very moment, it struck me that if I was an actor like Dad, I could skip that adult responsibility thing and just stick to the silly stuff.

Five years later and as many inches taller, my theory was put to the test—right back at St. D's. The casting folks were pulling their hair out because a young actor had fallen ill. They very quickly had to find a replacement for the role of Prince Chululonghorn in their production of *The King and I.* For some unexplained reason, I was snatched from the chorus of kids and handed the role of the king's son.

Destiny plays a hand. Mom coaches me through a Lincoln-Mercury ad to be used in the King and I *program.*

Surely, the old man must have whispered in someone's ear.

Next thing I knew, I was having body wash (affectionately called "Texas Dirt") applied to my entire body and I was changing in a real live actor's dressing room with adults.

The adrenaline rush of waiting for my cue in the "green room" was a new experience, and getting shoved on stage to sing in front of an audience terrified me, but call me crazy—I liked it.

That summer, I picked up acting tips from the "veterans" at St. D's. A tongue-limbering exercise (one that I use to this day) came from a Ford Motor Company executive; a clothier coached me on a projection technique, but the most important tip of all came from a garage door salesman:

"Don't drink soda before you go on stage, kid. You don't want to burp during the climax of the play . . ."

Theater was the great equalizer—I changed clothes in the same damp, concrete room as CEOs from Fortune 500 companies. Seeing their pasty, half-naked bodies and knowing that they were just as nervous as I was made everything all right somehow.

The following summers, I managed to act my way toward adulthood. In *Fiorello,* I itched like hell as a World War I soldier (Michigan + July + wool = misery), and drenched myself in Body Wash #7 as "Chang," the servant boy.

I could hear the casting folks musing over this one: "Let's get that kid who played that Siamese son. Maybe he can do Chinese."

When *South Pacific* rolled around, I was cast as a servant again—a *Polynesian* one this time. I began to think that the casting gods were plotting against me. Type cast at fourteen—a sure sign of things to come.

During this production, I got a peek at the relentless dedication an actor can have toward his craft. The flashy role of "Luther Billis" went to Ed Guest, a man who had been known to take a drink or two—or five or six. Well, the day before our last performance, Ed was nabbed for drunk driving. He had the misfortune of being brought before Judge Gilbert, "the hanging judge." With no tolerance for what was his third of-

The Greek Theater moments before the SWAT team stormed the place.

fense, she ordered him to serve time in the county jail—effective immediately.

Word of this got out to the folks at St. D's. Bear in mind, a number of "actors" at this humble community theater group were really high-powered professional people. One such member, Isabel Himelhoch, happened to pal around with a Michigan Supreme Court justice and put in an appeal to get Ed released for that one remaining show.

Meanwhile, my dad was collared to replace Ed if things didn't go through. He had been cast in a number of "character" roles at St. D's, but the big spotlight had swung around in his direction. I'd never seen Dad sweat so much as during that twelve-hour period. With script in hand, he circled our back deck, mumbling Luther Billis's many lines repeatedly.

Fortunately for Charlie, Ed was granted a release for that Saturday show, but we weren't out of the woods yet. Since the summer shows were all mounted at the outdoor theater, weather was a huge factor. Michigan is prone to summer thunderstorms and a big one was forecast for that night.

If Saturday got rained out, Ed would remain in jail, a rain performance would be mounted that Sunday evening, and Charlie would get the nod.

As the curtain rose that night, Ed sang and danced his way across the stage while Mother Nature kept us on pins and needles. Wind raced through the pines surrounding the stage and thunder rumbled in the distance. There was no question about it—a storm was gonna happen, it was just a matter of *when*.

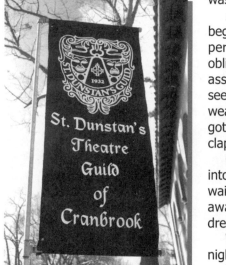

My "flagship" theater.

Act III began, and tiny drops of rain began to descend. Ed, giving the best performance of his life, was totally oblivious. Even the two burly police officers, assigned to monitor his every move, seemed to enjoy the show. Thankfully, the weather held until the final curtain and Ed got quite an ovation. I'm sure Charlie clapped harder than anyone.

Once off stage, Ed quietly changed back into civilian clothes and was escorted to the waiting patrol car. As the sedan pulled away, the heavens opened up and drenched all the well-wishers.

We toasted Ed at the cast party that night.

"To Ed! An *Actor's* actor!" someone shouted.

As I raised my glass of punch, I looked around the room. I had never before seen people so passionate, particularly about an amateur play, and I realized that this was the life for me.

I'm sure Charlie wasn't surprised when I announced that I wanted to be an actor. He also had dreams of becoming a painter, but my grandfather talked him out of it. Eager to see me free from a similar trap, Charlie encouraged me to get involved as deeply as I dared.

With this endorsement in hand, I set off to find out what this "actor" thing was all about.

THE ASSEMBLY OF LIKE-MINDED INDIVIDUALS
FORMATION OF THE "DETROIT MAFIA"

3

Michigan is surrounded by the largest supply of fresh water in the world—hence the nickname of "the Great Lakes state." But there must have been something more to the water of southeastern Michigan, something that caused half a dozen young men to throw caution to the wind and pursue the film business.

Meet "The Boys":

Mike Ditz and I date back to pre-kindergarten. Our mothers drove neighborhood kids to various events and we shared company at a birthday party or two. Mike's dad documented many of these events with a hand-cranked, Kodak Brownie double 8mm camera.

We found this "adult toy" much more interesting than your average G.I. Joe. You had a choice of three lenses, mounted on a revolving turret. The film inside was actually 16mm, mounted on a twenty-five-foot roll. After exposing one side, you flipped it over and exposed the other side. The processing laboratory would split the film down the middle and voila—you had 8mm home movies.

There were a few gizmos on this camera that just begged to be exploited, such as single-frame exposure. This allowed us to do magical things with the touch of a

Mike Ditz: Paparazzi of our past.

23

button. We could disappear, "animate" ourselves skidding across the ground, or change into Richard Nixon (my favorite mask at the time).

Mike's interest was primarily behind the camera, since he knew how to operate the damn thing. This was fine with me because it allowed me to jump in front of the lenses—all three of them. In the early experiments we did, the concept of telling a story hadn't captured our imaginations yet—that's where Scott Spiegel came in.

Junior high school hooks you up with kids from strange new lands. Scott was one of them. He lived near Walnut Lake, where my family had summer swimming privileges. Scott and I bumped elbows unknowingly at Gene's, the local candy store, buying *Spree* or banana-flavored Turkish Taffy.

Scott Spiegel: Three Stooges fanatic.

In eighth-grade study hall, when Mike Ditz wasn't borrowing *Mad* magazines from him, Scott and I talked about movies and TV almost all the time. We both agreed that the new film, *The Poseidon Adventure,* was about the coolest disaster movie ever and that *The Ghoul,* a local TV show, was very funny. The gag of this cheesy show was to air a really bad horror film and the host, Ron Swede, would dub in his own disgusting sound effects and put on skits during commercial breaks. One of his favorite pranks was to blow things up with M-80s, and Scott was impressed that a prop I had sent in got blown to smithereens.

As it turned out, Scott also made 8mm films, but by the time I met him in 1972 he was a veteran. His first film, *Inspector Klutz Saves the Day,* was cranked out in 1969.

"It was the plot of Dr. Frankenstein who wants to find a normal brain to put into his monster," Scott remembered, matter-of-factly.

"I was Igor the monster. I guess we killed somebody or something and then planted the brain in the monster, but then monster comes alive and kills us, then Inspector Klutz comes in and kills the monster . . ."

Convoluted yes, but Scott's films at least had a plot. He was a Three Stooges fanatic, as were most of my male peers at the time (go ahead and sneer, girls—pain is funny, I don't care what you say), and he was keen on redoing some of their classic shorts.

Scott's buddy, Matt Taylor, had a screening room in his basement. There, Scott showed me his latest effort, *Night in the Sanitarium.* This wasn't some handheld, out-of-focus piece of crap, it was a real movie with sets and costumes and even stock footage.

I couldn't help but be interested, and I mooched my way into Scott's world, appearing first as a thug in his *Three Smart Saps.* I had access to my very own wardrobe (courtesy of St. D's), so I came with a few tricks of my own.

Josh Becker, whom I sat behind in study hall, was absolutely insane about movies. His tastes leaned toward Hollywood's golden era of cinema and his knowledge of motion picture trivia was (and still is) dizzying.

Josh and I both got parts in the eighth-grade play, *The Lottery.* Josh was an early bloomer, and snatched a plum role from me simply because the bastard could grow a full beard.

As a school project, Josh filmed an early adaptation of *Oedipus Rex* in 8mm. Mike Ditz photographed it and I played King Creon. I think Josh was impressed, not with my acting abilities, but because I brought my own embroidered toga.

"Jane Gordon baked baklava for her project," Josh remembered. "She got an 'A' and I got a 'C.' Admittedly, it was good baklava and it was a bad movie."

But Josh was undeterred—his next production, *Super Student,* was much more ambitious. To pull off the story of a student with super powers, he got permission to film all over the school and even got teachers to play themselves.

The finished product was screened for the entire school in the auditorium. I remember thinking—*that rat bastard!*—I was making stop-motion stuff with Mike Ditz and was lucky if my parents would watch. This guy got the whole school to see his movie.

Josh's neighbor, Sam Raimi, recalled seeing it as well.

"That was a great movie," Sam noted. "The audience cheered because he made the assistant principal disappear, then he made the whole school disappear. He was the Steven Spielberg of the year."

Josh Becker: Bearded Wonder.

Josh and Sam had actually met many years earlier, at their bus stop.

<u>Bruce:</u> Did you, like, torment Sam at the bus stop?

<u>Josh:</u> No, no, no, I never tormented Sam. Sam tormented *me* for years.

<u>Bruce:</u> How did he do that?

<u>Josh:</u> Sam had too much energy first thing in the morning. He never seemed to shut up. All I wanted to do was sit and smoke cigarettes, but he had to either practice his magic tricks for me or knock over the stop sign.

<u>Bruce:</u> What do you mean?

<u>Josh:</u> There were those poles that were white and then black at the top—

Bruce: They're, like, to keep you from going over into a ravine or something.

Josh: Right. He would stand on top of that, put his foot on the stop sign, and shake it—

Bruce: Why would he do that?

Josh: He was trying to knock it down without going to a lot of effort. Each year, the county would come out and do road work and they'd find this thing bent in half. And so they'd take it and they'd shove it deeper and each year it would get shorter.

Sam Raimi: Bane of My Existence.

Sam Raimi was a different bird entirely.

My first glimpse of him, in eighth grade, was in the middle of the hallway, dressed as Sherlock Holmes, playing with dolls. Sam claims that he was just making a film.

"It was a shot of me being confused," he insisted. "I think I was hit on the head. The crook hits me on the head, I'm knocked out and I wake up and I don't know what's happening and all the people are supposed to be walking by me or something . . ."

I met Sam officially in drama class at Wylie E. Groves high school in 1975. An assignment to perform a pantomime made fools out of us both. Sam decided to portray a man on a unicycle. To do this, he stomped his feet on the stage rhythmically, as though he were pedaling.

Novel, I thought, *but the guy is one weird wolf.*

My pantomime depicted the intangible concept of "tension." I figured if I pulled on an imaginary rope long enough, something would be conveyed. James Moll, our teacher, couldn't figure out what the hell I was trying to achieve and gave me a "C."

Sam didn't fare any better that day and we exchanged condolences.

"Hey, pal, that was good," Sam said. "Whatever it was you were trying to do . . ."

Sam had been making films in his own neighborhood since 1972. As it turned out, he had access to a strange new toy—a video camera. A neighborhood friend of his owned a black-and-white, reel-to-reel setup. The concept of seeing images immediately after doing a "skit" was remarkable—no need to hound the photo department at Kmart for days on end. Even so, it was eventually abandoned because of its lack of portability.

Sam first met Scott Spiegel in high school biology, but they didn't become friends right away.

Sam: Yeah, I was aware of Scott.

Bruce: Did you sit next to him?

Sam: No, I didn't sit next to him. Scott and I didn't get along quite at first. We slowly got to know each other.

Bruce: Scott was kind of a joker, right?

Sam: He was a real joker. I asked him for Moe Howard's address (of the Three Stooges) and he wouldn't give it to me.

Bruce: He had it, though?

Sam: I knew he did, but he wouldn't share it with me. I thought that was really rude.

Eventually, Scott coughed up the address and Sam joined this expanding group. His first role, as was almost always the case, was a thug in *No Doughboys*—a gag fest about wayward delivery boys.

I met John Cameron relatively late—in high school home room. John was impossibly tall and thin—sort of like John Cleese if you stretched him out of proportion. John had a biting sense of humor, perhaps

John Cameron: "The Biggest Jerk for the Longest Time."

because he was a fellow Scot, and he wound up specializing in ill-tempered customers in our early Super-8s.

John also met Sam in high school.

John: I was on a lunch break. I was hanging out in a courtyard with Mike Ditz and eating my brown bag lunch, peanut butter and jelly or whatever, and Sam ambled by and Mike knew him and he introduced us—whatever that means at that age. And I recall acting like a jerk because Sam seemed like a fake name. We used it when we played Army. I thought he was lying, so I tormented him for the rest of the time we were in this little courtyard. "Okay *SAM*. No problem *SAM*," and he has since told me that he thought I was like the biggest jerk for the longest time.

Bruce: You were being horribly mean to him.

John: I didn't believe him. He seemed like a wisenheimer and was pulling my leg.

By this time, John had also met Josh outside the C-9 bathroom—the designated smoking area at school.

John: I saw him every day. I didn't know his name or anything, but Josh was always good for a free butt. He also had the longest hair of anybody that I ever knew.

Bruce: Did he have a beard then, because when I met him in eighth grade, he had a beard.

John: Yeah, he had the beard and he always wore a pinstriped suit jacket with jeans.

Eventually, Sam, Josh, John, Mike and I all merged with the Spiegel camp. Now, between us, we had cameras, projectors, editing equipment and lights—everything we needed to do more fully blown projects. It wasn't Hollywood, but a lot of film was being shot.

We got serious enough to form the Metropolitan Film Group and even issued business cards, but it was an operation where many of the traditional film jobs overlapped. Whoever bought the film and made the most phone calls became the producer, and anyone who came up with a basic concept was considered the writer. Directing was often handled by more than one of us at the same time.

Sam, Josh and I filming the Final Round.

Aside from the usual adolescent bickering, things ran smoothly with the exception of scheduling. A pie fight in Scott's *No Doughboys* on Friday night might require the actors Josh was using in *The Topanga Pearl.* Likewise, Sam's *It's Murder!* might need the same camera that John's *Shemp Eats the Moon* was using—such were our teenage problems.

Birmingham, Michigan, the nearest "city," became our back lot. Sunday afternoons resulted in empty alleys and a lower traffic volume—ideal for filming. Police were routinely called to our film set to investigate reports of some "person" being thrown off a parking structure. After several years of this, the police knew us by sight.

"Oh, it's *you* guys. That's a better dummy than last time."

"Yeah, we fixed this one so the legs won't bend backwards!"

The woman at the local Kmart photo department got to know us, too.

"Scott, how did *Three Pests in a Mess* turn out?" she'd inquire.

We owed a lot to expiration dates. With Scott and I working at a local IGA, any excuse to end a film with a food fight was good enough for us. The plea to our boss, Danny, would go something like this:

"Hey, Danny, these Boston creme pies are all expired. You're gonna pitch them, right?"

"Let me guess—you guys are filming this weekend."

"Yeah."

"(sigh) Go ahead—take 'em."

The Walnut Lake Market also provided us with an endless supply of boxes. If the plot didn't require pies, it surely would have some guy's car ramming through a pile of boxes—our idea of a "stunt." As our approach to filming became more ambitious, pies and boxes weren't enough anymore.

Sam's house had the best stairs to fall down. The sweeping staircase in his foyer had a good "grade" and was carpeted—always a plus. There, Sam and I perfected the art of the "stair fall."

Sam: That staircase had just enough slope.

Bruce: It was perfect—curved and so you couldn't get too much speed.

Sam: You could use the wall as a brake sometimes. You could rub your elbows—

Bruce: Or drag your heels. As soon as your legs go over your head, you start dragging those heels. You could control the speed.

Sam: Arcing.

Bruce: Right, the shoe scrapes left on the wall would be in an arc.

Other types of falls were to follow: the cliff tumble, the soapy floor wipe-out, the bicycle dump and the parking structure bail-out.

Moving vehicles offered up a whole new challenge. As an indestructible teenager, I thought nothing about leaping from car to car as they raced down the street or, when needed, being dragged by one—but smashing my head into concrete was a different matter.

For Sam's *Bogus Monkey Pignut Swindle,* a crime caper, I took a dive into what I *thought* was a stream. Eighteen inches below the water, however, my skull met with a slab of discarded concrete. Nonetheless, my credo remained the same: As long as it was captured on film, it was worth it.

Eventually, out of the need to film in a different law enforcement jurisdiction, we explored new territory. As suburban kids, the idea of venturing thirty miles into the heart of Detroit to film was intimidating, but we did so on several occasions. We never had any problems from the police in that city—stopping a bunch of yahoos in ill-fitting suits was the *least* of their problems.

Detroit is the land of teamsters, so the chance to reenact the abduction of former boss James Hoffa seemed like a good idea. Filming at the actual restaurant only two weeks after his disappearance was not, however, and it got us kicked off the property in twenty minutes.

"YOU WILL NEVER KILL MY CLASSIC"

Sam Raimi's family owned a 1973 Oldsmobile Delta Royale. For some reason, it became the all-purpose car that appeared in almost every Super-8 film we ever made.

When Sam began to make feature films, he kept

This damn car has been in more movies than I have.

using it—from *Evil Dead* in 1979 to his Kevin Costner film, *For Love of the Game,* twenty years later.

Sam began to adopt a strange attachment to this car and brazenly dubbed it "the Classic." My crappy car, an Opel Isuzu, had also been in several of our shorts, but Sam would only refer to it offhandedly as a "pseudo foreign sub-classic." The best any *other* car could hope for was "sub-classic."

David Goodman, a longtime friend of the Raimi family, offered his take on Sam's object of desire:

Sam's love nest?

"I think he got laid for the first time in the Classic, that's why it's so important to him."

The Delta was everywhere—aside from numerous Super-8s, it drove the kids to the *Evil Dead* cabin, engaged in a high-speed chase in *Crimewave,* absorbed the shock of Liam Neeson slamming into it in *Darkman* and became the "Deathcoaster" in *Army of Darkness.*

Wouldn't this piece of crap ever die? I wondered to myself.

Not if Sam could help it.

For *Evil Dead II,* Sam had it brought down from Michigan to North Carolina on the back of a flatbed truck because it no longer ran. By this time, Dave Goodman was the transportation coordinator and the car became the bane of his existence.

"It was just a pain in the ass. Sam needed specific things in the car to work because he had certain shots within the car that he needed and he would never bend. I said, 'Sam, you can't do it this way it's going to cost you this much money,' and he says, 'I don't care. I want it the way I want it.' It was almost like he was crazy about it."

As a result, our deal with Sam, starting with *Evil Dead II,* was this: anything over the amount of money in the budget to repair his car had to come from his pocket.

On *Crimewave,* I ordered the Classic to be killed. A rear screen projection sequence called for the chase cars to be mounted on sliding rails. In order to do this, the vehicle had to be stripped of excess weight. At the end of a long shooting day, the mechanic, Pat, approached me with a dilemma.

Pat: Hey, Bruce, I've got to prep one of the Deltas for tomorrow (there were several needed in the film) and the only one with the right interior is Sam's personal car.

I could barely contain my smile.

Bruce: Gut it, Pat.

Pat: Really? You sure?

Bruce: Sure I'm sure. The continuity has to be right, doesn't it?

With that, Pat proceeded to remove the engine, the transmission and he welded the wheels up in the wheel wells.

The next morning, Sam sauntered over to the car, now up on the rails, and began to direct Sheree, the lead actress being chased.

Sam: Okay Sheree, you're driving like mad, see, and you . . .

Sam's gaze shifted to the interior of the car—to the creamy white, *original* interior.

Sam: Hey . . . hey, is this my . . . ?

Instinctively, he turned to me.

Sam: Is this my car? Is this the Classic?

Bruce: Can't you tell?

Sam: You gutted my car! You tried to kill the Classic!

Bruce: No, Sam, I figured that for this important sequence, you'd want the only car that had the proper interior . . .

The Classic even has stunt doubles.

Knowing that I was bullshitting, Sam raised a finger at me.

Sam: Hard as you try, you will *never* kill the Classic . . .

God only knows how much Sam forked out over the years to keep this rusted hulk in front of the camera. I'd love to have an auto supplier checklist of every new part issued in the name of Sam Raimi.

Bruce: What percentage of that car is still original, Sam, like five percent?

Sam: No, there's more. The basic body and frame is still original.

Bruce: *And . . . ?*

Sam: Well, okay the motor is not original. Most of the working engine parts are probably not original. The wheels are not original. Some of the upholstery is not original, but it's got the original dash, the steering wheel. The body has a lot of Bond-O, I will admit.

When asked where the Classic was now, Sam cagily responded, "In a warehouse somewhere in southern California." He knew if I ever found out, an army of mechanics would be dispatched to destroy it.

THE SEWED SEED

Looking back, I wondered what propelled each of these guys to get involved in such an oddball profession. Not surprisingly, each could remember their first moviegoing experience vividly.

Mike had *The Music Man* indelibly imprinted in his memory.

"My mother knew that I enjoyed the film because it was the first one I had stayed awake through."

For John, a fourth-grade field trip to see *2001: A Space Odyssey* stuck with him.

"You'd get out of class to watch moon shots and takeoffs and things like that, so space was a big deal," John recalled. "But also I think that just the feeling of being transported to another world and being taken away from your own miserable existence as a fourth grader—it created a world that sucked me in and didn't let me go. I remember coming home and saying that I would like to do that."

Scott's family regularly attended the Oak drive-in in Royal Oak, Michigan. His experience watching the 1963 version of *Phantom of the Opera* was unlike any other.

"That really freaked me out and it really had an impact . . ."

Josh was taken to see *How the West Was Won* and immediately insisted that his parents take him again the following week. He still owns the commemorative, hardcover program.

"The thing that I still love about movies is that, for the course of the time you are watching the movie, you can absolutely believe that there's a God," Josh explained. "There's a hand of a creator leading these people to their logical conclusions. I think in life, we want to believe that. From that point on in my life, reality seemed paltry and small and meaningless."

Sam has never forgotten the opening disclaimer of *Fantastic Voyage,* warning of the amazing things he was about to see. Sam's father read it aloud to him.

The Birmingham Theater.

"It sounded very serious, like a nuclear war warning, or a warning that he would read aloud off of a can of poison," Sam recounted.

His father used to document birthday parties in 16mm. When Sam saw the footage projected, it all began to make sense.

<u>Sam:</u> Just to see yourself and your friends in a movie which had formally been reserved for that frightening, intense experience in the theater and suddenly you could be a part of it—that was a heavy experience.

<u>Bruce:</u> In that now you could do that same thing?

<u>Sam:</u> Yeah. I think so.

Personally, I was struck by those Walt Disney live-action films of the mid-sixties, like *Swiss Family Robinson* and *Flubber.*

Watching people fly and ride down the side of a mountain on a block of ice jolted a part of my imagination that hadn't been touched before—the images were larger than life and so powerful that it seemed more real than real.

These events contributed, no doubt, to our collective interest in experimenting with films. Amazingly, to this day, each of these guys still makes a living in some form of media.

High(jinks) School 4

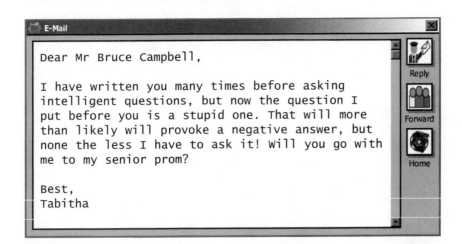

> **E-Mail**
>
> Dear Mr Bruce Campbell,
>
> I have written you many times before asking intelligent questions, but now the question I put before you is a stupid one. That will more than likely will provoke a negative answer, but none the less I have to ask it! Will you go with me to my senior prom?
>
> Best,
> Tabitha
>
> Reply
> Forward
> Home

If you saw me walking down the hall in high school, you would have grinned to yourself, muttered "loser," and never given me a second thought. The reason will become self-evident. For starters, I never wore blue jeans—not even once. Those were for cowboys and I didn't see any of them walking around suburban Detroit. To me, they were too damn tight to serve any other purpose and wore through at the knees and butt too quickly. Instead, I opted for the classic fit and rugged elegance of Montgomery Ward's work pants. Ninety-nine percent of them were sold to custodians, but I couldn't have cared less—they were mostly polyester, so wrinkles weren't a problem, and they came in four different colors.

I also refused to wear tennis shoes. I never played the game or jogged, so I figured why bother? With durability the rule of the day, I wore black, navy-issue shoes almost exclusively.

The other constant in my wardrobe came in the form of a dirty brown smoking jacket. I *started* wearing it long after Dad left it for dead, so by the end of high school it was eligible for the Smithsonian.

It's no surprise, then, that by the end of high school I could count all my dates on one hand. However, that didn't reflect a lack of interest, just experience. Because I didn't know what dating was all about, or how one went about it, my idea of a good time was to take Ann Zeh to the film, *Man in the Wilderness.* The story of a man being mauled by a bear and left to die in the middle of nowhere was about the farthest thing from a "chick flick" I could have chosen, but that didn't compute—I just wanted to see it again.

The closest I ever came to being a swinger in high school was on film. In our Super-8 flick *James Bombed,* a 007 spoof, I got to chum up with Christy Gritton, a tanned Robo-Babe who went out exclusively with the hunkiest jocks in high school.

On a school day, Christy wouldn't have given me the time of day, but the chance to be in a "movie" made it cool enough for her to hang out with us. It also helped that her boyfriend, Tim Quill, was the lead bad guy.

Prom came and went and I never even knew it—that's how disconnected I was from the dating scene. Still, it didn't keep me from trying to get the attention of women, and I would do anything to get it—even streaking. Yes, I too was suckered into that lame seventies fad.

Polyester Man to the rescue.

One night, neighbor Judy Feldman was home alone babysitting her little sister. The elements were ripe for a "streak," so Scott Tyler and I ran through her backyard, buck-ass naked, and bounced on her trampoline while she looked out the rear window. To prove that we did it, Mike Ditz came with camera in hand to document the entire thing. Streaking did nothing to further my relationship with Judy, but she never looked at me that same way after that. I'm not sure if that's good or bad. . . .

The smartest thing I ever did was drop Typing 101 for Radio Speech. From the minute I sat among thirty other typists, most of whom were able to type already, I knew this wasn't a place I *needed* to be. I paid the price eventually, of course, in writing this book—hunting and pecking my way from start to finish.

36

The other fringe benefit of this brilliant decision was that it put me in another class with Sam—did I say that was a good thing?

Sam was seated behind me in Radio Speech and one of his favorite pastimes was to inflict torture without getting caught. He'd lie in wait, until Mr. Moll called on me to answer a question. As I began to speak, Sam would place a sharpened pencil into the square of my back and apply pressure, testing to see how long I could speak normally. Afterward, when I threatened to stab his eyes out, he'd come out with, "What? I tried to help you," utterly convinced of his innocence.

This one-sided abuse became the basis of our professional relationship. Bear in mind, this is the same guy who went on to direct Gene Hackman and Kevin Costner.

Sam was a master at planting insidious little seeds. He took Modern European History from Chester Guilmet one period before me—all the time he needed to tell the serious teacher, "Bruce Campbell does a *great* impersonation of you."

As I settled into my seat in Mr. Guilmet's room, the first words out of his mouth were, "Mr. Campbell, I'd like to see you after class . . ."

Sam and I doing our impersonations of Mr. Guilmet.

Cut to me, red-faced, well after the bell, as Mr. Guilmet reamed me out for a crime I didn't commit. The scary thing about all of this was that Sam didn't do this because he hated me or anything—he did this type of thing to people he *liked*. I knew right then that he was an agent of the dark side.

As an outgrowth of Radio Speech, Sam and I teamed up for a live show that aired during Friday morning home room. Our "broadcast" reached an entire school and we enjoyed a captive audience—students couldn't have turned us off if they wanted to.

The show chronicled the misadventures of Captain Nemo and his band of pirates. Sam played the captain and I was Wood-Eye, his trusty First Mate. Enlisting the services of our Radio Speech teacher, Mr. Moll, as the announcer was a great way to keep our show on the air for the better part of a year.

Another sideline of being a Radio Speech student was providing music for the lunchroom study hall. Acid-rock lovers patronized the place and Kiss was always high on the request list. With influences more along the lines of The Carpenters, I wasn't about to play ear-bleed music, so I'd play a Kiss song, then place a thumb on the turntable and drag it to a slow death.

THE *PLAY* IS THE THING

From the day I enrolled in high school, I wanted desperately to be a part of the plays, but getting in wasn't as easy as I'd hoped. Theater, at least in these circles, was very clique-oriented, and if you weren't in drama class, you weren't gonna get in any plays—it was as simple as that.

This became obvious when Josh Becker, John Cameron and I auditioned for the spring musical, *Promises, Promises.* If you've ever heard me sing, you know what my chances were. Fortunately, Josh and John weren't any better. John sang the Beatles song, *Help,* and he needed plenty of it. Josh charged through *Gigi* until Mr. Moll cut him off halfway through with, "That's enough!"

Pick me . . . pick me!

My audition song was *Love*—you know, the one that spelled out the word: "L is for the way you look at me . . ." Mr. Moll attempted to cut me off around the letter O, but I was undaunted and finished the song. It didn't make any difference because I didn't get the part I was after . . . or *any* part.

The following fall, I took drama class and it changed everything. Mr. Moll got a better sense of what I could and could not do, and it eventually led to a role as a crazed Russian in the farce, *See How They Run.* At the risk of perpetuating a cliché, I must admit that seeing my name on the casting notice outside the drama classroom was a huge rush.

I didn't have much hope for the musical that following spring, but membership had its privileges and I snagged a nondescript role in the chorus of *Funny Girl.* That was fine with me, because my dancing partner was Toni Wylen, one of the most beautiful girls in school. I can't say that we fell madly in love, but it was enough to know that she *had* to dance with me.

Senior year, our little troupe ruled the roost. The fall play was Neil Simon's *Plaza Suite* and the boys were thick as thieves in the cast. John was the angst-ridden businessman in the first act.

"I was the serious one," John lamented, "which has always been my lot in life."

I played a Hollywood movie producer in the second act, and Bill Kirk, the school star of his day, headlined the farcical act three. Sam portrayed the bumbling bellhop throughout all the acts.

The spring musical was George S. Kaufman's political satire, *Of Thee I Sing.* I didn't get a role in that because I assumed the duties of assistant director. That job provided a great vantage point to watch a play develop.

For some strange reason, I was also assigned to design the set, something that I was loathe to do, and for good reason—the end result was embarrassing. Sam and John remembered it fondly:

Sam: You designed it? I didn't know you designed it.

Bruce: Yeah, there were the three tiered bleachers—

John: What do you mean, you designed the set? Did you get credit for it?

Bruce: Yeah, Set Designer and it was these horrible plateaued tiers—

Sam: A musical on those four-foot bleacher step downs—I almost killed myself on those sets.

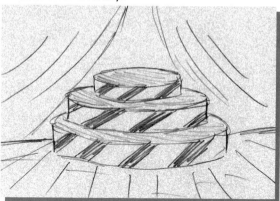

Bruce Campbell: Crappy Set Designer.

Bruce: No one really knew who did it, but everyone kept saying, "Those are the ugliest sets I've ever seen in my life." I kept hearing it and I was like, "Oh no."

John: And you never lived up to it.

Bruce: Hell no. They had like a red, white and blue stripe on them. They were papier-mâché—

John: Looked like painted cheap boulders. Yeah, that set sucked.

An actor fell ill the night of a performance (déjà vu all over again) and I was enlisted to fill in his role as chief justice of the Supreme Court. He only had a few scenes and didn't sing much, so it seemed doable. The wild card was a fellow Supreme Court justice—played by Mr. Sam Raimi. He was like a bad rash, this guy—you just couldn't get rid of him.

Everything was going fine until the justices huddled to discuss the merits of the First Lady's corn muffins. We had just sampled the crumbly things, and as we gathered, I could see almost an entire muffin hanging off Sam's fake beard. I started to giggle, but managed to contain myself until Sam, out of the blue, blurted a non sequitur that did me in.

"These muffins taste like shit," he said, spitting out crumbs. "I'm gonna shove 'em up the president's ass."

I couldn't hold my laughter anymore and the fake beard sprang from my face. The giggles are a curse for any actor, and are impossible to shake once you get them—especially when the cue for your singing number is immediately after this incident. So, before a packed auditorium, I whirled around, clamped a hand over my beard, and laughed my way through the longest twenty seconds of my life.

Around this time, Sam suckered me into a talent show, hosted by the Franklin Village Junior players. We were billed as the Bonzoid Sisters and our costumes were comprised of long underwear and gym shorts. The idea was to perform lame gymnastic routines and demand applause—sort of like Cirque du Soleil, minus the talent. In between these routines we would often hurl ourselves in every direction for no apparent reason.

<u>Bruce:</u> I remember the bruises on our bodies—I've never seen bruises before or since like those.

<u>Sam:</u> We were like bruised bananas.

<u>Bruce:</u>—I'm sure that I screwed up my elbows. I mean I know I've done something bad to them . . .

<u>Sam:</u> I didn't screw up my elbows, but my muscle and skin there was so damaged. It was so—

<u>Bruce:</u> My elbows were purple. It was horrifying. There was no concept of padding whatsoever.

The moment of truth for our act was auditioning for Cedar Point, a theme park in Sandusky, Ohio. Obviously, the organizers didn't share our enthusiasm and we were dismissed without comment.

Little did they know that they were passing up the opportunity to work with Douglas Sills, Sam's boyhood neighbor, the third man of our act. He has since become quite the Broadway sensation in *The Scarlet Pimpernel*, among others.

SUPER-DUPER-8 5

As our ambitions grew, so did our budgets. The average film cost of around a hundred bucks soon ballooned to four or five hundred. Eventually, a question began to loom: *Can we actually make money with these things?*

In his first year at college, Sam shot a film called *The Happy Valley Kid*, starring his roommate, Rob Tapert.

In Sam's words, "He was a student just like you. His roommate abused him, his girlfriend dumped him and his professor hated him. Then, the week before finals, his mind snapped. He became—the Happy Valley Kid."

The film was shot on the campus of Michigan State University, featuring Sam and Rob's actual professors. Josh, Scott, John and I came up on weekends to fill in the various roles of snotty desk clerks, mean-spirited classmates, security guards, etc.

The finished *Kid* cost $700—something like 2.5 million in 1978 dollars. The film was advertised in *The State News* and shown Friday and Saturday nights on campus for $1.50. Word of mouth spread and it became a hit—grossing well over $5,000 (I'll let you do the math).

"It was a really weird experience for us," Sam recalled. "Every night the place was packed and every night we'd split this tin of dollar bills—fifty dollars for Ivan (Sam's older brother), fifty dollars for me and fifty dollars for Rob. It was like, 'What the hell's going on here?'"

Eventually, after forty-four screenings, the film began to fall apart.

"We finally had to retire it just to preserve what was left of it," Sam explained. "But it was hard to say good-bye to two hundred and fifty dollars a night, I will say."

If the *Kid* succeeded, we figured, a bigger film would do even better. What followed was the mystery/comedy *It's Murder!*—the *Heaven's Gate* of Super-8.

Sam and Scott wrote a story that was feature-length—the first of its kind. To get a richer look with better sound, they also decided to shoot at twenty-four frames per second, as opposed to the standard eighteen frames. This was a huge decision—according to Sam, "it was like going Cinemascope because it required another thirty percent of film stock."

In addition, this script required a large cast and plenty of stunts. A climactic car chase ruined Sam's family Ford Grenada. His father tried to trade in the car several months after filming, but he had a hard time.

"It's funny, the guy at the dealership said it had a cracked engine block," Mr. Raimi told Sam. "I wonder how that happened?"

Another car, a 1962 Cadillac, was purchased so it could be destroyed intentionally. This was a good news/bad news scenario, because afterward, we had to get rid of it.

The cast of It's Murder!

Sam: We couldn't drive away, nor did we know where to put it.

Bruce: No. The concept of having, like, a wrecker come and salvage it just wasn't in the cards.

Sam: I don't think we had the right papers anyway. There was no title. There was no nothin'—we had to dump it.

Bruce: Off of Walnut Lake Road.

Sam: We hooked up a chain and towed it in a very herky-jerky way—I was driving the wreck.

Bruce: Yeah, and someone had to steer from behind. It was a horrible jury-rigged system.

Sam: We pushed it off the cliff, remember?

Bruce: Yeah, knowing that eventually someone from the county would go, "All right, we'll get the car out of there." It was there for like a month.

Even with cost-saving measures like that, the budget of the film went well over two thousand dollars. Worst of all, it dragged into the fall, when student actors returned to school.

Not having a college to return to that fall of 1978 (more on that later), I was available and eager to double for any actor who was missing. Scott was working a forty-hour week, but at least he was still in the state. The lead bad guy, Matt Taylor, was long gone. He was a burly, sandy blond-haired guy who was clean-shaven. I was a lanky, dark-haired guy with a moustache, but who were we to be choosy?

After limping to a halt, *It's Murder!* was "released" at MSU that winter with great fanfare—a custom poster was created and more expensive ads were run in *The State News*.

"I was killing myself with ads," Sam said. "Two hundred dollars for these big ads and renting the place was one hundred dollars for janitorial services. The whole thing was very expensive. I had to lug the big speakers there in the car and the projector and the sound amplifier and the films, extension cord and the speaker wire. The heavy-gauge speaker wire was like garden hose. It was a lot of stuff to carry and pack up. It was not how you wanted to spend Saturday nights . . ."

The effort proved to be a fruitless affair. A handful of the cast and crew were on hand that opening night, but we turned out to be the only patrons. The next night, there was only one paying customer. Sam shares his pain:

"About thirty minutes in—it wasn't quite halfway and I saw the shadow of

The flier promoting It's Murder! *at Groves High.*

a hand come up on the screen, throwing his hands up in the air saying, 'This sucks. I don't even want my money back.' Then, he stood up and the chair went *bappity, bappity, bappity* and I heard his *clump, clump, clump,* down the steps, then the door opened and I was left alone in there. I thought, 'I could watch the rest of the movie which is forty more minutes, or I could rewind it which is thirty.' I remember just rewinding it for thirty minutes backwards sitting in the balcony and I was thinking, 'I gotta somehow figure out a way not to be in this position again.' "

FIRST LOOK UNDER THE HOOD   6

High school ended right out from under me. I was having a good time as the leading man of Super-8, but reality descended like a Midwest thunderstorm and I was forced to ask myself the question: *Can you do this for a living?*

A serious attempt to answer that question came during the summer of '76. A "Star Theater" up north in Traverse City Michigan was looking for apprentices during their summer stock schedule. I never really expected to get a job there, since the Cherry County Playhouse employed professionals, but I sent the application in anyway.

After salting the butcher block at Walnut Lake Market (one of my stock boy duties), I called home to see if any letter had arrived. I had been tracking the household mail pretty intensely the last few weeks and that day, one showed up. I insisted that Mom read it to me on the spot.

"Dear Bruce—Congratulations! Your application has been accepted," Mom read, as happy as I was about the news.

It wasn't until I got home that the ramifications began to sink in. With the exception of a three-week camp outing when I was ten, I had never been away from home for very long, and certainly not alone. This payless job required me to stay, at my own expense, for three months in Traverse City, Michigan—cherry capital of the world. To be honest, I never once thought about the money—I would have *paid* for the opportunity to work in real theater.

Initially, I rented a room in a boardinghouse not far from downtown. Even in 1976 this was a Dickensian concept. Pretty quickly, I tired of tiptoeing around, but the price was right, and I was a free bird. I must explain that I was never the "I gotta get away from home" type since there was nothing about my teenage life that particularly compelled me to rebel.

Still, it felt great to know that for the entire summer, I got to make my own decisions.

I got a taste of this freedom walking to work the first morning. A light rain was coming down, so I wore a green plastic poncho. If Mom had been around, I would also be carrying an umbrella and wearing boots. The rain increased and my head and feet got soaked, but I was bent on savoring my independence, so instead of ducking under the elms along the street, I deliberately slowed down and walked in the open, tilting my head up toward the rain.

A normal day for apprentices started at 9:00 A.M. Dave Bodenstedt, the apprentice coordinator, had a Zero Tolerance for tardiness. His policy, which I endorse, is that if you were supposed to be at work at 9:00, you were *ready to work* at 9:00. You didn't grab a cup of coffee and shoot the bull—you hit the ground running.

THE MOTLEY CREW

1976 Apprentice Company

(Seated left to right) Bruce Campbell, Sue Noling, Chris Lemmon, R. Bruce Haustein, Deborah Kaskinen, Jerry Smith, Kevin Kearns. (Standing left to right) Janette Crawford, Terri Singleton, Nancy Uffner, April Scott, Susan Connor, Matt Roney, Mark Dawson.

Cherry County working stiffs.

It was an eclectic mix of apprentices to say the least. There were ten of us: a Coca-Cola addict, whose rotting teeth stood as testament to the habit; a movie star's son; past-their-prime hippies; sons and daughters of distinctly blue-collar parents; rich suburban kids; and me, Mr. Middle-of-the-Road. The apprentices were straight and gay, young and old, but we were the backbone of that theater.

The technical staff was a combination of imported and home-grown talent. John and Patricia, director and stage manager respec-tively, were a husband and wife team from New York—both were very seasoned hands at this demanding format.

Louis, the technical director, was also a resourceful guy from the East Coast. One play required the sound of a teapot whistling, and as I passed by one day, he stopped me with, "Hey, Bruce, can you whistle?"

"Heck yes," I said.

"Good, come over here. You're gonna be a tea kettle."

The final effect was a little on the cheesy side, but that's the way things were done in the fast and loose world of summer stock.

The assistant technical director, Bill, was from Traverse City. I thought Bill was pretty darned cool, because he did voice-overs for local radio commercials. He drove a hand-me-down Mercedes, complete with a "car phone." In reality, it was a regular phone that would "ring" from vibration when Bill's car got up to forty-three miles-per-hour.

"Works great on first dates," Bill proclaimed.

I wondered how many of his first dates were also his last.

WORKING STIFFS

Look up the term "apprentice" in the dictionary, and you will see it defined as "schlub, whipping boy, and/or low man on the totem pole."

We got an early whiff of the way things *really* were behind-the-scenes—the first three days were spent folding 16,000 promotional flyers. My job was pasting a sticker of Doug McClure over George Maharas's face. Apparently, ol' George had to cancel at the last minute and we paid the price.

Once that mind-numbing chore was done, we set up the theater. By this, I mean the *entire theater*—bleachers, stage, lighting grid—everything. It was theater-in-the-round, so the stage was situated in the middle of a circular seating arrangement. Therefore, each play had to be presented in an almost invisible format and it demanded a unique approach to lighting, set design and blocking for the actors.

It was my first taste of a twenty-hour day. I'll let a diary entry sum up the feeling:

FRIDAY—JUNE 18TH—'76

IT'S LATE FOLKS, SO THE MESSAGE WILL BE BRIEF, I THINK. WE WORKED OUR BUNZOLAS OFF AGAIN TODAY—HAULING WOOD, PLATFORMS, AND JUST GOOD OLD JUNK TO OUR STORAGE AREA SO WE CAN HAVE A CLEAR REHEARSAL HALL FOR THE STARS—BIG DEAL! I AM GETTING PROGRESSIVELY ANGRIER AT THESE "HOB NOBS" WHEN I THINK OF ALL THE WORK WE DO FOR THEM—FOR NO PAY—EXPERIENCE IS WHAT WE GET AND BROTHER—THAT WE ARE! WELL, I SUPPOSE IF I EVER BECOME A HOB NOB, THEN I CAN LOOK AT THE WORK DONE FOR ME AND REALLY APPRECIATE IT—I SHALL, I HOPE. IF I DON'T, I WILL BE TOO "HOB NOBBISH" TO CARE, I GUESS—LET'S HOPE NOT. BRUCE...

I guess my Midwest roots were starting to show.

Eventually, a number of the apprentices banded together and rented a generic condo outside of town. It became our groovy commune and I had an executive suite in the basement.

Aside from getting wet behind the ears in the real world of make-believe, it was also a very personal coming-of-age. I turned eighteen that summer and took immediate advantage of the then-current Michigan drinking law—piña coladas were the order of the day. However, since I was also working for free, this self-financed summer resulted in gallon-sized, strawberry-scented shampoo and daily doses of Egg McMuffins.

The schedule required us to mount an entirely new play, from rehearsals to performance, each week for the next seven weeks. When the first play was ready or, even if it wasn't, it would run for a week while the next play began rehearsals.

Summer stock, I realized, is where *Prime-Challenged* thespians spend their twilight years parading in front of retirees every week. Our star-studded lineup was Doug McClure, Vicki Lawrence, Pat Paulsen, Abe Vigoda, Tom Smothers, Allen Ludden and Sally Ann Howes.

Apprentices didn't always have contact with the actors, something I was desperate to do, because it was dependent on your assignment. Thankfully, we rotated every week, and by the summer's end, I had more than my share of interaction.

As a stage crew member for *A Thousand Clowns,* I witnessed an acting technique that was new to me. The lead actor, Doug McClure, scanned the crew during a rehearsal.

"Anybody have a pen?" he asked, matter-of-factly.

"Heck yeah!" I volunteered, and raced to the stage with it.

I watched, slack-jawed as my favorite cowboy actor scribbled his lines across the entire set—on props, furniture—anything. Apparently, Doug used these catch-phrases to jog his memory to the next batch of dialogue. The amazing thing was how seamlessly he used these written reminders during performances.

At the time, I was shocked at what I considered to be a lack of professionalism. Ironically, years later on the set of the TV show *Homicide,* I found myself in the very same predicament. Legal restrictions forced the writers to change the names of characters and locations constantly (so as not to offend any similarly named entity) and I was handed a

In jail on Homicide: *"Anybody have a pen?"*

new name for a bank just before filming a scene. I knew right away that it wasn't going to stick in my head, no matter what association tricks I tried. So, with a nod to Doug, I wrote the name of the bank on a napkin and glanced at it as needed.

The great Karma wheel turned the following week, and I was rewarded with a key position—that of dresser. This may seem unremarkable, but a dresser interacts more closely with an actor than any other job in theater. For me, that's what it was all about—to find out what made these famous people tick.

The show was *Play it Again, Sam,* and the star was Tom Smothers. For such a wacky guy in public, he was amazingly shy and reserved in person—another myth shattered.

Play it again, Tom.

Our intimate relationship was sealed that first weekend of rehearsals at the local laundromat. There I was, washing the underwear of a famous man I barely knew.

I began to understand, in retrospect, why some celebrities demand that assistants sign nondisclosure agreements during their employ. Think of the damning information that could otherwise be leaked to inquiring minds: *So-and-so wears little purple Speedos, so-and-so's T-shirts have armpit stains, so-and-so has really smelly socks!*

As Tom and I became more comfortable with one another, I gathered the courage to invite him to a Super-8 marathon at our condo. Scott, Sam, and Matt Taylor were in town and we were all eager to show our stuff to a "professional." To my amazement, he agreed. What was an eighteen-year-old punk to think as this man spent the night with us, laughing his famous ass off at our films?—my diary answers that:

> IT WAS BY FAR THE—I REPEAT THE MOST AMAZING, ELATING, AND STIMULATING EVENING I HAVE EVER SPENT IN MY ENTIRE LIFE . . .

As an asterisk to that story, this kind man later sent us five hundred dollars toward furthering our Super-8 career.

The occasional role would crop up in the main theater that could be filled by a younger person and the apprentices provided the talent pool. For some unknown reason, my audition for a speaking role had to be in the form of a song. I couldn't hit a note if there were a gun to my head, but I had already learned the words to the hopelessly daffy, *Love.* Chris Lemmon, classically trained in piano, provided the accompaniment. What I wouldn't pay for a video of that performance.

The audition ultimately led to a speaking role in Neil Simon's *The Sunshine Boys.* I was the voice of a TV director and threw my lines from a side booth. Not quite on stage, but it was fine by me because, technically, it was my first "professional" job.

Lunch was often spent at the local diner, Stacy's. The food wasn't so remarkable, but the style of management was. As I sat eating a gravy-drowned turkey sandwich, I couldn't help but notice local businessmen lined up at the cash register—they weren't waiting to be cashed out, they were *doing it themselves.* I asked the waitress what that was all about. Very casually, she explained that at Stacy's, you cash yourself out.

"Come on up after you eat, sweetie, and I'll show you how."

The lease on our condo ended before the season did, so the last week of work I resided in what could only be called a flophouse. One night, while watching *The Sand Pebbles* in the lobby of the "hotel," I was asked to vacate my seat—they had rented out the couch to an elderly transient and he was ready for bed.

This period in my life was an intense mixture of fantasy and hyper reality—sort of a jump-start to adulthood. In a footnote to all of this, I ran into several of the "stars" years later.

Tom Smothers was waiting for a car at the Detroit airport.

<u>Bruce:</u> Howdy, Tom! Bruce Campbell. Hey, you remember that summer of 1976?

<u>Tom:</u> Uh, no, not really.

<u>Bruce:</u> In Traverse City . . . I was your dresser and we showed you those wacky films of ours?

Tom's blank look told the whole story. Clearly, his gig in Traverse City was one of many that year.

Doug, the Western star, had the same nonreaction when I collared him after a screening in Hollywood. The summer may not have been a memorable one for them, but it certainly was for me.

"College Schmollege"
Six Months in Limbo

7

The person who dragged himself to college that fall was a changed man.

Three months in a dark theater left me pale, rail-thin and *convinced* that this was the life for me, and this damnable "college" thing seemed like a traffic jam on my road to the big "H."

I was so busy over the summer that I wasn't able to register for college classes at Western Michigan University. In a panic, I begged my cousin Nancy to do it for me since she already lived in the college town of Kalamazoo.

"Just sign me up for a bunch of theater stuff," I told her over the phone from Traverse City. I ended up with four classes—all but one related to the theater.

My dorm was Draper Hall. Some clever frat boy had removed a few key letters from the building and it became Raper Hal. As a starving, ex-apprentice struggling to get back to his fighting weight, this was the right place to be—though not known for its selection of stunning coeds, Hal boasted the best food on campus.

The Hall of Shame.

The dorm also housed a fine array of quirky collegiates. Richard, a dope-smoking guru, would wander daily into our four-man room at the end of the hall, plunk down on a vinyl chair and expound on the mysteries of life—the most mysterious of all being how he managed to stay in college.

My six-month alma mater.

Every college kid is required to endure an insane roommate. I was no exception. My roommate, Brian, had suffered a traumatic motorcycle accident a few years earlier. I made the mistake of asking him why he limped slightly, and he explained in lurid detail.

"One afternoon, I was pulling my bike out of the driveway. The sun was low, so I couldn't see if a car was coming or not—that's when I got hit head-on."

Brian was quick to produce grisly Polaroids of his motorcycle and point to the large dents in the gas tank, courtesy of his knees. One of his all-time favorite things was to lay the hand of an unsuspecting hall mate on his knee and demonstrate the nonaction of his shredded cartilage.

This life-altering incident left Brian in a fragile state—he would defiantly skip tests, opting to drown his sorrows in pints of low-grade bourbon. At night, he would sooth his tortured soul to sleep with a stack of Barbra Streisand records. He used headphones, but my lower bunk was close to the record stylus and a tinny "The Way We Were" haunted me for six months.

It's safe to say that Brian got on my nerves.

One night, after I challenged how bad he really had it, Brian insisted on wrestling. This was not the same as those playfully adolescent, big brother/little brother matches, this was worthy of a Cage Match. Brian was so serious that when he got the advantage, late in the fight, he groped for the location of my kidneys—presumably so he could focus his punches there. In utter terror, I managed to elude this, along with his attempt to belt my hands behind my back and inflict God-knows-what on my person.

Brian turned out to be his own worst enemy and eventually fell off the face of the earth when year-end finals rolled around. If you ever come across a guy offering to show you dubious Polaroids of a 1974 Honda 350—*run.*

My college sexual experience consisted of turning down an advance from a male theater classmate. His words, "I just don't want to be alone" resonated with me, but not enough to experiment with sexual orientation—I was far too bent on unraveling the female gender.

College wound up being a blip on the radar screen—six months to be exact. As thankful as I was to Cousin Nancy for enrolling me, I found college to be a step backward. I had tasted the real enchilada and felt betrayed by preliminary theater classes—I knew the difference between "up-stage" and "down-stage" and couldn't see how "trust" exercises were going to help me in the real world. After semester finals were done, I called it quits.

LOW MAN ON A GREASED TOTEM   8

Near the end of my college career, I got whiff of a guy who made commercials in Detroit. As an ad executive, my dad worked with this fellow, Verne, on several occasions and spoke highly of his creativity.

In Verne's youth, he had served as a "gofer" (go-fer *this* Verne, go-fer *that*) for Hollywood director, George Stevens—fortunately for me, he was eager to take a young filmmaker under his wing. Thus began the real-world tutelage that I craved, so Friday afternoons, I'd head home from Kalamazoo via Greyhound bus.

Our driver, Roy, nicknamed "Mr. Excitement," was famous for his interminable monologues over the loudspeaker—he loved to rattle off the list of stops and reprimand dope smokers in the back of the bus, but his shining moment came when our bus hit a deer. We didn't just bump it, or wing it—we *destroyed* it. I was sitting above a wheel well and shuddered as I felt what was left of Bambie flap underneath.

"Now, you folks saw that I couldn't avoid it," Roy explained. "I can't endanger the lives of my passengers for a deer. Michigan's got plenty of them—that's why they extended the hunting season this year. As a matter-of-fact, my brother-in-law and I went out last weekend . . ."

"Good God, make him stop," I begged the stranger next to me.

The following Sunday morning, I'd find myself at Verne's house learning the basics of filmmaking—often with Sam Raimi, Scott Spiegel or Mike Ditz in tow. We started by showing Verne our Super-8 films. He enjoyed them very much, but still offered tips on how to keep action flowing from shot to shot (otherwise known as screen direction), as well as editing and camera techniques. This went on for many weekends and I consider it to be the most valuable "schooling" I've ever had.

As soon as college and I parted ways, I put the word out to Verne about my official availability—within a month I was holding up cue cards for Ronald Reagan's daughter, Maureen, on a national Chevrolet commercial. My diary will explain:

> I RAN CUE CARDS AND CHAUFFEURED THE ACTORS AROUND. A GREAT DAY—12 HOURS LONG, BUT AS I LOOK BACK, IT SEEMED ONLY LIKE ONE. THEN, THE AMAZING PART, I WAS TO WALK AWAY WITH $75.00 FOR THE TWO DAY SHOOT! I WENT NUTS AND PROFUSELY THANKED VERNE AND HIS PARTNER KAREN...

What can I say? I was young . . .

A production assistant had the privilege of being the ultimate fly-on-the-wall—I was everywhere, virtually invisible, yet had no official job description. When not getting Dunkin' Donuts and coffee for the crew, or dropping exposed film off at the laboratory, I could be driving Verne's kids to the dentist.

Aside from the indignities, it was a wonderful opportunity to see just how fake advertising was—we tweaked, manipulated and fudged the look and performance of lawn sprinklers, fertilizer, motorcycles, appliances, pizzas and even Cyalume Light Sticks.

Verne was doing well in the commercial business, but his heart wasn't in it—his dream was to put together legitimate film and television projects so he didn't have to do commercials anymore. The idea behind it all was sincere, and Verne's sights were set on a musical fantasy called *The Magic Balloon,* a bittersweet tale of a child's trip to a zoo.

Funding for this production was hardly in place when we began, but Verne, the consummate salesman, managed to get equipment, personnel and post-production support for virtually nothing. I was upgraded to some form of assistant director, but the bulk of my inflated salary was deferred.

Shooting progressed well, until the day came to film the actual balloon ride. Hoping to cheat the effect, Verne tied this volatile thing to the back of a pickup truck and expected his actors to jump in.

The lead actress would have none of this. She locked herself in her car and refused to come out, so Verne did what any committed director would do—he dressed his partner, Karen, in the actress' costume and put her in the balloon.

Little did Verne know, he was about to get the footage of a lifetime—a gust of wind caught the balloon on the upswing and the guide rope snapped like thread, sending the balloon toward the heavens. Fortunately, the pilot was aboard and he went into action—his first job being to keep the lead actor from leaping to his death. Once that crisis was averted, he hit the gas, hoping to get above the low treeline, but he miscalculated and the entire balloon went crashing through the trees.

The entire time, Verne bellowed to Steve, his cameraman, "Keep shooting! Keep shooting!"

Rushing to the scene, we found the balloon's inhabitants ruffled, but unhurt—and about a hundred feet from the lion's den.

The Magic Balloon led to the demise of Verne's company and subsequently to my unemployment, but this professional experience was a crucial dose of reality. I learned that actors were but the tip of the production iceberg and that the world most certainly did not revolve around them, as much as they liked to think so. Most importantly, I got to learn the nuts and bolts of film production and it stoked the fires of my ambition.

DRIVING MISS CRAZY 9

Ever since the film *Taxi Driver* came out, a lingering romantic image of the lone driver stuck in my mind. Obviously I wasn't alone. In all, five of the boys took up the call and "hacked" to make ends meet during this post-college, *what are we gonna do with our lives?* transitional period.

Josh Becker, Mike Ditz, John Cameron and I all took up the wheel under the auspices of the Southfield Cab Company. Rob Tapert enjoyed a very brief stint with Detroit Cab—an entire day. Scott Spiegel and Sam Raimi held more reasonable jobs during this time, those of stock boy and busboy respectively.

The rest of us worked the night shift from about 5:00 P.M. to 5:00 A.M. The great thing about this type of truly "odd" job was the fact that if you couldn't show up for work, they really didn't give a rat's ass—they'd simply fill the cab with another warm body.

Mike Ditz, John Cameron and I seemed to vacillate between #11, #98 and #99, all owned by the Beezaks, the cab company honchos. Thankfully, I usually managed to avoid #98 and its dreaded carbon monoxide leak—in order to live through the night, you had to drive with the windows rolled down.

Josh was the odd man out, driving #33—a Wyler cab. Ben Wyler was the dirtiest man I had ever seen. He was a human version of the *Peanuts* cartoon character, Pig Pen. It wasn't necessarily a hygiene problem with Ben—it was just that he did all of the maintenance on his cars.

In this freakshow job, I wasn't sure who was the stranger group—passengers or drivers. Flip was a Vietnam vet who dated a stripper. Lee lived at the Blue Bird Motel not far away. The only reason he drove was to support a serious racing habit. You haven't lived until you've seen a fifty-

59

year-old man, failing to secure yet another loan, break down in the office and bemoan his misbegotten life.

Mary was the three hundred-pound queen bee dispatcher with a heart of stone. If she liked you, IBM, the new dream client, was yours for the taking. If you pissed her off, you'd be picking up ice cream, cigarettes and Diet Pepsi for her at all hours of the night.

A regular client of mine claimed to work for the Carter administration in a "top-secret" capacity. Many a night, I'd take this anonymous man from his favorite watering hole to a street corner and drop him off. I was never allowed to take him all the way home because that was "strictly need-to-know."

Cab drivers, I learned, are invisible. Extremely personal conversations played out in the backseat, all within earshot of the nonentity behind the wheel. I particularly enjoyed listening in on the drunken ramblings of a man desperately trying to lure a woman into an affair. He was well on his way, since our destination was a motel. I was so naïve I was actually shocked to learn the true nature of those seemingly benign motels I had passed on Woodward Avenue all the years prior.

Cab drivers are also surrogate priests—taking confessions from businessmen who have sinned against their wives. One fellow felt obliged to overly rationalize an affair that I wasn't even witness to.

"Look, I'm gonna tell my wife eventually," he reasoned. "Just not today . . . "

One of my "clients."

Cab drivers are easy targets as well, because it's assumed that we are morons—why else would we be driving a cab? As a result, I declined many in-kind services of prostitutes headed home after a long night of tricks.

<u>Hooker:</u> Can I eat my fare, baby?

<u>Bruce:</u> Sorry, ma'am, I've gotta buy my own gasoline and, well, you know how prices are these days.

Other nights, when the woman was attractive, it wasn't as easy to decline. A beautiful hooker stepped out of my cab in front of her modest Detroit home.

<u>Hooker:</u> Want to come inside?

<u>Bruce:</u> Well, gee, I . . .

<u>Hooker:</u> We'd just call it even, how's that? That's a good deal, honey.

Twenty-three dollars for the time of my life seemed like an *incredible* deal, but my bank account was low enough to decline.

Sometimes, cab drivers are targets of a more insidious nature. John's cab karma wasn't good—on one occasion, his cab was egged, then stoned.

Later, he was held up at gunpoint just outside the city of Detroit. Our cabs didn't have what we referred to as "ghetto glass" between ourselves and the passengers. Fortunately for John, he wasn't injured—just scared to death, and he quit that night.

My tour of duty in the metropolitan Detroit area lasted about a year. At this point, I was three years out of high school and a college dropout. As a cab-driving actor, I was a cliché on wheels. It was time to get on with things.

THE HUMBLE BEGINNING OF THE HUMBLE BEGINNING 10

Cut to January 1979.

I had a low-rent apartment in Royal Oak, Michigan. Rob and Sam were in East Lansing, attending Michigan State University where Sam was studying literature and Rob was finishing up an economics degree.

Rob had become very involved in *The Happy Valley Kid,* since he played the lead role, and was equally fascinated with the *It's Murder!* debacle. Sam brought the film up to MSU to finish it during school and he enlisted Rob to help—to the extent that he was soon missing final exams.

This experience opened up an entirely new world for Rob, something infinitely more interesting than economics, so he proposed that Sam do a feature film next. Initially, Sam didn't share his enthusiasm.

Sam: I didn't tell Rob what was really going through my mind. We had talked about this for years, but we never could get together to really do it. We had all those conversations in your apartment about how to do it.

Bruce: Yeah, no kidding.

Sam: So, I figured I wouldn't even tell the poor bastard. I won't dampen his spirits. I'll just let him figure out for himself that it's impossible. So I played along, you know what I mean? Okay I'll ride this boat as long as I can take it, but I really didn't think we

Life on the other side of the tracks.

63

Rob Tapert: Optimist.

were going to get the money together for this, but I've never been one to say no.

Preliminary phone calls between the three of us centered on the inevitable question: *Can we make a real film for the real world?* None of us had the answer, but we had nothing to lose either. *I could always move back home,* I reasoned.

For Rob and Sam, it made just as much sense. Rob was in the process of a changing his economics major to fisheries and wildlife, so his future wasn't exactly written in stone. Sam was doing the college thing to avoid what seemed inevitable.

"I wanted to be a filmmaker," Sam admitted, "but I thought that it wasn't going to be possible. I just thought I would run from reality as long as possible until they dragged me back to my dad's store."

The other "boys" were wrapped up in other interests and obligations at this time, so it wound up being the three of us against the world.

With the "can we?" question answered rather swiftly and painlessly, we had to focus on the next ones: *Where, what kind* and *how?*

Starting with *where,* we couldn't answer that one without asking a few questions of our own. Should we move out to Hollywood? Do we *need* to? In retrospect, that issue never really needed much discussion—you were simply a traitor if you ever abandoned Michigan.

In reality, I think the prospects of moving across the country were just too daunting. Josh Becker was out in Hollywood already and was feeding us monthly tales of woe. Hell, the poor bastard came down with a case of— and I'm not kidding—*scurvy,* because he survived on a diet of macaroni and cheese while trying to get a film made.

THE MIDWEST IS THE THING   11

So, we decided to root ourselves in the Great Lakes State. We would conquer Hollywood by having nothing to do with it.

The next lingering question was, *What type of film should we make?* That was harder to confront than the decision to do a feature. Our film library at that point consisted almost exclusively of sappy comedies. For some reason, the idea of doing a feature-length yuck fest just didn't compute. The comedies of 1979, *Manhattan* and *1941,* among others, were headlined by well-known comedians or directed by the likes of Woody Allen and Steven Spielberg. Our goofy films, with titles like *Booby Bartenders, Shemp Eats the Moon* and *The Great Bogus Monkey Pignut Swindle,* didn't seem to measure up.

But something that happened during the screenings of the murder mystery flop, *It's Murder!,* made us take note. A suspense scene called for what we later would term a "scare." This played out when a heinous criminal leapt upon an unsuspecting victim from the backseat of a car. Screenings of the film were always met with a lackluster response, but that scene always delivered—people never failed to jump out of their seats.

"It worked great," Sam noted. "When we showed it, that was the one part, the *only* part of *It's Murder!* that really worked well."

Aside from comedy, "scares" were the only other guarantee of provoking a strong reaction from the audience.

This prompted Sam to write a short film called *Clockwork*—a creepy little tale about a woman in a home alone who is tormented, for no good reason, by a demented man. It was nothing new, but the end result was very effective and represented a new direction that our films could take—a turn toward horror.

We decided to do some low-budget, grass roots research into the genre, and one destination seemed requisite—the *drive-in* theater. Even in 1979, this mode of exhibition was a fading cultural phenomenon. The first-run family films were no longer being shown. Most drive-ins showed either kung fu flicks or horror.

Wading through countless "two films for two dollars," we got the chance to document the behavior of what would become our target audience. If the pace of, say, *Massacre at Central High* dragged, the horns of cars all around us would honk in unified disapproval. If *Revenge of the Cheerleaders* had cheesy effects (which it did), headlights came on and the screen would be washed out for several punishing minutes. The message was loud and clear—keep the pace fast and furious, and once the horror starts, never let up. "The *gore* the merrier" became our prime directive.

The other thing that stood out among all of these lame-ass films was the fact that very few, if any, boasted the requisite "name" actors, fancy clothes or exotic locations associated with other genres. Aside from ample amounts of blood, they didn't even require that many special effects. For three guys who never managed to come up with more than $2,000 for a film, this was really encouraging news.

Scott Spiegel terrorizing Cheryl Guttridge in Clockwork.

With three questions down, all really theoretical, the last one was a quandary: *How would we make it?* What proof did we have to show that we could pull it off? *Clockwork,* for all of its effectiveness, was really just a test.

That's when the idea of filming a "prototype" sprung to mind. By doing so, we could prove not only to ourselves, but to our potential investors, that it was possible.

We decided to make *Within the Woods.*

At MSU that year, Sam had been studying H. P. Lovecraft in his literary classes and the *Necronomicon,* or "Book of the Dead," caught his fancy.

<u>Sam:</u> I read a short story in a class, yeah.

<u>Bruce:</u> Called?

<u>Sam:</u> I can't remember what it was called. It was just a writing exercise.

<u>Bruce:</u> Was it about the "Necronomicon"?

<u>Sam:</u> No. It was just about being alone in a cabin—a scary short story about being alone in a cabin. And at the same time I had a class in ancient history where we studied the "Necronomicon."

<u>Bruce:</u> So it was a combination of creative writing and ancient history.

From these rough concepts, he concocted a short story where a group of kids unwittingly dig up an ancient Indian burial ground and unleash some nasty spirits.

THE "PROTOTYPE" 12

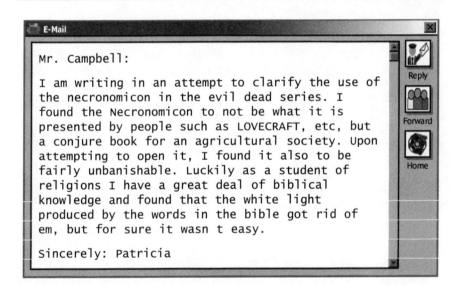

E-Mail ✕

Mr. Campbell:

I am writing in an attempt to clarify the use of
the necronomicon in the evil dead series. I
found the Necronomicon to not be what it is
presented by people such as LOVECRAFT, etc, but
a conjure book for an agricultural society. Upon
attempting to open it, I found it also to be
fairly unbanishable. Luckily as a student of
religions I have a great deal of biblical
knowledge and found that the white light
produced by the words in the bible got rid of
em, but for sure it wasn t easy.

Sincerely: Patricia

Reply

Forward

Home

By this point, staging a Super-8 film was old hat. We mustered a cast of regular characters in the spring of 1979 and headed to the Tapert family farmhouse outside of Marshall, Michigan.

One of the many constants in horror films of that day was that the lead *had* to be a woman and she *had* to be terrorized. Ellen Sandweiss was the natural choice as the starlet/female victim. Ellen had been in numerous Super-8s and expressed a sincere desire to be an actress. I was cast as her innocuous boyfriend who would later become possessed and stalk the others relentlessly.

Scott Spiegel, who demonstrated a gory flair in *Clockwork* as the psycho, was cast as the obnoxious boyfriend of Mary Valenti—daughter of a friend of the Tapert family who also had stars in her eyes.

The film, pieced together over a very hot three-day weekend, would serve as the first hint that films weren't always gonna be as easy as chuckin' pies around in our spare time.

To pull this $1,600 film off, we needed special makeup effects. Up until this time all of our makeup needs were met by a trip to the local costume shop, Van Beau's. This outfit, with astonishingly rude attendants, specialized in Halloween costumes, but also stocked your basic moustaches, spirit gum and derma wax. Between that and liquid shoe polish (which we got at the local drugstore) we had everything we ever needed to age, change identity or die.

Tom Sullivan's handiwork.

But this time, we had to go a little further. Sam's story called for knives into necks and abdomens, mutilated body parts and possessed people. To do this, Rob and Sam enlisted the help of artist-turned-makeup man, Tom Sullivan.

<u>Sam:</u> Tom saw the ad for *The Happy Valley Kid* at MSU. He wanted to see who these student filmmakers were, but hesitated because he saw the name Raimi and he thought it was Iranian. This was when the United States was on very bad terms with Iran.

<u>Bruce:</u> Is that really what he thought?

<u>Sam:</u> Yeah.

<u>Bruce:</u> That's horrible.

<u>Sam:</u> I said, "I'm not Iranian, I'm American," so he goes, "I'm a filmmaker, too, and I do art work and makeup." So, Rob and I went over to his apartment to see his effects.

The shoot began innocently enough, but it soon proved to be much slower than the other Super-8 films. There were new factors, like attempting to do realistic dialogue, special effects and a stepped-up visual design from Sam. Where horror films allowed for simplicity with regard to setting, cast, etc., they more than made up for it in their demand for heightened visuals.

The weekend dragged on, sometimes grinding to a halt while we attempted to attach an "I've-been-stabbed-in-the-chest" rig to Scott's indescribably furry chest. Tom had provided the half-knife prop, but it still had to be secured, wiggle free, to the actor. That's when one of the great staples of Super-8 films came in handy—duct tape. This hard-to-tear, all-purpose tape had been used to secure everything from lights on ceilings to cameras on car fenders—it most certainly would suffice to keep a blade plastered to Scott's torso.

The scene you really want to replay, though, is two or three of us huddled around Scott, attempting to get the horrid tape off without exfoliating him more than necessary. Scott decided that only he really knew his own threshold for pain, and yanked the sticky substance off. The end results were far too horrifying to put in any film.

Another Super-8 standby was brought up to Marshall courtesy of Scott's employment at the Walnut Lake Market: canned cherry cobbler. This provided a perfectly thick, pulpy substance for Mary Valenti to vomit out upon being stabbed in the neck. *Titanic* can have all of its fancy computer graphics, I'll take a good off-brand pie filling any day.

This shoot also required my first full-on monster makeup. During the course of the film, my character is found horribly mauled in the woods and later I appear as a possessed creature. Without the luxury of an extended shoot, our scheduling demanded for shooting horror at night and horror in the morning—roughly translated, it meant that Bruce slept in his makeup. I was still on the waning edge of that "perceived indestructibility" teenagers are blessed

A happy scene from Within the Woods.

with, so I didn't think much about it . . . at the time. . . .

When the shoot was over, however, I realized that my skin had undergone a disturbing change—of the DNA variety. Where the latex makeup had been applied, fascinating patterns began to emerge. Coincidentally, they were shaped exactly like my latex appliances. These rashlike apparitions remained with me for months—a lingering reminder of blatant stupidity. I also found out, after the fact, that the stuff I was almost always drooling as a monster was actually black latex paint. Hell, who needs a functioning intestinal system, we had great-looking bile!

Within the Woods, as well as serving as a prototype, allowed us to experiment more extensively with the concept of "fakery." It was the first time, in the interests of getting the most out of our schedule, that we blacked out windows to provide the false illusion of night. It also was one of the few times that we actually filmed outdoors at night . . . *all night.*

Despite the newfound hardships, the film came together very well. It was our first collective effort to actively pursue a genre and it worked. Sam had clearly made strides as a filmmaker, and I began to get a basic grip on this elusive, *acting* thing. Well, okay, it wasn't acting, per se, but I had taken a baby step beyond the "mugging for the camera" phase. . . .

Once assembled, we did our own brand of test marketing to see if *Within the Woods* would get a response from regular civilians. What could be a better proving ground than our old high school? A screening was arranged and the feedback was good . . . and *loud.* Hell, this film got a better response than *Six Months to Live.*

We weren't experienced filmmakers by any means yet, but this audible feedback was all the encouragement we needed to take the next leap.

THERE'S NO BUDGET LIKE LOW-BUDGET   13

We had a useful prototype, but what was the next step? The *how* question still fluttered about. With Michigan, you had to plan months ahead, just to factor in the weather. Summer 1979 became the target for shooting, but we had to get our act in gear—May flowers were already in full bloom.

Before we attempted to raise any money, we had to figure out how much was needed. For the first time, we had to determine, in advance, what our film might cost. This was an entirely foreign concept to us, since we had always casually pooled our loose cash and shot whenever we could and with whomever was available. A "professional" endeavor like this would call for renting equipment that wasn't ours, using a real film laboratory and, yikes, even *paying* people.

In my year as a production assistant not long before this, I had become reasonably familiar with a number of motion picture suppliers in Detroit who catered to commercial producers. Technically, we were just doing a long commercial, so we gathered price lists and began to jot some numbers down.

Long before the days of budgeting software, we started with a blank sheet of paper. Not knowing any other method, we proceeded to make the film in our heads, reviewing every phase of production.

"Okay, we gotta rent equipment . . . *what* equipment? For how long?"

"What do you pay production assistants? Should we pay them at all?"

There were the odd "how to make an independent film" guides available, so we got our hands on whatever we could at the local bookstore. Our little hand-hewn budget began to grow . . . and grow. Eventually, it reached an inconceivable $150,000. For all we knew about raising money, it might as well have been a million.

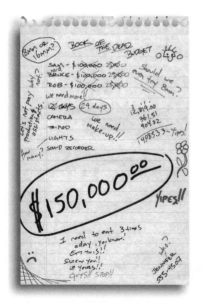

The budget grows . . .

Being so immersed in the Super-8 format, we convinced ourselves that we could save lots of money if we shot our feature in that same format and blew it up (enlarged it) later to the industry standard of 35mm. Was this an insane idea? We had never seen a film in a theater that had originally been made in Super-8, but there was always a first time. . . .

A company in San Francisco (Inter-format Labs) could fill the obscure request. The fellow in charge, Mike Hinton, sent us a test of a film that was shot in Caracas Venezuela on Super-8mm and blown up by them to 35mm. When the test arrived, we marched down to our local Maple 3 theaters in Birmingham and screened it.

The print looked okay, but *just* okay. We asked the projectionist what he thought about the quality of the film. He assumed it was a blowup from 16mm, a fairly standard process. This was very encouraging to us, but we proceeded to test it for ourselves—this turned out to be good idea.

What resulted was *Terror at LuLu's*—as in LuLu's Lingerie. Sam's mother had recently opened a string of these shops and it seemed like the perfect place to stage a *Clockwork*-like film.

We cast another aspiring actress, Liz Dennison, as an unsuspecting woman working late at night who is terrorized by a mysterious man/thing. This wasn't so much a story as a technical test, and it only took one night to put this small sequence together. We merely wanted to assemble enough shots—light, dark and in between, to satisfy our curiosities of how each exposure would hold up in a blowup process.

On the advice of the San Francisco lab, we used a Boleau, the very best Super-8 camera we could find with a very specific film stock. We rented professional lights, for the first time, and used professional cameraman, Steve Mandell, to shoot the thing. In short, we did everything we could to make it work.

The results, once back from the lab in San Francisco, were nothing short of disastrous. Screening it again at the same local theater we stared, slack-jawed, at an image that was obscured by enormous globs of grain—it looked like the action was taking place in a hailstorm.

This was a real blow—our budget, meager as it was, didn't seem to support the jump to a more expensive format. On a hot, depressing day in June, the three of us sat on Rob's screened-in porch trying to make the decision to go forward or stop dead in our tracks. We reasoned that a number of the then-classic low-budget horror flicks had been shot in

16mm. By making the leap to that millimeter we were, in reality, merely making it all the more possible to pull off.

We decided, after some wailing and gnashing, to blast ahead in the new format.

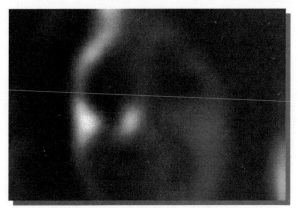

A frame from the disastrous blow-up.

THREE SCHMOES IN SEARCH OF A CLUE   14

We reasoned that another impediment to raising money was credibility. Three guys with no professional experience, questionable education, and a dream to make a film in Detroit wouldn't exactly make the average investor dive into his pocketbook.

We had to shake the "flaky" image of filmmakers and conquer the Midwest, "kick-the-tires" mentality. If we were going to immerse ourselves in the world of business, we had to *look* like businessmen. Mostly, this meant that we had to dig up, dust off or just plain buy a suit.

Fortunately, a love of "cool old suits" gave me a leg up. I had already accumulated three or four vintage, double-breasted wool outfits. My basic theory had been to haunt Salvation Army stores with a methodical zeal, and soon I knew when and where to look for the good stuff. An annual church bazaar in a nearby wealthy neighborhood produced a great bounty as well—castaways from the Detroit elite. Hell, if it was good enough for the Fords and the Fishers, it was good enough for me.

My usual layout for a primo suit was twenty-five bucks. Dump another $15–20 on top of that for tailoring, and $10 for some two-toned wing-tip shoes, and you've got yourself, on average, a $50 masterpiece. I was stylin' in the Motor City.

We also needed briefcases, so it was off to Montgomery Ward. I opted for the "double wide," while Rob and Sam took the sleek "slim line" models.

Aside from all the trimmings, we needed confirmation that we were for real. Of course, *we* felt qualified, but a second opinion from someone actually in the film business who could bless us from on high seemed like a useful thing.

The only professional person we knew, a family friend of the Taperts, was a film exhibitor at Butterfield theaters in Detroit. We set up an appointment at Andy Grainger's downtown offices.

Walking into his lobby was like stepping into a time warp. His receptionist still used the forties-style plug-and-patch phone system and the walls were adorned in a rich wood paneling. Appropriately, I was wearing one of my aforementioned vintage suits.

Andy's advice was simple: "Fellas, no matter what you do, keep the blood running down the screen." As a tribute to him specifically, there is a scene in the finished film where an old film projector whirs to life and "projects" blood running down the screen.

Most importantly, Mr. Grainger provided the name of a distributor in New York City whom we could approach for possible distribution—Levitt-Pickman films. Their claim to fame had been *Groove Tube,* featuring a very young Chevy Chase.

Rule #1: Dress for success.

Little did we know that a letter of "intent" was all one could really expect without a finished film, but that was good enough for us and we set up an appointment to meet with them. I'm not sure what dream world we lived in, but we were convinced that the only way to get to New York was by train.

Bruce: Wasn't that kind of an absurd concept?

Sam: We didn't have a car that would make it.

Bruce: No.

Sam: "We'll take a train."

Bruce: "We'll take a train to New York City."

Sam: It was affordable. I think the tickets were like forty bucks each.

We arranged to stay at Andrea's apartment. I had met her on a Chevy industrial shoot and we hit it off very well. So well, in fact, that as we prepared for bed in her New York apartment, she came on to me like I'd never experienced before.

Sam: How did she come on to you? Did she just put her arm around you or something?

Bruce: No, she was like, "You're sleeping in my bed and that's going to be that." She was giving me *the look* and even though I didn't know shit about women, I knew something awful was going to happen and I knew I had to get out of there.

Sam: And you left that night.

Bruce: I told her, "I have to drive back tonight 'cause I've got a lot of stuff I have to do."

This remains a great source of amusement to Rob and Sam. My only consolation was that Andrea's cat slept on Sam's face, and by morning, his eyes were swollen shut.

Humiliation aside, we came back to Detroit with a letter of intent to distribute.

"DO YOU VALIDATE?" 15

The next step was to get some notice of our abilities *artistically*. We had a pseudo seal of approval from a "major distribution company in New York City," but there was no outside opinion about our capability as *filmmakers.*

In August of that year, we got whiff of a theater on the east side of Detroit (the Punch and Judy) that ran *Rocky Horror* every weekend and whose management was "open and flexible." We approached them with the idea of showing *Within the Woods* just before *Rocky Horror.* To our shock and delight, they agreed.

The only real battle with this screening was a technical one. A Super-8 projector has limited bulb power, so we had to set the thing up halfway down the aisle of the theater. It became a game of:

"The image is too dim, move it closer."

"Well, if we move it closer, the picture isn't big enough."

Eventually, with the help of a new, $21.10 EFR Halogen 150 watt, 15 volt bulb, we found a happy medium. A trip to Radio Shack provided the hundreds of feet of audio extension cable needed to patch our feeble projector amplifier into the theater sound system. The distance, combined with lousy source material, resulted in a slightly annoying hum, but hey, we were in a legit house.

The "cult" crowd gathered to see *Rocky Horror* seemed to share enough basic interest in real horror to enjoy themselves. To combat the fact that we scored the film with music we didn't own the rights to, we decided to donate the proceeds to the American Cancer Society. A week after the showing, I dropped off all of $11.40 to the Cancer Society—about half of what the new fancy bulb cost.

On a side note, I had a chance to discuss the "cult" thing with *Rocky Horror's* star, Tim Curry, several years later, at the top of the Iruzu volcano between shots of the film, *Congo.* I told him how, indirectly, I was grateful that *Rocky Horror* provided us with such a good springboard. He explained that I wasn't alone. He had gotten a number of thank-you notes from independent theater owners across the country applauding him for being involved in a film that eventually proved to be the difference between success and failure for their theater.

The "net benefit" of that weekend was bamboozling Michael McWilliams, a reviewer from *The Detroit News*, to come and see *Within the Woods.* It was refreshing to know that even in Detroit, people still got excited over "home-grown" stuff.

Several days later, we saw what would become our calling card printed in the *Lively Arts* section of the *Detroit News.* It was the first, best and perhaps most important review we've ever gotten. Nothing felt better than to slap that review on the desk of a potential investor and casually ask, "Read the paper today?"

By MICHAEL McWILLIAMS
News Special Writer

It probably will never be advertised alongside the glossy, big-budget horror movies of our time, but you won't easily forget a locally produced litle film called "Within the Woods."

In just 32 minutes, it provides more chills, thrills and squeamish giggles than such recent professional duds as "Prophesy" and "The Amityville Horor" combined.

"Within the

THE QUEST FOR MOOLAH **16**

Okay, the big ball was rolling. We had a prototype, a budget, a decided millimeter, a bogus letter from a "professional" and our "art" had been validated. Now, we had to get to the heart of the matter: *THE RAW STINKING CASH TO MAKE THE FILM.*

"How *do* we raise money?" we asked ourselves.

Within the Woods cost a whopping $1,600. We needed an amount that was exponentially more. A bank wasn't gonna just fork over $150,000 unsecured. Our friends and family weren't "fat cat" rich.

What to do?

Enter Phil Gillis—the Tapert family lawyer. Phil had helped a younger, wilder Rob get out of trouble a time or two, and he walked us through the steps of forming a business "entity" whereby we could raise the dough.

He recommended a limited partnership because of its simplicity. Simplicity? That's a good one. This Private Placement Memorandum used terms like "Fiduciary Responsibilities" and "Willful Malfeasance"—not exactly common usage for us. Reading the Agreement of Limited Partnership for the first time was like taking a fistful of Melatonin—a one-way ticket to Snoresville.

Phil and his partners were unimpressed with our prototype, letter of intent, or our cool review—it merely represented the *good* news. An offering like this had to be very careful about "hype." Phil suggested that other items would serve us better in the eyes of an investor—things like "financial projections" and a "tax statement."

I've got to tell you, that first meeting with our new CPA, Charlie Bosler, about financial projections was a joke:

Charlie: Well, fellas, how soon do you think you'll recoup?

Bruce: . . . Recoup?

Charlie: Get your money back . . ."

Rob: Uh, well, it's gonna take the better part of six months to make the thing.

Charlie: Better make it a year.

Sam: Yeah, a year, sure—that should be plenty safe.

Charlie: Now, how much money do you think you'll make with the film? What do you project?

Bruce/Sam/Rob: Well . . . that is, I . . .

The reality was and still is that a finished film lives on a 35mm strip of negative—it could be worth nothing more than the stock it's printed on, or it could be the next *Titanic.*

Bruce/Sam/Rob: What the hell? They'll *double* their money in two years.

If we had to live or die by the accuracy of the projection we came up with, I wouldn't be typing right now—I'd be drinking Woolite on a street corner in downtown Detroit. The truth was, we broke even exactly six years later.

Investors, we came to learn, also got really pissy about taxes. *What's the fuss all about?* I wondered. *I didn't even qualify for a bracket.* Folks with something to lose, however, needed a Tax Opinion.

"Hello, my name is Rob Tapert, and I'm calling with an exciting investment opportunity . . . Hello?"

Once these items were in place, we had to scrape together a resumé for the offering—you know, one that showed things like . . . *experience.*

"Let's see . . . I worked as a newspaper delivery boy for a year and earned enough to buy a black-and-white TV set. How's that? I swept studios out for a year and took my boss home when he was drunk . . . that good enough? I was a cab driver for a year—wanna see my chauffeur's license? Oh, *acting* experience? I'm a veteran of *several* community theater productions, and I also starred in at *least* thirty Super-8 films!"

You can almost see the investor's jaw drop. . . .

We slapped the lawyer-approved document together and found, much to our shock and utter horror, that we had exactly thirty days to raise the cash or the offering would expire.

On top of that, because it was a *private* placement, we couldn't advertise in any way whatsoever—no radio ads, no newspapers, no mass mailings . . . *and* there was a limit to how many people you could even *approach*. These strict guidelines were designed to protect the average schmuck investor, but it certainly didn't do us any favors.

As a potential investor, the first thing you were treated to on page one was:

WARNING

The securities offered by this document are highly speculative, will have no market and should be considered only by an investor who has no plans to resell the security, and fully and adequately understands the risks involved and
CAN AFFORD TO LOSE HIS ENTIRE INVESTMENT!

We also had to disclose anything that might go wrong for any reason. These were known as risk factors. We quit listing them after 11—it seemed embarrassing enough. They were as follows: (translation included)

1. *New Venture*: (We haven't done anything yet)
2. *Limited Financial Resources*: (It's a really low budget)
3. *Lack of Distribution Agreements*: (We have no real commitment from anyone)
4. *Reliance on Management*: (Come hell or high water, investors were gonna be stuck with us)
5. *Failure to Engage Certain Key Employees*: (We haven't hired a single person yet)
6. *Liquidity of Investment*: (As an investor, you were in for the long haul. You couldn't sell your share in this venture, even if it smelled like a stinker)
7. *Federal Tax Consequences*: (You can't write off anything)
8. *No Guarantee of Completion*: (If we go over budget, we're screwed)
9. *Lack of Diversification*: (We're only doing one flick and it's a very specific genre)
10. *Production Risk*: (Bad weather, bad planning, bad anything could and *will* shut us down)
11. *Conflict of Interest*: (We can do other stuff at the same time)

Makes you want to whip out the ol' checkbook and fire off ten grand, doesn't it?

Basically, an investor might as well have drilled for oil in the Arctic Wildlife Refuge with his or her bare hands, because it was a total crapshoot.

Combine these factors with the very practical sensibilities of Detroit businessmen, and you've got a Grade A challenge staring you in the face. If we had even a prayer of answering questions from a savvy investor, we had to know this prospectus in and out.

This became shockingly clear after the first few meetings:

Mr. Turner: How much can I write off in the first year?
Bruce: Uh . . . *a fair amount* . . . ?
Mr. Gates: What's my liability?
Sam: You're *liable* to . . . make money?
Mr. Trump: How do you handle "Phantom Income"?
Rob: Very, very carefully . . .

Later, we learned to put an artful "spin" on our answers.

Mr. Buffett: How much can I write off in the first year?
Bruce: That's an excellent question . . . for your tax attorney.
Sultan of Brunei: What's my liability?
Sam: You might want to consult your attorney on that.
Mrs. Gotrocks: How do you handle "Phantom Income"?
Rob: I'll bet your CPA has all kinds of ways . . .

Here I am looking up the definition of the word "amortize."

The unspoken rule of raising money was simple: Start with the people closest to you and branch out from there. My father was investor #1. A brave man, but I think Mom browbeat him into it. From relatives you digress to friends:

"Hey, Stu . . . we had some great times in high school, didn't we? Who would have thought you'd be the king of scrap metal today? Hey, listen, I want to talk to you about something . . ."

From friends, you move on to relatives of friends:

"Try my uncle, he's always doing crazy things like this . . ."

One particular uncle was a dentist. He ran in a pack with a bunch of other dentists and they invested money in numerous ventures, a certain percentage of it "crazy."

You really haven't lived until you've screened an unrated Super-8 film at a dinner party for four dentists and their wives, watching them squirm as a possessed creature (me, in this case) bites his own hand off. The bad news was—we ruined their meals. The good news was—we got some moola.

But, let's not forget the friends of friends:

"Hello, Mr. Stevens, this is Bruce Campbell. I'm a friend of Larry Dorfman who is a friend of a woman who used to babysit for your family. Anyway . . ."

Finally, you're stuck with the *enemies* of friends and you realize that those people turn out to be your relatives, so you go back to them again.

Last on the list, and arriving all too soon, were the cold calls. A shiver ran up my spine as I word-processed this recollection. Just getting past the secretary of a potential investor was an entirely fresh hell.

"Hello, my name is Bruce Campbell and I'd like to speak with Mr. Jennings . . . No, he *won't* know what this is regarding, but I'm sure . . . what's that? This number? Oh, I got it out of the phone book and I . . . hello . . . *hell-oooo*?"

We met an amazing array of people that ran the gamut from honest professionals who were willing to sit through our clumsy pitch, to the "I could write you a check right now for the whole amount" blowhard that deserved a slap in the face.

One sales pitch was conducted during a football game:

"So, guys, if I invest in this thing— AWWW, come *on* Sanders, what are they payin' you all that money for?!"

Trying to put the squeeze on a young dad while his kids played in the backyard was also extremely productive:

"You guys really think you can pull this— Billy! That thing could put your eye out! I'm, sorry, what was the question?"

We once screened *Within the Woods* at our old haunt, Walnut Lake Market, for the owners—in the soap isle. I had mopped it many times while working there after high school and at least knew where the power outlets were.

Merchants turned out to be the toughest sell of all. They were used to getting something very tangible for their money, like a shipment of frozen chickens, so something as ethereal as a film didn't compute.

Walnut Lake Market: An "ideal" screening room.

It was always a special treat to screen our prototype, now badly scratched, in a corporate environment. Sam met a potential investor at the Kmart Photo Processing counter.

<u>Sam:</u> I was bringing in rolls of raw stock to be processed and he was there, I think getting back some of his kid's pictures. He wanted to know why I was developing so many rolls of Super-8 film. I said, "It's for a horror movie—we're making a feature version of it eventually." He said, "Well, gosh, I've got some money, call me if you guys ever need an investor." He gave me his card. I couldn't believe it.

<u>Bruce:</u> The funny thing about that guy was that he never saw the movie.

<u>Sam:</u> Why not?

Bruce: He didn't want to. He said, "This is not my kind of movie. I can't handle this kind of movie—show it to my colleagues." So, we showed it to a group of guys in suits in his fancy boardroom. He invested blindly on the advice of his associates.

The silver lining of this maddening process was the occasional "domino effect," whereby one hard-fought investor led quickly to a multitude of others. One such investor happened to casually mention our film to a buddy of his while golfing.

"Sounds good," his friend said, with a stroke of his pitching wedge. "Count me in."

Gain credibility, grow a beard.

He sent us the investment check sight unseen. To this day, we have only spoken to him on the phone.

Living on the edge of a fading industrial city did have its advantages—Fortune 500 companies were easily within reach. Another investor, heir to the Delta three-way faucet fortune, chipped in and several relatives followed suit without question.

We also got some fairly clinical investments. One investor wasn't a person at all—it was a law firm pension fund. In this case, it was *entity* investing in *entity.*

We also got what would now be called "soft" money. We preferred the term "in kind." Our lawyers agreed to invest their fees into the film. When this wasn't enough, we managed to get hard currency out of them as well.

Another fellow, clearly a man who had earned every dollar the hard way, informed us very casually that his investment was his Vegas gambling money and that he simply would refrain from going out West that year.

Hundreds of screenings later, the summer had passed us by. November was knocking at our door and the prospects of filming in northern Michigan during winter seemed like a *really* bad idea.

At this point, we did have some money in the bank. At $85,000 it was *almost* enough to start shooting. Unfortunately, our anal-retentive legal document stipulated that all funds would be held in a special escrow account until $90,000 was raised—enough to "get it in the can."

Having hit this virtual cash wall, we were left with no other option than to beg. We sent a thinly veiled "plead" letter to the investors, asking to release the funds early.

"There would be no adverse effects at all," we wrote.

None except the fact that this was not nearly enough to make the film and we had no prospects for getting another nickel out of the Motor City. Praise the film gods . . . the investors agreed and we were on our way.

What Else Have I Got to Do for the Next Six Weeks?

17

With a bank account filled with investors' cash, it was time to get the big ball rolling. Phase one: find actors . . . *real* actors.

Casting in Detroit became an interesting process. There were certainly actors, but all the legit folks I had run across as a production assistant were in that damnable Screen Actors Guild. Their "type" was *way* too expensive for our meager budget.

The trick was finding qualified actors who wanted desperately to be in the union, but just hadn't figured out how yet. Theater wasn't huge in this culturally-challenged town, so it took some research.

Our first round of calls led us to agencies like Affiliated Models, the Weist/Barron School of Acting, and the ever-popular Specs/Howard School of Broadcasting. Had we needed a good DJ, this would have been the place—but actors? Not quite . . .

Sam: We took out an ad in *The Detroit News*—a little tiny ad. It probably looked like a porno picture and they were supposed to meet in my basement. The whole thing sounded so seedy.

Bruce: Yeah, I remember a lot of them came with their boyfriends.

Sam: And with good reason with you there.

Getting willing participants was anything but easy. Personally, as an actor, I was flabbergasted. Since when do you have to talk an actor into *anything*?

"C'mon, Betsy, it'll be cool. You'll turn into a monster and we'll cover you in all kinds of horrible makeup. Then, you attack your boyfriend and he, *get this* . . . cuts your head off and your decapitated body writhes all over him . . . sound good?"

Most of our meetings took place in very public places. We met Theresa at the Nugget restaurant. Betsy Baker and fiancé met us at Pasquales, an

Italian joint, where Loretta and her "escort" met us twenty minutes later. On the other hand, Carol and her muscular mate preferred the upscale Bloomfield Charlies.

The Big Boy restaurant chain became the mainstay for future interviews. With bottomless cups of coffee and a killer lemon meringue pie, you couldn't have a better "office."

"Casting again, fellas?" the waitress would inquire. "You know, I've done a commercial or two . . ."

THE CAST

By early October, we held official "scream tests" at Sam's house.

"We had readings and they had two chairs and they pretended they were driving in a car," Sam recalled. "Then we had them scream and shriek."

From the trickle of hopefuls, we culled our actors. They were:

Teresa Seyferth—daughter of the accountant who did our financial projections. Because she was a member of the Screen Actors Guild, and this was a decidedly nonunion shoot, she felt compelled to change her name. She started with Theresa Tilly, then T. Tilly. We urged her to "class it up" a little and concocted the name Sarah York. Either way, it didn't work. The union found out and fined her. She was last heard of in Chicago, working as a DJ.

"Hal-Del-Rich"in monster mode

Betsy Baker—back in the Motor City, she had done some "Industrials" as a spokeswoman and was cast for her girl-next-door demeanor. After *Evil Dead,* she abandoned the acting life entirely and got into the motor home rental business. Hey, made a hell of a lot of sense to me. . . .

Rich Demanincor—with a "What else have I got to do for the next six weeks?" attitude toward the whole thing, Rich dove in. He also had "union" jitters, so Rich adopted the stage name, Hal Delrich. This was the result of combining the first names of his roommates at the time: Hal and Del. Rich also got nabbed by the union and eventually worked his way out of the business. Last seen: driving a truck in rural Michigan.

Ellen Sandweiss—as an old high school pal and former Super-8 starlet, she was a natural for the part. Ellen also phased out of show biz after this film (I'm sensing a pattern here). She is currently living a respectable life as a married mother of two in Michigan.

That guy named Bruce—a "veteran" of those same Super-8 films, but never did anything other than "schtick" acting. The concept of creating and maintaining a "real" character was a totally new concept.

All actors were contracted to make a staggering $100 per week. Fortunately for us, this was well before the age of overtime, forced calls, meal penalties, night premiums and residuals. It wasn't about money. An actor *acted* . . . period.

The first read through at Sam's house was a little on the clumsy side. It was really hard to get a sense of the film, when the dialogue in the climax consisted of:

"Ahhhhh! Grrrr. Noooo!!! Hellllp! I can't feel my legs!"

New Guineas

Had these poor actors read the fine print at the bottom of their contract, they would have seen the disclaimer: "In addition, you will also be the guinea pigs for makeup testing. These heinous products have not been tested on animals, because they will be tested on you . . ."

The actors destined to portray possessed monsters in the film (four out of five), had to be fitted for Scolero contact lenses. These weren't your basic "soft," or "disposable" lenses for "sensitive eyes," these suckers were glass and, covering two-thirds of the eye—*big.* To get the idea, run to your kitchen and shove a Tupperware lid over your eyeball. Because the glass lenses prevented the eye from breathing, they could only be kept in for fifteen minutes at a time. Of course, *getting* them in took a full ten minutes, so this was a pretty neat trick.

As bad as it got during production, I could always nod to myself and chuckle, *At least I don't have to wear those stinkin' lenses.* I nodded a lot over the next twelve weeks.

Because a number of these possessed characters ultimately were dismembered, it was necessary to make plaster molds of various appendages. The make-up techniques we used at the time were not that far

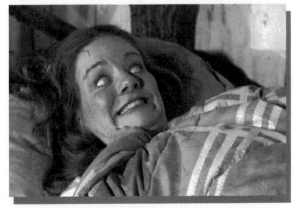

At least I didn't have to wear those stinkin' contact lenses.

off from those used on the original *Frankenstein.* When things called for a plaster mold, we simply poured plaster of paris directly on top of Vaseline-coated skin—who wouldn't?

Now, if you've ever had any experience with this form of plaster, you'd know that it heats up as it sets—not a little . . . a *lot.* Betsy Baker, head coated in this stuff, unable to see, hear or talk, began to jot furiously on a pad of paper:

"Getting very warm . . . how much longer?"

Betsy's scrawls soon became more urgent: "Getting very light-headed . . . must get out *soon*!"

Using implements the Three Stooges would have been proud of, we liberated her from her tomb only to find a full set of eyelashes perfectly preserved in the plaster. Needless to say, we had some explaining to do.

And so the makeup tests plodded along, resulting in raw limbs from excessive heat and unwanted hair removal, and strained eyes from numerous attempts to "wear" Scolero lenses.

It was unquestionably an omen of things to come.

CREW WHO?

Rob, Dart, Sam, Tim and Josh on Swamp Patrol.

The ragtag behind-the-scenes group we conned into this adventure came from all walks of life:

Steve "Dart" Frankel— he was very good with his hands. By way of carpentry, he became our art director. His hammer was affectionately referred to as "Uru." Sam had first met this mythical man at Camp Tamakwa, situated in the Algonquin Park of northern Ontario, Canada. Dart was last seen in the South Island of New Zealand, working as a chiropractor—still using his hands.

David "Goody" Goodman—a longtime Raimi friend, Dave went all the way back.

"One time Sam was really being a pain in the ass. In their backyard they had those prong type fences, so once Ivan (Sam's brother) and I hung him on the fence by his pants and started spitting at him and hitting him and he was stuck on the fence and couldn't do anything. The housekeeper saw what we were doing and came out with a broomstick and started chasing us until we took him down."

During the course of this shoot, Dave will earn the dubious title of "the Filmmaker's Burden." His official job was chef.

Don "I wanna break stuff" Campbell—Brother Don was a yahoo in search of an adventure. With no true interest in filmmaking, this was one of his few experiences on a set. His driving desire to work with us stemmed from the fact that "a lot of stuff was gonna get wrecked." Production assistants made $50 a week, so we couldn't be really picky.

<u>John Mason</u>—sound man. He was an old teacher of mine during a very brief stint at Wayne State University, in Detroit. John quit teaching and left his family behind to work on this film. Go figure . . .

<u>Tim Philo</u>—cameraman. He came from the same university as John Mason and had actually shot the better part of a feature film before. *What the hell,* we thought, *he seemed like a nice guy.*

Foggers: Never leave home without them.

<u>Josh Becker</u>—obviously, Sam and I had already "worked" with him for years. As the shoot intensified and crew members began to drop like flies, Josh, in his own irascible way, became a key player and distinguished himself as one of the few who went the distance.

<u>Rob Tapert</u>—Mr. Producer. In those days, producer meant doing anything that nobody else was doing, or *would* do. This ran the gamut of fogging the background of a shot to pushing the wheelchair dolly.

That's the real beauty of having no budget—the lines of *who does what* get very blurry. During production, when I wasn't acting, I'd toss a coat over my sticky, blood-soaked shirt and haul lights around.

<u>Tom Sullivan</u>—makeup man. Tom was merely expanding what he had learned from our prototype, *Within the Woods.* Aside from baking actor's body parts and subjecting them to noxious substances, he was a nice, quiet guy.

<u>Sam Raimi</u>—writer/director/boy genius. He was technically a teenager when we started the project and had just turned twenty when filming began. This film was his rite of passage. It was always fun to see what shade of gray Sam turned on any given day, depending on how few hours he had slept. I got a perverted comfort in knowing that as hard as he pushed the cast and crew, he always pushed himself just a little bit harder.

Rob, Sam and I were contracted, as executive producers, for $35 a week in expenses, which we never collected. We had never been paid on anything else, why start now? I recall attempting to buy a pack of gum during the shoot and realizing that I simply had no money to pay for it.

PICK A STATE, ANY STATE

We now had the cast and the crew, but where would we shoot the film?

Michigan had never been big on the "let's get Hollywood to film here" thing, so there were no formal agencies to assist in finding a location. We needed a house on a hill, a chasm and winding, rural roads.

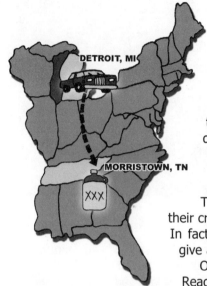

We contacted the Michigan Travel Bureau, but nothing came of it. We even checked out a creepy suburban house we used to pass on our high-school bus, but since it was on the corner of two very busy streets, we decided to keep looking.

Michigan was rapidly becoming out of the question—daily frost and incessant drizzle confirmed that. It was the end of October already, and the only way to avoid assuredly inclement weather was to head south.

The Tennessee Film Commission, much to their credit, made the best case for shooting there. In fact, they were the *only* state that seemed to give a rat's ass.

On November 9, there was no going back. Ready or not (emphasis on *not*) we loaded up several cars and a truck and pointed the convoy south on Interstate 75.

Sam and Rob had scouted a location in the town of Morristown, Tennessee, about forty miles northeast of Knoxville. I'd like to say that it was sleepy or quaint, but it wasn't—it was just a small town in rural America.

We managed to find a fairly large house several miles outside of town where everyone stayed—thirteen people in all. With six bedrooms, it would work if most of us slept in groups.

Josh and Goodman became unlikely bedfellows:

<u>Bruce:</u> Where did you sleep?

<u>Josh:</u> I slept in that back bedroom with Goody. We were in the same bed.

<u>Bruce:</u> Ugh—you shared a bed with Goodman?

<u>Josh:</u> I finally got to the point where he was so aggravating, I pulled the box springs out and I slept on the box springs and let him have the mattress. He was like some horrible monster.

When the crew later ballooned to seventeen, the accommodations became downright collegiate, averaging 2.83 persons per room. With actresses each rating a single room, we had to break out the cots and the living room took on a whole new meaning. Tom Sullivan, the odd man out, claimed the laundry room—more on that later. . . .

DEEP IN THE HEART OF . . .

One day, during our rushed preparations, I had to withdraw a chunk of cash from the local bank. It had the funniest smell.

"This money smells like dirt," I said to the teller.

"Makes sense," she explained. "Folks around here still bury it in their backyard."

We weren't in Detroit anymore.

A cabin that had been secured from the previous scouting mission fell through at the last minute. This led to a mad rush to find a new location.

Enter Gary "Here's-the-deal-I-worked-out" Holt.

This man was our first introduction to the South, circa 1979. He was classic in every sense. His "entrepreneur" background consisted of record producing, "previously owned" cars and "Dwarf tossing." His "client," Percy Ray, was a diminutive black man who specialized in a mean "Mr. T" impersonation. Gary circulated Percy as a "tossee" in local bars. Apparently, good ol' boys were more than happy to pony up for the chance to chuck ol' Percy Ray as far as they could.

"It was all in good fun, y'unnerstand . . ." Gary would explain.

Gary had also worked as a chauffeur in Memphis way back when and had the privilege of driving Elvis on one mystical occasion. He explained it this way:

"Now, I ain't queer or nothin', but as I drove him around, I could feel that he had a . . . a *magnetism*. But, I ain't queer or nothin'."

We were later treated to a song he produced in Memphis. A woeful tale about Vietnam, this spoken song lauded the soldiers of the United States Marine Corps:

"He was a *real* Deer Hunter . . ." the lyrics droned. "Not like that *Fonda* Woman . . ."

Gary Holt: "I ain't queer or nothin'."

As much as we appreciated his efforts, the quality and presentation of the song were so low-grade, that if any of us had made eye contact with each other, it would have been all over. Snickers were hastily disguised as coughs and sneezes.

Still, when Gary wasn't masterminding some self-serving event, he led us around to various backwater places to find a cabin. In more *really* remote areas (as opposed to *regularly* remote), Gary would insist that we wait in the car while he "hollered" at the prospective owners. We were fine with this.

One location, a former first-class resort in the twenties, was now overrun by squatters. As a semi-sheltered suburban boy, I had never encountered anything quite like this. Inside a former "guest cabin" sat the scruffiest, most rampantly bearded, dentally challenged folks you've ever seen. But they were gracious hosts, urging us to "set down awhile" with them on their orange crates or springless mattresses to chat.

Home Sweet "Home"

The manure capital of Tennessee.

Eventually, November 13, a day before the shoot was to begin, the search led us to a cabin not far from our rented house. Visually, it was ideal. The rustic homestead boasted an overgrown driveway, easily a quarter mile long, that wound down into a feral, isolated valley. It was storybook Tennessee—something Ma and Pa Kettle would settle into. Practically speaking, however, the place was a bad idea waiting to come to fruition.

As we soon found out, this was no ordinary cabin. There was something of a history to the old place. In the thirties, so the story goes, a young girl named Clara lived in the cabin with her family. One night, a terrible thunderstorm swept through the valley. During that storm, her parents were both brutally and inexplicably murdered. Our stunned girl, escaping that grim fate, wandered aimlessly until she was taken in by neighbors.

To this day, apparently, every time there is a terrible storm, Clara would wander from the Morristown Manor resthome, looking for her parents. She was found, just days before we arrived, wandering in the hills behind our cabin.

Well, Clara or no Clara, the reality of it all was that there was no electricity, no running water and no telephone service in the cabin. Cattle had the run of the place and had managed to deposit easily four inches of manure in every room. There were no doors, the rooms were very small and the ceilings were claustrophobically low. This sucker needed work—a lot of it. Art Director Dart reckoned it would take about a week of pretty hard work to get it in shape.

But we had a film to shoot, so it was decided that the cabin would be prepped while some simple exterior shots were done. The general edict came down that anyone who wasn't actively filming had to work in the cabin—*actors included.* There were walls to be knocked out, ceilings to be raised, a trapdoor with a partial basement to be hollowed out and years of newspaper-based wallpaper to be stripped away.

Dart with a circular saw was something to behold. He cut out windows, evened out the front porch and built furniture with "Hitchcockian" flair— tilted at cock-eyed angles. Ma and Pa Kettle would have been proud.

Brother Don seemed to have a talent for stonework, so he was assigned to put a new craggy face on the fireplace. Sam encouraged him to position the stones above the hearth like angry, jagged teeth.

Eventually, power and telephone lines were installed and the basic work was completed. Our single, rotary telephone sat in a bare, back room. We never did get any kind of plumbing worked out, but it was all part of the charm.

"On Your Marks, Get Set..." 18

November 14, the race began.

Right from the get go, filming was a comedy of errors, or *terrors,* if you will. Within minutes of leaving for the first location, an abandoned bridge, the production van got lost and we spent a half-hour trying to locate it. No sooner had we found it than Sam drove his "Classic" into a ditch and we had to get a tow truck to haul it out.

The next location was an isolated dirt road. Sam felt that a high, wide shot would be best. We weren't versed in the etiquette of location shooting, so no effort was made to get permission of any kind. We just hopped the fence and set up the camera. Things were going pretty well, until Josh spotted a large bull glaring at the crew.

"Sam . . . there's a bull." Josh stated, flatly.

"Yeah, hang on," Sam replied, focused on the shot at hand.

"No, Sam, you don't get it. The bull is coming this way."

Sam got it in a hurry and he was chased about a hundred yards by the angry bovine.

Man, what next? I thought.

A *cliff* was next. About two hours later, Brother Don, scouting for an additional vantage point, lost his footing and tumbled

A "vantastic" way to shoot.

101

headfirst off a nearby cliff. Apparently he was well enough to get up under his own power, but he was taken to the hospital for some tests.

Other than that, day one was very productive.

A week later, shooting a night scene at the same bridge location, Sam had a little run-in with a tree branch. A construction winch was drawn around the side of the bridge to bend a steel girder into position. Unbeknownst to anyone, the cable was also around a large tree branch that promptly snapped when tension was applied to the cable. It flattened Sam—a limb of easily fifty pounds. He staggered back and sat on the wrecker, dazed.

"Sam, you okay?" I asked.

"Why wouldn't I be?" he asked back, a blank look on his face.

At first glance he seemed fine, but upon closer inspection he was pale, his lips were white and crusty, and a small amount of blood trickled from his left nostril.

"Sam, you okay?"

"Well, you don't look so good. What the hell happened?"

"Oh, I just needed to sit down for a . . . for a little bit . . ."

With that, he rallied himself and carried on shooting. On the way home that night, he passed out cold.

During the next three months, *Evil Dead* left a path of destruction through the South as wide as Sherman's march to the sea.

Among other things, we destroyed the paint job of a white pickup truck, bent the housing of our 16mm camera, ripped the roof off a rental truck with the help of a low-slung tree branch, and crushed the septic system of my folks' house in northern Michigan.

SAM, I AM

When not plagued by Murphy and his endless series of laws, we did manage to get some work done. For instance, Sam made some remarkable strides as a visually oriented director.

Early on, his directing style became evident. He was never big on shooting a "master" (usually a wide shot, allowing the scene to play from beginning to end). He was much more apt to break scenes down into a series of shots, based on his own indecipherable thumbnail sketches, and shoot only the pieces he needed. This afforded him a great deal of precision, but it's not a method that's applauded by your organically inclined actor. The funny thing was, the actors were all so green (myself included) that none of us really knew the difference.

Sam also wasn't one for the standard medium shot, close-up, over-the-shoulder angles that most film and television shows use to "cover" a scene. As an actor, I found myself being photographed from every conceivable angle. If Sam could have put that camera up my nose, I think he would have done it.

There is an entire sequence in the film where every shot was photographed at a forty-five-degree "Dutch" (tilted) angle. That's quite severe. I must admit, we all thought Sam was crazy when this scheme was revealed, but he was the director. The results were very effective and hold up pretty well, even against the cock-eyed, "MTV style" used regularly today.

As a result of Sam's boldness, this shoot spawned a number of low-tech but unique camera rigs. Early "tracking" shots were easily accomplished from a wheelchair. When the moves needed to be smoother, or more precise, the *Vas-o-Cam* was used.

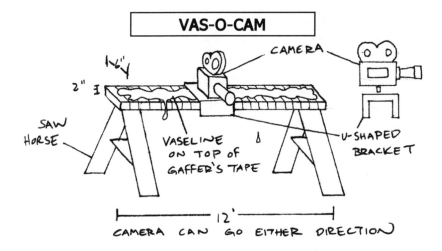

This was basically a poor man's dolly. It consisted of several two-by-fours, placed on top of saw horses. The two-by-fours were covered with silver duct tape, thereby providing a smooth, knot-free surface. The tape was then "greased" with household Vaseline. Next, the camera was bolted to a "U"-shaped wood device that laid on top of the Vaseline. Now, the camera could smoothly proceed along its track, stopping on a dime if need be. This device was lightweight, very portable and, even better, *really* cheap.

The next invention-of-necessity was the *Shaky Cam*. This was the polar opposite of its big-budget (hence completely unavailable to us) brother, the *Steadi-Cam*. Our version was merely a three-foot hunk of two-by-six board with the camera bolted in the middle. The cameraman slapped on a wide-angle lens, grabbed the board at either end and ran like hell. On film, the end result was an evil, roaming entity that could leap tall shrubs in a single bound.

103

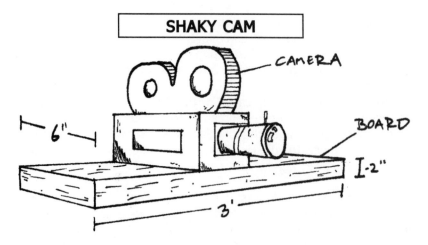

SHAKY CAM

CAMERA

BOARD

6"

I -2"

3'

Then there was the *Ellie-vator,* named after its first victim, Ellen Sandweiss. This rig was based on an old magic trick and allowed her to float in the air, as if possessed, without wires. Sam, a former Bar Mitzvah–style magician, often used simple trickery in his films. To him, motion pictures were the ultimate sleight of hand. He once explained it this way:

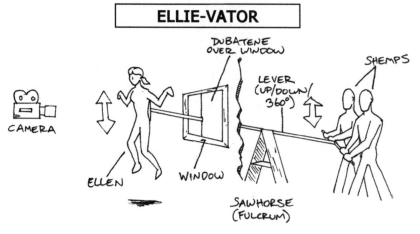

ELLIE-VATOR

DUBATENE OVER WINDOW

SHEMPS

LEVER (UP/DOWN/ 360°)

CAMERA

ELLEN

WINDOW

SAWHORSE (FULCRUM)

"The point isn't to just make the film, it's to amaze yourself and everyone at the same time. If you think what you're doing is neat, chances are everyone else will too."

But who could forget the *Ram-o-Cam*? Need an evil entity to ram through a plate-glass window? No problem. This rig consisted of a two-by-four (what else?) with a "T-Bar" at the end which would prevent injury by smashing the glass well ahead of the probing camera. With a total wholesale price of around $3.50, it also prevented costly budget overruns.

When all else failed, we just taped the damn camera to Sam's hand. The opening shot of *Evil Dead* consisted of me pushing Sam in a rubber raft across a swamp while he leaned out, skimming the camera across the water and swooping over decaying branches.

RAM-O-CAM I

Lest you forget, the number one rule of the B jungle is: "When in doubt—make it up as you go along."

"BRINK"MANSHIP

Given the factors of inexperience, a distant location and the early arrival of an unusually harsh winter, our "perfect" plan of a six-week shoot rapidly turned into eight, then ten, then twelve weeks.

Sam's script called for the main characters to endure countless woes during the course of one interminable night. It kind of worked this way: If you weren't possessed by a demon, you were chased by one. If you weren't killed, you were at least caught and soon wished that you had been. If killed, however, your character would come back to life as an unstoppable monster. As you might imagine, the actors were pushed to the brink of human endurance very quickly.

One such scene called for Teresa Seyferth's character to be hacked apart with an axe. Because the film had no rating, and we really didn't film any scenes to meet MPAA guidelines, Sam figured it would be cool to see her "parts" flopping about on the floor.

This required Theresa to be placed *partially* under the floor, with very specific boards fitted carefully around her neck. This way, she could remain an animated, decapitated creature and torment those around her—torment being the operative word.

Rob Tapert, who foolishly agreed to play her disembodied leg and arm, had to get into position next to her. Underneath the floorboards, their intertwined bodies resembled a perverted game of Twister.

By the time everything was put into place, which was several hours later, Rob was getting horrible leg cramps. Theresa also felt that she had been uncomfortable long enough, and was ready to get out. Sam, in a rare moment of compassion, agreed. That's when I had to step in.

"Look, the whole thing sucks. Everyone's uncomfortable, but getting out right now isn't the answer because we're just gonna have to put you back in again. Let's just shoot the damn thing right now and be done with it!"

105

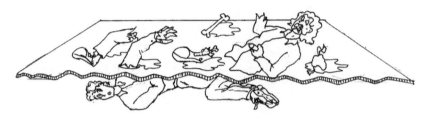

The perverted game of Twister.

After we shot that scene, Theresa never looked at me the same way again.

Then, it was Ellen Sandweiss's turn to endure the hardships of stardom. A scene in the film called for her to race through the woods, dressed only in a nightie and slippers, hoping to escape the evil "force." This entailed an entire night of clawing her way, literally, through the dense foliage around the cabin. Oh, did I mention that it was about forty degrees outside?

After the twenty-second take, Ellen fell hard and gashed her leg. She began cursing and stated flatly that she couldn't film any more that night.

Shooting came to a halt.

Rob pulled Josh aside while the crew wrapped to point out drops of blood left in Ellen's wake.

"I like it when an actor bleeds," he exclaimed. "It makes me feel like I got my money's worth..."

Later, it was Betsy Baker's turn. Her big scene took place in a makeshift graveyard up the hill from the cabin. Betsy Baker, as Linda, had just come back from the dead (you've all downloaded the script off the Internet, right?). As she attempts to kill the dim-witted Ash (me), he defends himself by smashing *It's Murder!* beams over her head. These Styrofoam "beams" (whose normal use is to create a "rustic" look in mobile home dens across America) were used extensively in Sam's epic Super-8 film, *It's Murder!* and became identified with the same.

The scene was to progress like this:

Betsy approaches. I swing. The beam cracks over her head and she spits out a milky bile. Hoping to avoid putting in the cumbersome white contact lenses, we applied white makeup to her eyelids instead. As long as she kept her eyes closed, you wouldn't really notice the fakery in the middle of a scuffle. Therefore, Betsy had no way of really knowing what was going to hit her, when, or how *hard.*

For her close-up, Sam and I lined up on both sides of the camera with beams to get the maximum number of hits without stopping to reset. Upon

"Action," I would swing my portion of the "beam" and break it over her head. Sam would then follow this with a blistering SMACK that would send Betsy into a rage. Sam would apologize, set up for another take, and do the exact same thing again. Here's what you got:

Got milk?

> Sam: "Action!"
> Bruce's hit: *Whack!*
> Sam's hit: *CRAAACK!*
> Betsy: "Goddammit, Sam!"

After the third cranium-rattling blow, Betsy defiantly spewed milk (a bile substitute) in every direction, mostly into the camera lens. This, in turn, pissed off the cameraman, Tim Philo—so went a typical night.

I wasn't left out of the torment loop—not by a long shot. In fact, since I shared a longer working relationship with Sam than anyone else on the set, I became the very *least* of Sam's worries. Sam knew too much—*way* too much—and it worked against me.

I'm not crying "foul," but I can guarantee that Theresa, Ellen and even Betsy were nodding to themselves, thinking, *Hey, I gotta wear these damn contact lenses, but at least I don't have to get the living shit beaten out of me every day.*

One occasion got out of hand—after filming yet another vicious graveyard encounter, I ran down a steep hill, rejoicing that we had finished the scene. On the way down, my foot caught a root and my ankle turned in a direction that was diametrically opposed to the way I was going. I hit the ground, curled up in pain.

Sam and Rob thought this was particularly hilarious, and prodded me to get off my ass—there was more to shoot. I managed to get to my feet, but that was about it. Next thing I knew, Sam had a pretty good-sized stick.

What the hell is he gonna do with that? I thought.

Then Rob appeared with one of his own. They circled me, like Amazon tribesman around a downed animal and began poking my ankle.

I couldn't help but laugh at the insanity of it all. This misinterpreted angst only spurred them on and I was soon huddled in the corner of a back room begging—no *pleading*—for them to stop.

The scene we filmed later that night recorded a very visible on-camera limp and now you can tell the world why. . . .

THE WRONG STUFF

Then there was the blood—that damnable stuff. Fake blood is one of the staples of horror films and ours was no exception. We needed gallons of the goo, and most of it had one destination . . . *me.*

LOW-BUDGET C...

FAKE BLOOD

So, you're making a low-budget horror film, and you need gallons and gallons of fake blood? Then, this is the recipe for you!

INGREDIENTS *(coats two thespians)*
6 pints clear Karo Syrup
3 pints red food coloring
1 pint non-dairy creamer
1 drop blue food coloring

EQUIPMENT
Large ceramic bowl
Medium sized bowl
Spoon
Cleaning products

1. The Karo Syrup is your foundation, the base of your blood. Pour syrup into large ceramic bowl.
2. In the medium bowl, stir the non-dairy creamer until it turns into a nice paste. This will provide opacity.
3. Gradually fold the non-dairy paste into the syrup.
4. Stir in red food coloring. Add drop of blue food coloring for density.
5. Test on white surface.
6. Coat aspiring actor from the top down.
7. To remove, place actor into hot shower, fully clothed, and let sit for 30 minutes or until clean.

CAUTION: Do not attempt to scare members of your family who have heart conditions—this blood looks real!

Within weeks, we had cleaned out every local Quik Pik, Gas n' Go, and Bait Shop of the essential ingredient: Karo syrup. This harmless substance, beloved by pancake-eaters across America, became my nemesis. As it dried, Karo (or "Kay-ro" as it's pronounced down South) became the inbred cousin of Super Glue.

One night, my shirt "broke." Hoping to make my life easier, I hung my Karo-soaked shirt on the back of a chair and placed it directly in front of a space heater. *If I just dry the thing,* I reasoned to myself, *it won't cling to me so horribly and wrench the very hair from my arms.*

Within minutes, it seemed to be dry. That was an understatement, because my science experiment had created something just a little harder than peanut brittle. Upon thrusting my arm into the shirt, a sleeve snapped off and fell to the floor. I tossed the rest of it into the fire.

After each night of carnage and mayhem, I'd jump into the back of our rented pickup truck, soaked in blood like a mass-murderer, and ride home. One Sunday morning, we passed a series of spit-polished families, bound for church. There really wasn't anything I could do but smile and wave like nothing was wrong.

Back home, I'd walk straight into the shower, fully clothed, and let the hot water work its magic—the only true solvents of Karo syrup were heat and time.

WHERE THE FUN NEVER SETS

It would be incorrect to portray these twelve weeks as a mirthless exercise in agony. Somewhere along the way, maybe once a month, we managed to have some fun.

Our first official reprieve was Thanksgiving, and we celebrated Southern style. I have never had a meal like it before or since. A small army of women, all related somehow to Gary Holt, took three days to prepare the fixings. In case you're skimming, that was three *days.*

The food was laid out on card tables, buffet style, and ringed two large rooms. I tried to taste a little of everything, but this was physically impossible—the sweet potato dishes alone came in five varieties.

Events like this tended to bring out the best of the South. You would be hard-pressed to find a single family in other parts of the country that would so willingly and happily prepare a veritable feast for seventeen people they didn't know, or even *like* for that matter.

I'm including moonshine under the category of "fun," but that was debatable. Mr. Holt introduced us to its charms after weeks of constant prodding.

Bridge over troubled shoot.

"C'mon, Gary, you gotta get us some! Ya *gotta*!"

"Y'all sure you want me to?" he'd warn. "It ain't fer kids, this stuff . . ."

"Aw, phooey! We're from Detroit!"

The moonshine that Gary produced didn't really make you drunk. It was too powerful for that—it made you *crazy.* Gary explained that to test a batch of "shine," you'd pour some into the lid of the mason jar (the only true receptacle) and light it on fire. If it burned a soft blue flame, it was good stuff, but if it burned an orange color, you'd better pass—it was most likely distilled in a car radiator.

Armed with "shine," one night we decided to go clubbing. In the small burg of Morristown, we had to adjust our big-city expectations. The place Gary steered us to was small, really small—okay, downright clandestine. Across the dim room, we saw a smattering of Southern belles and I knew I had to get something going.

Brazened by a gut full of home-brewed nitroglycerine, I approached a girl and offered what I was thought was a unique line.

"Pardon me, ma'am (we learned to say *sir* and *ma'am* a lot down there), but have you ever danced with a Northern boy before?"

The woman rolled her eyes, but stood up and offered her arm.

"No."

With that, we stumbled to the dance floor. As drunk as I was, I think she actually had a head start on me. We'd dance a step or two, fall to the dance floor, help each other up, attempt to dance again, and go right back down.

Helping her up for the umpteenth time, I detected a pleasant odor.

"Excuse me, ma'am, but what's that lovely scent you're wearing?"

"Ivory Soap," she explained, as if I were a moron, and promptly collapsed.

A DEEP AND DARK DECEMBER

manufacturing industries. Population, 143,485.

win·ter (win'ter) *n.* A period of inactivity or decay.

winter aconite *n.* Any of various Eurasian herbs of the genus

By the end of November, winter was in full swing. Later, we found out that Tennessee had logged one of the harshest winters in recent memory, while Michigan posted a positively balmy one.

The rural Slip 'N Slide.

The muddy driveway to the cabin froze, rendering this difficult-at-best road impassable by car. The daily "long march," lugging equipment and food down the quarter-mile, slick road became positively gulag-like. At the beginning of the shooting day, gravity was our friend. At the end of a sixteen-hour day, the last thing you wanted to do was haul equipment up that rural Slip 'N Slide.

The cabin, lacking any hint of insulation whatsoever, became astoundingly cold inside. A roaring fire and two space heaters didn't seem to help any. Under duress, I developed a theory about personal comfort that dogs me to this day. I reasoned that it was better to keep myself in a mild state of *dis*-comfort, rather than give in to the false impression of warmth provided by the space heater. By mid-December, I had sworn off any "external" heat source and preferred instead to shiver uncontrollably.

Equipment, as well as personnel, began to freeze. On the seventeenth take of an exterior dolly shot, the synchronization cable (between the camera and the sound recorder) froze and we were forced to go inside and let it thaw by the fire. As weeks rolled on, this problem became kind of moot because the *camera itself* would freeze.

When In Doubt, "Shemp" It

By late December, our original termination date, actors and crew members began to leave in droves. Prior commitments to "real" jobs, or school made it impossible for some to stay.

Tim Philo, the director of photography, had to return to Wayne State University in early January. That was all well and good, but Tim had borrowed our main camera, the Arriflex BL, from their film department, and it was his responsibility to return it.

Sam, as captain of this sinking ship, could never allow that to happen.

Sam: But Tim, without the BL, we don't have a backup camera.

Tim: Okay, but if I leave it, you promise not to use it?

Sam: Absolutely.

Tim hadn't been gone five minutes when Sam turned to Josh.

Sam: Josh, unpack the BL.

Other cast and crew members simply had enough. Faced with this, we were forced to employ an old Super-8 trick: "Shemping."

Being fans of the Three Stooges growing up, we discovered that their shorts of about twenty minutes in length were filmed two or three at a time—thereby capitalizing on sets from the big, Columbia A pictures, currently in production. It allowed them, for example, to use a large castle set (and shoot a pie fight or something) before it was torn down. As a result, they often shot overlapping scenes from different shorts.

One day, Shemp (the really ugly one with long, stringy black hair) had a heart attack and the rest of the Stooges, distraught as they were, had to finish off scenes from several shorts.

To do this, a "fake Shemp" was brought in. The double, actor Joe Palma, was the wrong height and weight and lacked the true Shemp mannerisms. Even as teenagers

Kurt Rauf AKA Ellen.

Cherly Guttridge AKA Betsy.

Ted Raimi AKA Rich.

Barbara Carey AKA Betsy.

Rob Tapert's best side.

Sam's "Pudge Paw," Shemping for Rich.

watching the Stooges after school, we could tell whenever the *fake* Shemp made his appearances (which amounted to four shorts) and it amused us to no end.

We then began to use the term "Fake Shemp" for any actor in our Super-8 flicks who didn't have any lines, or was doubling for someone else, (which seemed to happen a lot when you couldn't pay actors to stay around). With *Evil Dead,* we decided to elevate "Shemping" to an official, on-screen credit category mainly because they soon constituted the bulk of our cast.

Former film student, Kurt Rauf, was a monster leaping into frame. Super-8 starlet, Cheryl Guttridge, allowed us to cover her with peat moss in Sam Raimi's garage for a dramatic, out-of-the-grave lunge. Sam's brother, Ted, did his best to imitate a pair of tentative feet, shuffling across a blood-strewn floor. Local Tennessee actress, Barbara Carey, endured many nights of wigs, latex applications and broken fingernails to play the long-departed Betsy Baker. Dorothy Tapert, Rob's sister, spewed blood during a reshoot in a suburban Detroit basement. Even Rob, Mr. Producer, donned a monster wig and doubled for Ellen Sandweiss.

The term Shemp has since expanded in our vocabulary to include much broader applications:

Shempish—anything that is cheesy or second-rate—"Man, throw that shirt out, it looks really Shempish."

Shemping—doing nothing of any importance—"I have no plans Saturday night, I'm just Shemping . . ."

Shemp Alert—sighting a Shemp; being "Shempish."

THE DOG DAZE

The month of January began to take on a *Lord of the Flies* feel. We were now a full month over schedule. Gone were the days of zany antics—we had entered the darkest, oddest days of the shoot.

To kick things off, a "fogger" fire nearly burned our entire woods down. These hand-held, portable fog machines ran off electricity and relied on a volatile oil-based substance to create the clinging mist you see in horror films. The effect was great, but foggers tended to spit flames every so often. Tall, dry grasses surrounded the cabin and created a recipe for disaster. Next thing we knew, a fire appeared out of nowhere and only a mad stomping session put out the conflagration.

When you get tired, you become careless and lose the ability to sense danger. Late one night, after securing a light, Josh jumped down from the rafters and impaled his foot on a sharp, upturned spike. He yanked his foot off the nail, dragged himself over to a couch and curled up into a ball. For the next several days, we'd peek into his room before shooting and see how he was doing.

"Josh, are you coming to the set today?"

". . . No."

"Okay . . ."

Josh's diary, kept faithfully, chronicled the collapse of our youthful enthusiasm:

Sunday, November 11, 1979—

It's a real strange grouping together of people. I'll wait to see how everyone functions as a team. Nevertheless, we're all here, all the equipment is here, so I guess we're making movies.

Sunday, Nov. 18th, 1979—

Five more weeks—lord god this is going to be trying.

Monday, Dec. 17th, 1979—

Soon we'll be leaving for the location again and once again I'm dreading it. Last night was unquestionably the coldest yet, possibly zero and just absurd weather to be doing extensive exteriors in. Aside from the fact that it's awful to be out personally, both lights and cameras resent it, too—the Arriflex BL

freezes up regularly now and has to be thawed by the fire.

Wednesday, Jan. 16th, 1980—

Today's shoot was plain stupid. In about ten hours we got two shots. One shot took one hour, the other took nine. Two more weeks of this will ruin me.

Wednesday, Jan. 23rd, 1980 (scribbled on the back of a continuity log)

I'm going insane! Nothing makes any sense! I can't keep my mind focused on a single thought! My mental processes have no continuity at all! I just want to have one uninterrupted day of thought, but "Book of the Dead" (the original title) will not end!

The cabin was so rural that we never thought anything of leaving the equipment in place and going four miles "home" to eat lunch or dinner. The driveway had become so inaccessible that only a damn fool would try and steal anything—or so we thought.

Returning from a late night lunch, we discovered that our power tools were missing. The loss: a skill-saw, saber-saw, drill and chainsaw. The ironic thing about the whole incident was that a $20,000 Arriflex camera, sitting out in the open, wasn't touched. Value is a subjective thing, particularly in rural Tennessee.

This incident led us to post a watchman at the cabin after wrapping each night. That lucky person got to shiver on a hard floor next to the dying fire until someone relieved them the next afternoon.

Just when our defenses reached an all-time low, we came face-to-face with an indescribable substance known as Goody's chili. We returned to the house for "lunch" (at 2:00 A.M.) only to find Goody sound asleep in a La-Z-Boy chair in front of a TV test pattern, surrounded by Snicker's Bar wrappers. When we asked him where lunch was, he groggily pointed to the stovetop.

Dave: You guys had been working really hard for six or seven nights, so I said, "just come home and I'll make you guys a real meal." I made this chili—a really intensive meat experience—three or four pounds of beef and I threw in some lamb and beans and a lot of jalepeños and Tobasco sauce and a lot of seasoning. Everybody comes home and they eat and I've got bread and cheese and sour cream and it's like a real meal and everybody's hungry and they start eating like animals.

"Goody, this chili sucks, and so do you!"

Bruce: That's when the trouble began. . . .

Dave: I went to bed and then I came up the next morning and I saw Sam. He was asleep, with his head on the table. You were underneath—

Bruce: I was underneath the table.

Dave: You were snoring and Rob was passed out in his chair.

Bruce: No one was able to move after that meal.

Dave: I woke everybody up and Sam turned to me and he goes, "You drugged me and violated me, didn't you?"

As if that wasn't bad enough, there was so much left over that we had the same meal the next night and the same thing happened—two nights of work, down the crapper because of Goodman's chili.

With Goodman, you never really knew what kind of sustenance you were going to get from day to day. Another night, he confused baking powder with baking soda and the crew was treated to "pizza cake." Most of us threw our portions in the fire.

As the weather became more volatile, so did Goody. After a while, he simply refused to bring the food down to the cabin.

Dave: The road is too slippery.

Bruce: No shit, Dave.

Dave: I'm gonna leave it at the top of the driveway. Fuck it. I don't care. You're not paying me enough to bring it all the way down. . . .

Bruce: Sure, whatever is convenient for you. We wouldn't want you to miss the soaps. . . .

Life at the house became surreal. Tom Sullivan slept in the laundry room. Apparently, he was fine with the idea of nesting among weeks of unwashed crew clothing. Eventually, a horrid stench began to emanate from the room. We secretly discussed Tom's hygiene, but someone had seen him take a shower a few weeks before, so it couldn't be him . . . *could it?*

After Tom returned home to Michigan, we discovered the source of the smell: rotting chicken bones that he had used for several ghoulish props.

About 3:00 A.M. one night, Sam awoke to an eerie wind, whispering through his bedroom window. Like the dedicated filmmaker that he was, he immediately rousted sound man John Mason.

Sam preparing me to shoot.

Sam: I woke John up and I asked him to record it because it was so scary and so unique.

Bruce: And so you got a couple minutes of that or whatever?

Sam: Yeah, we wound up using it in the finished film a lot, actually. I couldn't believe it was natural—it sounded so fake.

Reality Bites

Our back room telephone had been knocked off its perch so many times during the course of the shoot that to make or receive a call, you had to hold a delicate lever in place to keep from hanging up.

One frigid night, while shooting a difficult sequence, I got a cryptic call.

"Joe's Pool Hall, who in the hall do you want?" I answered, assuming that it was Goody, calling to complain about something.

"Who is this?" the irritated voice wanted to know.

"Who wants to know?" I shot back, not recognizing the caller.

"Bruce, this is Dad. When are you coming back?"

I rubbed my eyes and tried to make a joke. "Never. We're having way too much fun."

"Quit screwing around. Have you heard from your mother?" Dad asked, in an uncharacteristically stern tone.

"No, why?"

"Because she's not here. I don't know where she went or when she's coming back."

"What is that supposed to mean?"

"Just what I said." He sounded more sad than worried.

"Uh, well, God, I don't know, Dad. I'll be home in a couple of weeks, I guess. I'm not sure. What's going on up there? Is everything all right?"

"I don't know. We'll talk about it when you get back . . ."

"Okay. Bye, Dad. *Dad?*"

It was too late—the phone had hung up on itself.

On the home front, a problem that I didn't even know existed had reared its hydra head. The whole thing was too hard to grasp, so I went back to the set and got a bucket of blood dumped on me.

THAT'S A WRAP! SORT OF . . .

Eventually, our house rental agreement expired, and we were forced to vacate. Apparently, there were big plans for this house—it was to be converted into a country brothel. Hauling out hastily gathered clothing and equipment, we passed the shiny brass beds of the new inhabitants—for shame, Bible Belt, for shame.

The last few days of our shoot, the spent crew—all five of us—lived at the cabin. To stay warm, we burned any furniture that was no longer needed. There were still day shots and night shots to complete, so sleep wasn't really an option, but it didn't seem to matter—getting the *hell* out of Tennessee was the only important thing.

For sheer absurdity, nothing could top an incident with a man named Fats. This fellow, who single-handedly perpetuated the Red Neck stereotype, hailed from the bowels of Newport County. This was an important distinction, because it was one of the few "wet" counties in Tennessee and Fats, a drinker's drinker, lived up to its reputation. He had visited the set with his girlfriend and small child many months before. His boy, all of four, displayed a vocabulary that was about seventy percent expletives.

"Goddam sumbitch, goddam sumbitch" he would say repeatedly.

About 5:00 in the morning after our last night of filming, Fats's 1971 Plymouth Duster slid to a halt at the bottom of the driveway—the one that had long been impassable. He was drunk and *determined* to get into the movie business.

"How're all my friends gonna know I knowed you, if you don't put me in yer pitcher . . . ?" he slurred.

We could only stare at each other in amazement.

"Gee, Fats, we just wrapped for the night. Sorry." Sam explained, as rationally as he could for a man who had been up for almost two days straight.

"Wrapped, hell . . . *put me in yer pitcher.*"

We learned never to argue with a man who had a bullet hole in his car.

"Sure, Fats," Sam shrugged, "we'll put you in the movie."

With that, we mocked up a few props and proceeded to act out a scene from Sam's student film, *The Happy Valley Kid*. Fats was given the role of college professor and Josh was enlisted to portray the "Kid." Sam scribbled copious amounts of dialogue on the back of a script log and insisted that Fats adhere to every word.

"C'mon, Fats, you want to be an actor, don't you?"

"Well, I . . ."

"Let's shoot . . . Roll sound!"

"Yeah, but I don't know my—"

"Slate it!" Sam bellowed. For some reason I thought of Captain Ahab.

"Oh, shit, boy, I ain't ready fer—"

"Action, Fats—*ACTION*!"

His drunken bluster reached new heights as he vainly struggled with material way past his third-grade education, but by golly, Fats was a movie star!

With that, on Wednesday, January 23, 1980, filming was declared "kind of finished." Everything that didn't absolutely have to return to Michigan was placed on a stump and blasted to bits with the remaining ammunition. The scraps were then tossed on a giant heap behind the cabin and ceremoniously burned.

To close out this life-altering experience, we gathered around the trapdoor, exchanged a few solemn words, and buried a primitive time capsule deep below the floor of the main room. This cigar box, filled with a spent shotgun shell, a sample of fake blood and a hand-written "visual code" to the film, commemorated the culmination of twelve grueling weeks filming our first "real" movie.

AFTERMATH

19

Upon limping back to Michigan (my wrenched, poked ankle made this a literal thing for me), we found ourselves penniless and with an incomplete film.

The cryptic phone call with Dad came to fruition as soon as I walked in the door of my house. My mother informed me that she was, in fact, leaving for good. After a borderline Vietnam experience, this was about the last thing I wanted to hear. It had been a long time since I cried, but tears flowed freely that day.

Ironically, my oldest brother Mike was about to get married. The family picture at the wedding was a hoot—it was the classic Midwest, everything-is-all-right-on-the-outside portrait of a family in transition.

The prospects for additional funding were equally as grim, but life goes on—we had come way too far to give up now.

The nearby suburb of Ferndale provided cheap office space, and we settled into an old dentist's office—that seemed appropriate, since a good deal of our budget came from this profession and raising money was a lot like pulling teeth.

Ferndale was a quaint neighborhood. Tom, our building manager, lived with his Doberman, Duke, on the premises. I have no

American Gothic: Michigan style.

The Ferndale office.

doubt that our six years there led to his early insanity.

We attempted to adjust back to civilian life, with uneven success. For some reason, I refused to shave until the film was done. This absurdity became self-evident once we did reshoots and I *had* to shave. During this period, I slept on the floor of my room, insisting that it had been good enough for me during "the Shoot."

We half-heartedly attempted to reestablish contact with some of the cast and crew. Our relationship with the actors was strained at best. Theresa (her real name) invited us to see her new routine at the local Komedy Kastle. I barely recognized her with all of her appendages. After the show, we exchanged sheepish hellos, like two friends who had gotten drunk the night before and revealed some *awfully* personal things.

Bruce: Hey, Theresa—funny show. How's it going?
Theresa: Fine, now that I'm away from that hellhole in Tennessee . . .
Bruce: Yeah, that was a tough shoot, wasn't it?
Theresa: It was the worst experience of my life.
Bruce: Well, if it's any consolation, you don't know the half of it . . .

Anatomy of a Lemon

Going into *Evil Dead,* I had what could be considered a reasonable car— a 1976 Opal Isuzu (the "pseudo Foreign Sub-Classic" according to Sam). The seeds of destruction were sewn when Goodman, the belligerent cook, borrowed my Opal during the shoot.

"Bruce, I gotta pick up more film stock. Can I take your car to Atlanta?"
"Sure, Dave, go for it . . ."
Upon returning, Goody wouldn't look me in the eyes.
"The good news is . . . I got the film stock," he said, avoiding my gaze.
"Yeah . . . what's the bad news?"
"I ran over a cinderblock."
Nothing seemed *specifically* wrong with the car, but upon returning to Detroit, my Opal began to spew steam from the exhaust pipe. I'm not a graduate of Mr. Goodwrench, but I knew it couldn't be a good thing.

"Sorry, bud, you got a cracked block," the mechanic said.
"That's, like, tragically bad, right?"
"Nothin' worse. But, hey, what can ya say? These goddamn *foreign* cars suck."

He just had to slip that in. If I were a true Detroiter, he was intimating, I would have purchased an *American* car and I wouldn't be having this problem—cinderblock notwithstanding.

The next day, I dropped off my Opal's title and loan termination papers to the neighborhood junkyard and walked away with a fifty-dollar "scrap bonus." Typically, the month before, I had paid off my car loan.

It was time to bite the bullet and get a new set of wheels. Well, not a *new* set, *any* set—the Motor City wasn't big on mass transit.

Buddy John Cameron worked as a bartender at the local bowling alley, the Strike and Spare—known affectionately as the Sit and Stare for its high-class clientele. A waitress there had a "great" car for sale—only 150 bucks.

The odyssey began on a cold January day. I met Kathy outside her house to inspect her car—a 1973 Chevy Bel Air. It could have been a 1943 Nash for all I knew, because the car was covered by two feet of ice and snow. Between the two of us, it took so long to uncover the thing that the issue of whether it was a good car or a bad car became quite moot.

"Look, uh, Kathy, tell you what. I'm sure the car is fine. Let me get the money together and I'll call you."

Several weeks later, on another bone-numbing day, I returned with the cash.

"I just need to put a teeny bit of radiator fluid in it and she'll be ready to go," Kathy assured me, as she produced two jugs of generic antifreeze.

Since my last visit, the snow had melted off somewhat, revealing a very black car. Upon closer inspection, I saw what appeared to be a paintbrush bristle, stuck in the coarse layer of paint.

"Is that what I think it is?"

Kathy looked up from her refilling duties. "Oh, yeah, the car was painted with house paint."

". . . with a *brush*," I added.

"Isn't that weird?" she smiled, almost done.

Walking around the car, I noticed a rotted, bashed-in rocker panel. "How's the radio?"

"Well, I'm not much for the radio . . ."

I squinted at her. That was a very White-House-damage-control kind of answer. "Does the heater work?"

Kathy nodded vigorously, as if to make up for the last answer. "Boy, *does* it!"

Yeah, that's just what I thought . . . *Does it?*

Eventually, the paperwork was exchanged and I was out of there. The radio didn't work and the heater was either off or on full blast—there was no in-between for this excellent, *American* car.

My first stop was the gas station. After filling up, I turned the ignition key and nothing happened—no click, no whirr, no moan—*nothing.* Since I was at a full-service gas station, I enlisted the help of an attendant. As he popped open the hood, a wave of heat engulfed him.

"Whooh, she's pretty hot. Let me check the fluids . . ."

"Fluids? I just saw her add some," I mumbled to no one in particular.

Using a rag to protect his hand from the glowing radiator, he peered inside.

"Looks empty to me. Let me dump some more in."

The money pit.

As he did this, a three-foot stream of coral blue antifreeze shot back at him with a *fooomp*! The radiator was so hot it had rejected every drop of fluid. Apparently, it was so riddled with holes that Kathy's antifreeze had passed right on through. As it coagulated in her driveway, I'm sure she knew exactly where that frozen blue puddle came from.

A replacement, "slightly used," radiator would cost me eighty dollars. In retrospect, this was the point where any rational human would have paid for a tow truck, dumped the car on Kathy's lawn, and insisted on their money back, but I managed to convince myself that this was just a fluke. Aside from a little old radiator, what could possibly go wrong?

This was a Saturday afternoon—by Saturday evening, the transmission was a thing of the past—another testament to the craftsmanship of mid-seventies *American* cars. I remember thinking, *How odd, here I am pressing on the gas pedal more and more, and the car is moving less and less.*

I abandoned the piece of crap in a snowdrift on the side of the road. The next day, far too cold for any rational person to be rescuing cars, I let it sit. The following Monday morning, I forged out to retrieve it, but alas, there was no car to be found—it had been towed.

A hundred dollars later, between the towing charge and the impounding/storage fees, the car made its way to AAMCO for inspection. There, I had a lovely chat with the serviceman.

"Well, I can fix her for three hundred and fifty dollars."

"Junk the car," I said, without a moment's hesitation.

"What?"

"Yep, junk it. Do whatever you'd like. You don't really expect me to pay twice the amount of the car just to have it fixed, do you?"

"Well, now wait a minute, that was for a full warranty," he backpedaled. "I can do a *limited* warranty repair job for two hundred and fifty."

"Junk the car," I repeated emotionlessly. I wasn't acting, mind you, I was dead serious.

"Are you shittin' me? Really?"

"Absolutely. It's not worth it to me. C'mon, If I was made of money, do you think I'd be driving a car that was painted with *house paint*?!"

"Okay, okay. Tell you what—I'll fix the car for two hundred bucks, but there won't be any warranty or guarantee whatsoever."

"It's a deal . . ."

Little did I know that this was just the beginning of an epic journey of repair. Witness the embarrassing journal entries over the remainder of that year:

KittyLube
AUTOMOBILE SERVICE & REPAIR

CUSTOMER SERVICE & REPAIR JOURNAL

SO THAT WE MAY BETTER SERVE YOU, PLEASE LIST YOUR RECENT AUTOMOBILE SERVICE AND REPAIR HISTORY IN THE SPACE PROVIDED BELOW:

MARCH 20	TOOK IT TO MUFFLER PLACE 10:45. 2:00 GETTING REAR TIRES.
MARCH 23	MY CAR IS DRIPPING TRANSMISSION FLUID.
APRIL 8	CAR DIED—THIS WAS HARD TO STOMACH.
APRIL 15	ATTEMPTED TO RETRIEVE DEAD CAR AT MARKET. IT WAS TOWED. TO BANK TO GET BRIBE MONEY ($30). PAID BRIBE. FOUND CAR AT K-MART. HAD IT TOWED BACK.
MAY 5	CAR DIED. RESTED IT ENOUGH AND I GOT IT BACK TO THE OFFICE.
MAY 11	HAD CAR TROUBLES ON WAY HOME. READ SCRIPTS ON SIDE OF ROAD TO LET MY JUNKER REST A BIT.
MAY 28:	CAR DIED. FREON WENT CRAZY—SWELL CAR.
JUNE 16	BORROWED $100 FROM DON (AGAIN)—TOOK TO CAR PLACE—PICKED UP CAR—WORKING AGAIN.

Kiffy Lube
AUTOMOBILE SERVICE & REPAIR

CUSTOMER SERVICE & REPAIR JOURNAL

SO THAT WE MAY BETTER SERVE YOU, PLEASE LIST YOUR RECENT AUTOMOBILE SERVICE AND REPAIR HISTORY IN THE SPACE PROVIDED BELOW:

JULY 2	CAR TROUBLES. DIED ON WOODWARD AVE AGAIN.
JULY 6	CAR DIED ON I-75. BIG JAM. GOT TOWED TO 7 MILE RD. GAS STATION.
AUGUST 25	TO GAS STATION—ENGINE NEEDS TO BE CLEANED.
AUGUST 29	MY CAR IS SICK AGAIN.
AUGUST 30	SWITCHED CARS WITH DON—MINE'S A LITTLE NAUSEOUS.
SEPTEMBER 7	CAR GOT PINCHED BY COPS FOR UNPAID PARKING TICKETS, EXPIRED TAGS AND SUSPENDED LICENSE—IMPOUNDED CAR. TO FERNDALE 43RD DISTRICT COURT—PAID $50 TO GET LICENSE BACK—TO FOUR SEASONS INSURANCE—GOT EL CHEAPO $100 POLICY.
NOVEMBER 13	TIRE TROUBLES—FRONT LEFT. COP TOOK ME TO GAS STATION. GOT WHOLE NEW SET OF FRONT TIRES AND A NEW RIM.
NOVEMBER 16	TO FERNDALE 43RD DISTRICT COURT—PAID ABOUT $240 OF OLD PARKING TICKETS SO I DON'T GET HAULED AWAY—BORROWED MONEY FROM REN PIX TO HELP ($160).
DECEMBER 2	CAR DIED ON WAY TO JOSH'S—SAME OLD PROBLEM.
DECEMBER 8	DROPPED TIRES OFF TO BE REPAIRED.
JAN. 21, 1983	TO K-MART. GOT MY BOMB—ABOUT $300—GOT TUNE-UP—NEW FRONT & REAR BRAKES—OIL CHANGE AND SOME NEW MISC. PARTS.

In addition to the maladies listed above, I bought new tie rods and a drive shaft, and endured a particularly wet year with a rear window that leaked like a sieve every time it rained.

Other than that, it was a fine car. . . .

There is somewhat of a silver lining to this tale of woe. Later in the year, when I could afford to buy a real car, I donated the beast to Will, a member of my church. A list of disclaimers preceded the transaction.

"Now, Will, you can have the car. Just take it—I don't want a penny, but I gotta warn you. This thing could fly off the freeway at any time, or blow up or, or . . . *anything* . . ."

I saw Will at a church function about a year later and avoided any contact with him. When he cornered me at the punch bowl, I knew I was gonna get it.

"Bruce!"

"Hi, Will, hey long time," I said, not daring to ask about the car.

"Bruce, I gotta tell you something."

"I know, I know, look I warned you . . . how long did it last? A week?"

"The car is great!"

". . . *Is* great?"

"I still have it—it's in the parking lot! I haven't had a single problem with it and I just wanted to thank you for such a trouble-free car."

The Quest for Moolah–Part II **20**

Having sold as much personal stake in the film as the three of us could justify, we proceeded to the next option: loans. This word soon became a permanent part of our vocabulary and it manifested itself in every form: personal loans, corporate loans, temporary loans, emergency loans—even *bank* loans.

What resulted was a series of large, early eighties, point-and-a-half-above-prime-rate loans from the National Bank of Detroit. At nearly twenty percent interest on over a hundred thousand dollars, it became clear to me why banks rule the world. The loans were secured by a double helping of personally owned blue chip stocks—graciously put up by several long-suffering investors as a guarantee.

Investors were also invited to loan us money directly and reap the same rate as the bank. Much to their ultimate pleasure, this became the highest source of profit for some of them.

As the loans were deposited, some film gremlin kept sneaking into our checking account and throwing the money away with reckless abandon, or so it seemed. My Day Runner from that period told the whole story:

Pick up a check from Mr. O'Connor, take a check to the camera rental place. Sign the loan papers from Brian M., FedEx a check to the film lab. Pick up a quickie loan from Rob's folks, pay off phone bill.

When in Doubt, Keep Shooting

The loans, in all of their forms, allowed us to shoot the last third of our film in fits and starts. The first spring after our return, we filmed for two additional weeks in the Tapert Farmhouse in Marshall, Michigan. Here, Sam Raimi began what would become a series of salutes between filmmakers.

The "eyes" have it.

The Hills Have Eyes was a very effective independent horror flick and we had great respect for Wes Craven's ability to capture raw terror on the screen. In one particularly grisly scene, played out in a ramshackle trailer home, a psycho bites the head off a small bird and drinks its blood. Behind him, Sam noticed a poster of Steven Spielberg's film, *Jaws,* torn in half—as if to say, "As scary as *Jaws* was, what's happening in this film is much worse."

Not to be outdone, Sam put a torn poster of *The Hills Have Eyes* on the wall of Rob's basement, as if to taunt Wes with, "Oh yeah? *Hills Have Eyes* is nothing. What's happening in *Evil Dead* is true horror!"

This set off a tip of the hat from Mr. Craven in his film, *A Nightmare on Elm Street.* In it, a character is up late at night watching a film on television—none other than *Evil Dead.* When the sequel to *Evil Dead* rolled around, seven years later, Sam placed a torn poster of *A Nightmare on Elm Street* in a work shed—we'll see who ups the ante next.

That summer, we shot for four more days to fill in a few gaps in the film and provide what Sam would call, "a little kick in the ass." These "pickups" ran the gamut from shots of blood spattering on a wall to an entire sequence where a character gets raped, literally, by vines.

The end of the film required a climactic "meltdown" of the monsters when the character Ash finally defeats them—this required three months of animation shooting in the suburban basement of effects wizard, Bart Pierce.

Bart teamed up with Tom Sullivan, now speaking to us again, and their job was to give the end of the film a little "oomph." Sometimes it was hard to tell what these eclectic animators were up to. Witness a typical wish list: *fake arm, saber saw, fake blood, wig, white eggs, necklace, dowel rod, heater.* The heater was for them, since this sequence dragged on into the frigid months of Michigan in winter.

My final shot as an actor in *Evil Dead* took place in that basement. Sam felt it was necessary to show my character interacting with this meltdown, and Alpo dog food proved to be the best substitute for monster guts. Somehow, being splattered in the face with an entire can, complements of Sam, seemed a fitting end.

A CUTTING WE WILL GO

We had a mountain of footage—now the trick was to make sense of it all.

In Detroit, film editors worked on thirty-second car commercials, they didn't edit ninety-minute gore flicks. However, several times a year, full-length industrial films are shot and "feature" editors are brought in to do the work—one such editor was Edna Paul.

Through a series of referrals she became our editor, but she was based in New York, so if we wanted her to cut the film it had to be there. It was a lot closer than LA, so that was good enough for us. . . .

Sam was the only one who absolutely had to be in New York, so Rob and I stayed behind while Sam, Edna and her assistant, fledgling filmmaker Joel Coen, pieced the film together.

The editing process was fascinating—it was the first time that I realized how extensively you could manipulate film footage. Shots were often reversed, used out of order, or stolen from a different scene to make a sequence work.

<u>Bruce:</u> So that's when you met Joel Coen. Did you guys hit it off right away or what?

<u>Sam:</u> Yeah. He seemed like a nice, quiet guy. Some editors let their assistants cut a little bit, so he ended up editing the work shed scene, which he was really into because it was designed as a specific sequence. He made it better because he took two longer pieces and made them into four cuts and it looked even better.

The first assembly of *Evil Dead* came in at 117 minutes. This was quite an achievement, particularly since the screenplay was only sixty-five pages—some thirty pages shy of the industry standard. What impressed me most, how-ever, was Sam's ability to slice his own material with steely-eyed brutality. I recall arguing with him about several large cuts he wanted to make.

Working on the "Mean, Green Editing Machine."

"But Sam, you can't cut that out," I reasoned. "It took a long time to shoot!"

"Let me cut it out for now and next time we screen the film, tell me if you miss it."

This was the right way to go. On several occasions, he'd refer to a given scene.

"Notice anything missing?" he'd ask.

"No, I don't think so . . ."

"The wood chopping scene is gone."

"Oh . . . sure, I, uh, I knew that."

This kind of perspective allowed Sam and his crew to whittle the film down to a lean ninety-one minutes.

BLOOD? SIMPLE.

During the course of editing *Evil Dead,* Sam became good friends with Joel Coen, the assistant editor and his partner/brother, Ethan. The Coens had concocted an idea for a thriller but they too needed to raise money. The notion of filming some form of prototype appealed to them, but their twist was to do a coming attraction—like the film was already done.

So, on a frigid February in rural New Jersey, Sam, Rob and I pitched in to help. One scene called for a mortally wounded character to drag himself down a lonely road, refusing to die. That role, for reasons all too clear, was given to me—I was the current expert on blood and cold. The full-length film, *Blood Simple,* did pretty well for the Coens and, well, you know the rest.

LOUD AND CLEAR

Eventually, the "meltdown" animation was completed and the film was cut together. Now, we had to add sound—lots of it. Horror flicks, while very visual, need just as much attention in the audio department.

The concept of "looping" was relatively new to us. This is the process whereby actors replace poor or missing dialogue. In our case, there was plenty to replace. Looping, to the uninitiated, poses several challenges. One is synchronization—actors have to match the exact cadence of their original reading. This is essentially a mechanical thing and can be mastered eventually. The other more intangible aspect of looping is re-creating the urgency you felt in a wind storm, or the emotion as a friend dies in your arms.

In my case, first time out of the gate, I found out pretty quickly how fast a person's voice can blow out. After years of this vocal torment, I now book my looping sessions in half-day increments and always carry homemade throat lube—a concoction of herbal tea, lemon and honey.

Jumpin' Joe Masefield and the boys.

Then there was that thing called "Foley." Named after a sound pioneer, it is the nonvocal equivalent of looping, wherein organic sounds are added to enhance or fill in the on-screen activity.

Evil Dead had its own unique sound requirements—our characters stumbled through the woods, tramped across sticky floors and chopped each other to bits. To record this, Sam and I dutifully followed the anal instructions of Joe Masefield, the supervising sound editor. Joe was an old school New Yorker and lived on a diet of cornbread muffins (with extra butter) and coffee. Joe had mapped out, like an engineer, where each sound would go, complete with a corresponding number, and a basic idea of how each sound could be made.

Sam and I were the self-appointed Foley artists, so we brought in an arsenal of destruction, consisting of several uncooked chickens, a meat cleaver, a turkey baster, walnuts, a nut cracker, celery and actual props from the film.

Chickens substituted for any form of impaled, chopped or pounded flesh. The turkey baster was wonderful for blood spurts and gurgling of any kind. Walnuts and celery became staples for breaking appendages. We also discovered that quarter-inch recording tape very handily simulated the sound of dead leaves, and an added bonus was that it never decomposed.

Ask any of the old timers at the Sound One Corporation in New York City and they'll confirm that the stench of decomposing chicken flesh lingered for months in their studio.

A TRIP TO THE LIBRARY

Next on Joe's list were the "hard effects"—like train whistles, car honks or bird chirps—items generally impossible to create by hand and usually found in a prerecorded library.

I would be remiss if I didn't mention that Sam and I snuck in a few recordings from our own "library." *Three Stooges* sound effects, recorded directly off the TV, were "cleaned up" and proved particularly effective for eye-gouges and body falls.

Have mixing board, will travel.

Another item in great demand was the "Scare Chord." This was any sharp, disturbing sound that could be used to jolt the audience when something sudden or scary happened on screen—these wound up being anything from gun shots to cymbal clashes.

Sam, Rob and I became possessed with "enhancing" the sound track. After a full day of mixing the recorded sounds together, a numbing process, we'd spend the better part of the night editing additional effects or dialogue on secret tracks. Joe Masefield had no specific designation for them, so they simply became known as "X" tracks.

To break up the grind, Sam and I would routinely sneak away at lunch time to a video arcade called Fascination, and dull our senses even more by playing rounds of Asteroids and Berserk. Sam, with his innate ability to blow the living crap out of anything and anyone, excelled at both.

One day at the arcade, we were both surprised to see director, Brian DePalma, doing the same thing. Apparently, he had been at the same sound facility, finishing up his film, *Blow Out,* with John Travolta.

Sam brazenly approached Mr. DePalma and half asked, half challenged him to a round of *Berserk*. DePalma, not exactly Mr. Amiable, agreed, and I'm pleased to say that Sam kicked his A-picture butt from one end of Broadway to the other.

How Low Can You Go?

Pretty low.

With a finished 16mm film we could tour college campuses for years, we could screen our film on every aircraft carrier in the Pacific—but could we get it into theaters? No. To do this, we had to get the film enlarged ("blown up") to the industry standard of 35mm.

Our investments were all sold off—National Bank of Detroit turned its nose up at the prospects of any more business and every relative we knew had been tapped out. A phrase we began to hear a lot was, "Guys, no more means *no more.*"

Who could we swindle next? The answer was very close to home.

I spotted my recently divorced Dad whispering to himself in a lawn chair behind our house one summer evening. Mentally, he was on another planet. Prodigal son that I was, I went for the jugular.

Charlie getting broad-sided.

"Hey, Pop . . ."

". . . Huh?"

"Uh, now that you and Mom are . . . well, you know . . . do you have any plans for that property up north?"

"Not really, why?"

"Well, I figured since you might not be going up there as much, me and the boys could get some use out of it."

"Go on up whenever you want," Charlie said.

"Oh, uh thanks, Dad, but what I meant was . . . (wince) . . . if you'd be willing to let me put the property up as collateral, we could get a loan to finish the flick . . ."

As the words came out, I astonished even myself. I was sure the answer would be returned to me in the form of loud invectives, but Charlie, God bless him, without so much as a glance, tossed a hand in the air.

"Whatever . . ."

Conning Dad was the easy part—the real trick was getting the loan officer of the Mid-Michigan bank in Gladwin, Michigan, to understand the concept of a blowup.

The officer, tired of our confusing, technical explanation, finally stopped us with, "Look, fellas, I don't really give a rat's ass what a *blowup* is. It's pretty simple—you return the money when the loan is due, or you risk losing the property. In the meantime, blow up whatever you'd like. . . ."

THE FIRST PICTURE SHOW   21

Because of the time and effort it took to get our first film finished, we decided to throw a big premiere and pull out all the stops—this turned out to be a mini-production of its own.

Most importantly, we needed the proper venue. The Redford Theater, a grand old revival house, circa 1929, was ideal—it could seat over 1,000 patrons easily, had a gigantic screen and boasted a fully restored pipe organ that rose from the orchestra pit. As the lights of the theater dimmed, "stars" twinkled subtly in the painted "sky."

Many of my Saturday evenings had been spent there watching newly minted prints of *Ben Hur, Sound of Music* and *Bridge on the River Kwai*. It was a splendid place to launch our film.

We began to put together a show within a show—custom tickets, programs, and a creepy wind track to create the right tone in the auditorium. For giggles, we posted an ambulance and a security guard in front of the theater—in case any patron found the film too horrific to handle. Many thanks to pioneer shclockmeister William Castle for that idea. On top of that, you couldn't have a premiere without spotlights, limousines and tuxedos.

Just two weeks before the premiere, we finally saw what was then still called *Book of the Dead* in a local theater, late at night, on the big screen. The blowup looked good—really good.

As I watched the 35mm images flicker in front of me, the thought rolling around in my head was, *Crazy, man, crazy.* We had laughed in the face of disaster and pulled it off. It was one of the few times in this odyssey when we had a feeling of accomplishment. Sure, it wasn't sold yet, but at least the current crisis was over.

Our first audience lining up at the Redford Theater.

Turnout for the premiere exceeded our expectations. About a thousand curious relatives, investors and ex-high school pals seemed to enjoy themselves immensely and whooped it up in *almost* all of the right places. Essentially a melodrama, *Evil Dead* walked a very fine line—combine inexperienced actors with a primitive script and you're bound to get some unexpected laughs. We were happy to have any reaction at all.

Shortly after the show, we were told that an elderly woman wanted to see the filmmakers in the lobby right away. The screening was open to the public, so we figured we were going to get an earful.

"Did you fellows make this picture?" the octogenarian asked, in a tone that was hard to read.

"Uh, yes, ma'am," Sam replied.

"I just want to tell you boys that I was having such a bad day today. I saw the ad for your film and I thought I should get out and see what it was. Well, I'm glad I did, because now I feel great and I just wanted to thank you for it!"

Thus began our own "test-screening" process. We knew that the audience at the premiere was a deck stacked in our favor. We had to try *Evil Dead* in front of a pure audience and see if it still played. The decision was an immediate one—take it to Michigan State University.

Screenings at the State Theater at MSU proved that the film *did* play—the rowdier the audience the better. The one thing *Evil Dead* did was dish out the gore—by the shovelful.

BIRTH OF A SALESMAN 22

In a rudderless search for a distribution deal, we showed our film to any man, woman or child for advice. The first targets were filmmakers, just to get sage advice about the do's and don'ts of the big "D."

"Well, you didn't fuck up, but you didn't do great either," came the assessment of an exploitation filmmaker. "It's really crude."

From there, we progressed to booking agents, exhibitors, subdistributors, packaging agents and lawyers. As helpful as they were, we began to get the impression that we'd be lucky to get any deal at all and that we should take what we could get.

We dragged a print to larger distributors on both coasts and in Canada, but the reaction was the same: unanimous disinterest.

"Your picture is pretty bloody," said a distributor. "Have you submitted it for a rating?"

"Well, no . . . not exactly."

"Cause if it can't get rated, you're shit out of luck."

We needed help. Eventually, the name of a sales agent surfaced: Irvin Shapiro.

After doing some research, we saw that his company, Films Around the World, was connected to George Romero's early films. If this man was representing the filmmaker who brought the world *Night of the Living Dead,* he might just be the right guy for us.

Irvin Shapiro had lived a full life before we ever met him. As a young man in the 1920s, he handled the publicity for *Battleship Potemkin* by filmmaker Sergei Eisenstein. Seeing an opportunity to sell foreign films to the U.S., Irvin became one of the founders of the Cannes Film Market. He was also one of the first entrepreneurs to buy television rights to films and was involved with the company Screen Gems. Irvin often enjoyed pointing out a painting by Picasso, hanging on his apartment wall, that he had traded the young painter for a bottle of wine.

Irvin had been around.

On December 10, 1981, we screened our film for this living legend. As the lights came up in the screening room, Irvin cracked a smile.

"It ain't *Gone with the Wind,* but I think we can make some money with it. Of course, we're gonna have to change the title. If you call it *Book of the Dead,* people are gonna think they have to read for ninety minutes. I think we can do better."

Revelation #28c: Making a film and selling it are completely different birds.

Back in Ferndale, we kicked some new names around. Irvin sent some ideas to us and we sent some back to him. Among the classics on the list were:

Book of the Dead (the original)
Blood Flood
Fe-Monsters
101% Dead
Death of the Dead
The Evil Dead Men and the Evil Dead Women
Evil Dead

Big Bad Irvin Shapiro.

Evil Dead emerged as the *least worst* of the bunch. I recall thinking at the time that it was a piss-poor title, but changing it turned out to be the easy part.

"Where are your delivery elements?" Irvin asked.

Rob, Sam and I exchanged dumb looks.

"What's a delivery element?"

"The lab elements you need to sell your picture around the world."

"Like?"

"Like stills, a foreign textless, an M&E, a dialogue continuity, an inter-positive . . ."

This was a depressing prospect, because it led to the possibility that we'd have to scrape together even more money—a feat I didn't think we could do.

Fortunately for us, Irvin Shapiro was one of the few honorable men in the film business—his company fronted the necessary funds to create these delivery elements.

What followed was a lesson in sales from the Grand Master.

MADISON AVENUE IN DETROIT

In order to sell our film around the world, we had to provide not only the film but the technical tools necessary for foreign distributors to rerecord dialogue in a different language, change the title on the print and make a new poster. Even if your film was marketable, you couldn't close a deal without these items—and if you couldn't close, you couldn't collect money to pay back the investors.

During production, we had taken some pictures, but they were mostly behind-the-scenes stuff, or "Hey Sam, make a funny face!"—nothing useful for promotion.

Irvin suggested that we simply fake it, so early in 1982, we got back in action. Our photographer buddy Mike Ditz had his own photo studio just down the street from our offices and we concocted a number of poses. Armed with a shotgun, shovel and monster arms, we worked all night creating our first marketing concepts.

It was the first time we had to think about how an audience should view this film. Should we be explicit? Should we imply the evil? Because we had no idea what would sell, our photographs represented numerous themes: "Man vs. Demons," "Man and Woman vs. Demons," and even "Woman Overcome by Demons."

Next on Irvin's list was a trailer, or coming attraction—those slick highlights you see in a theater before the main feature. Sam pieced ours together in one of the cramped dentist cubicles with a Moviola editing machine that shredded more film than it put together.

The process of laying out the first advertisement was more technical than anything—it was all about the dimensions of the paper you were advertising in and how

"What's a delivery element?"
(A few of our concepts.)

LET'S LOSE THAT CROSS!

HAVE SOME BLOOD COMING OUT OF THE DAME'S MOUTH!

BETTER DROP THAT STRAP!

WE NEED THE HAND TO BE "SCARIER!"

CLEAN UP THAT STRAW!

BEFORE - The untouched photo from a Ferndale, Michigan, warehouse.

AFTER - The slick, new "marketable" ad concept.

many screen lines it had and how to make an original photo into a Velox or half-tone or transparency.

The idea of photo retouching was a curious peek into the world of advertising. If something in the original picture bothered us, like a visible bolt on the skeleton arm, or a lack of sheen to the chainsaw blade, we simply changed it.

The last items for our promotional shopping cart were easier to come by—let's face it, every city has a custom T-shirt shop. Our *Evil Dead* shirts were made at the same place that would have cranked out Biff's Bump Shop, or Big Al's Car Stereo Warehouse, so no big challenge there.

Blank match books, we found, had to be purchased from a wholesaler before a printing company could adorn their covers, and that buttons could be hand-made, as long as you bought a few basic tools. This all seemed like a lot of work at the time, but it wasn't until years later that we realized how good we had it. As filmmakers for a studio, you quickly become the fifth wheel once you hand over a completed print.

On *Evil Dead,* we had our fingers in every pie and remained connected to the film until the bitter end—for what was to be the first and last time.

Armed with 500 matchbooks, 150 T-shirts, 48 hats, 200 buttons, 1,200 brochures, and 500 invitations, Irvin could now do his magic.

First stop: the American Film Market.

JUST ANOTHER WIDGET

In case it's all a mystery, buying and selling films isn't all that different from buying and selling clothes hangers—you've got a product to sell and you want to find buyers. Manufactured products are exhibited at trade shows all around the country—you've heard the ads: "Don't miss the Home and Garden Expo, this weekend only at the downtown convention center."

The boys and their "widgets."

Films are sold the same way. Three time a year, in Los Angeles, Cannes France, and Milan Italy, films from around the world are bought and sold like slabs of meat—country by country.

In fact, the American "Meat" Market would be a more appropriate name. Chronologically, it is the first one of the year, usually in March, and it works like this: the market organizers take over several major hotels while the sellers, the foreign sales agents, each take a suite in which to hawk their wares. Buyers from around the world wander in and out of the suites, each with a budget and a laundry list of the type of films they are willing to buy.

Let's say Joe Germany walks into Acme Foreign Sales Company and he's looking for a horror picture to round out his purchases. By this point, he may have already seen ads in trade magazines like *Variety* or *Screen International* and knows that Acme represents several horror titles.

Acme would show Joe their racks of 8½" x 11" ad slicks (which look like mini movie posters) for the flicks available, and if one interests him, he'll ask for more information. It's an incremental thing—the sellers want to lure the buyer deep into their lair, where the arm-twisting can begin.

Joe the buyer might then wish to see a trailer (like the one Sam edited). If this keeps his interest, he'll arrange to see the entire film at a local cineplex that has been taken over by the film market. If Joe likes what he sees, he'll come back to Acme and they'll begin negotiations.

Having that useless information as a backdrop, enter the three Midwesterners.

LA-LA-LAND 23

March 24, 1982, Rob, Sam and I arrived in Hollywood.

Stepping off the plane, we got the first of many surprises—the weather was lousy. This was supposed to be the land of eternal sunshine, but during the first two weeks of our stay, it drizzled almost every day.

When the sun did come out, it was a lovely dry heat and the air would be clear, but not for long. Within twenty-four hours of any rain, an orange-yellow haze would build up until you couldn't see the mountains anymore.

Picking up our "Rent-A-Wreck" '65 Cadillac convertible, we took on the LA freeways and they certainly lived up to their reputation—some sections were eight lanes in *each* direction and made the freeways back in Detroit seem cute in comparison.

Still, with no public transportation to speak of, Los Angeles was a car town and traffic jams occurred at any hour of the day or night—a flat tire or an overheated radiator could start a chain reaction that stretched for miles. Few things were more disturbing than being stuck in a major traffic jam at one o'clock in the morning.

To my taste buds, cuisine in southern California was very exotic. In Detroit, Chinese and Italian were about the only "ethnic" foods available, so

Have wreck, will travel.

143

it was an eye-opener to sample Japanese, Korean, Thai, or even Mexican food.

I wasn't aware how lame the fruits and vegetables were back East until I set foot in a California supermarket. Suddenly, I had three choices of lettuce other than iceberg, and I could get strawberries the size of golf balls—but what surprised me most was the orange juice. In Michigan, I never liked the stuff—it was always bitter and awful, but I was led to believe that this was normal. In California, I could get fresh-squeezed orange juice at almost every restaurant, and it was sweet, pulpy, and wonderful.

Rob, Sam and I in front of Twentieth Century Fox Studios.

Sociologically speaking, LA was a crazy place—the mix of ethnicity was as startling as it was amazing. I had never seen anyone who was "Eurasian," or a mix of black and Latino. It also puzzled me that attendants at 7-Eleven, or even McDonald's of all places, had trouble with the English language.

When we wandered into trendier areas, beautiful people seemed to be everywhere. A native from LA explained that it resulted from generations of pretty people who had come to Hollywood to find fame and fortune mating with other pretty people who had come to Hollywood to find fame and fortune. What really struck me was the amount of attention that people gave to the human body. Working out was the religion of choice, and if that didn't result in the perfect body, they liposucked, body-sculpted, and breast-augmented themselves the rest of the way.

As twisted as it was, it made sense—this was Hollywood, the wannabe capital of the world, so why wouldn't every *Miss Boot Lick Arkansas* in the country gravitate there? The thing that saddened me was that the actors I met seemed far more concerned with outward appearance than with training or, dare I say, talent.

When we weren't attending screenings of the film, or meeting with buyers, we were at the beach, body surfing. I remember the sensation of diving into the Pacific Ocean for the first time—as I surfaced, I spit out a mouthful of water.

"Yuck, this is *salty* . . ."

As a person accustomed to fresh water, I found this an apt metaphor for Hollywood: It looks inviting on the outside, but if you dive in, you're in for a shock.

CAN I CALL YOU CHUCK?

The real stunner of that first LA experience, though, was the city of Hollywood itself. Nothing like the postcards I'd seen, Hollywood is a seedy place where the rich and famous are scarce and you're more likely to see hourly motels, hookers and burned-out rock 'n rollers. This Hollywood didn't represent the best and the brightest—it was a place where Hugh Grant could get a blowjob.

Having said that, I'm happy to say that I met my first movie star there. Rob, Sam and I strolled along the *Walk of Fame,* past the stars of Jack Benny, Dinah Shore, Charlton Heston . . . wait, that's no star . . . that's really *him*!

I ran after him, repeatedly calling out "Mr. Heston, Mr. Heston" until he had to look back, no doubt trying to gauge my particular level of mania.

". . . Yes?"

Taking advantage of this hesitation, I swung around in front of him and thrust out my hand. He was gracious and patient as I babbled incoherently about this film or that. After sufficient groveling, I let him pass.

Boulevard of broken dreams.

Charlton Heston would continue to crop up in my life.

Irvin's company got us special passes so we could roam the American Film Market, gawking at the immense amount of independent films for sale. In the evenings, the market organizers lined up a number of splashy "show biz" events to wow the prospective buyers. Being an actor in *Evil Dead,* I was put on the invite list to a swank bash at Universal Studios.

After assembling on sound stage 44, we were herded into an actors' only dining area and seated with other performers. You'll never guess who was at my table—that's right, the Chuckster. I took the opportunity to reintroduce myself.

"Mr. Heston, Bruce Campbell—how funny that we'd be seated together."
"Oh?"

"Well, recently we met on Hollywood Boulevard. I wasn't really an actor then, I was just a big fan."

Thinking I was a gate crasher, Chuck glanced at a nearby security guard before answering.

"Did we?"

"Yep. And now I'm an actor—*just like you*!"

". . . Indeed."

145

Seeing that my nametag actually matched the place setting at our table, Chuck realized that he had to deal with me.

"Uh . . . have you met my wife, Ben?"

"That's Bruce."

"Oh, yes . . . of course . . ."

Star of Chuck.

After a rushed piece of chocolate cheesecake, Chuck excused himself from the table, so I hooked up with Rob and Sam again and we gawked at all of the famous actors there, like Martin Landau, David Soul and Morgan Fairchild. She was there, hawking a film, and we huddled up for a picture. As I looked over at Sam, I soon saw why he had such a big smile on his face—he was giving Morgan the Rabbit Ears behind her head.

Recently, I had the opportunity to torment Charlton Heston again at a screening in Hollywood and I came a stutter away from calling him "Chuck." He still didn't recall meeting me, even after my detailed account of the other *two* times. I have a hunch that next time we meet, he'll either recognize me or have me arrested.

BEWARE THE SPORES 24

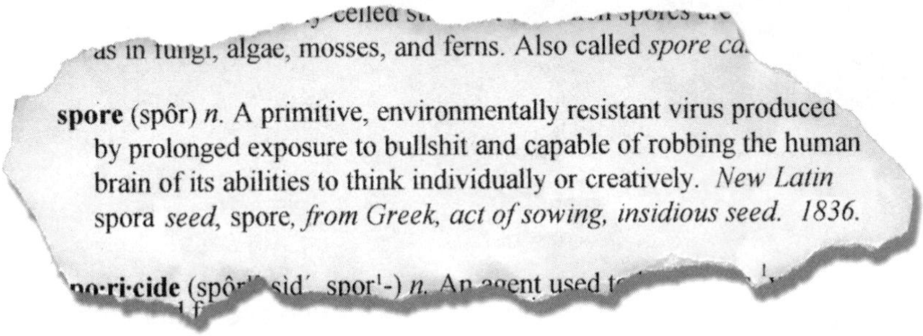

as in fungi, algae, mosses, and ferns. Also called *spore ca*.

spore (spôr) *n*. A primitive, environmentally resistant virus produced by prolonged exposure to bullshit and capable of robbing the human brain of its abilities to think individually or creatively. *New Latin* spora *seed*, spore, *from Greek, act of sowing, insidious seed. 1836.*

po·ri·cide (spôr'·sid´ spor'-) *n*. An agent used t

After just a week in Hollywood, Rob, Sam and I began to show symptoms of a bizarre disease, including wild mood swings that took us from lethargy to euphoria and back. We found ourselves less concerned with screenings or schedules and all we really wanted to do was go to the beach. Something had gone terribly wrong and we didn't know what it was or how to stop it.

After doing some independent research with experts in the field, we learned that the spores we had been infected with are a motivation-sapping virus that alters your perceptions of reality. If left untreated for five years or more, Chronic Spore Syndrome is likely to develop. Here is an example of this tragic condition:

Since we were in LA, I decided to look up my old boss, Verne, who had an office on the lot of Twentieth Century Fox. My tour of the back lot and subsequent meeting with him was exciting, but it wasn't nearly as educational as a conversation with a man on the bus bench outside the studio.

As I sat, waiting for Sam and Rob to pick me up in the Caddy, a well-tanned man turned his attention to me.

"Excuse me, do you have a few dollars for the bus?" he asked, unashamed.

As I fished through my pockets for loose change, he went on, jerking a thumb at the Fox lot behind us.

"That damn studio had me signed to a three-picture deal."

"Really?" I said, believing him.

"Yeah. They insisted that I do my own stunts and I got hurt on my first picture with them."

I looked at my tanned friend a little closer. He never made eye contact. A low Spore Count caused my Michigan suspicions to rise.

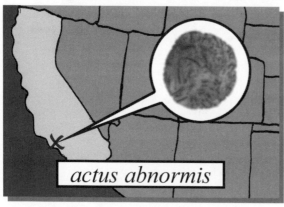

actus abnormis

Beware the spores...

"Really," I said again, this time a little less enthusiastic.

"Yeah. Now, they won't pay up and I'm out of work."

"That's tough," I said, letting the coins drop back into my pocket, but he wasn't done explaining.

"See, I was a famous child actor. I was one of the kids in *Lassie*."

"Oh," I said, looking for Rob and Sam in the Caddy.

"Good for you."

The odd thing about his last reference was that it was so specific. For all I knew, the poor sap was a child actor who was driven insane by a strange profession. I didn't really want to get into it and luckily the convertible arrived to save me from further discussion.

In my own effort to rid the world of spores, I have tabulated a few early warning signs:

YOU KNOW THE SPORES HAVE GOTTEN YOU WHEN:

• *Your day-to-day decision making process is ruled by fear instead of reason.*
• *You wear black to every Hollywood function.*
• *You deny the fact that you're from Gary, Indiana.*
• *You begin to despise your body.*
• *You attend parties hosted by losers, hoping to meet a winner.*

• *You entertain the notion of having a cell phone surgically implanted in your ear.*

SPORE SPEAK:

• *Look, I can't tie up the line, I'm waiting for* Paramount, Universal and Columbia *to call me back.*
• *Once I get my teeth fixed, I'm going to be a star!*
• Titanic *was the best film I've ever seen.*

Playing Kick the Cannes   25

The feeding frenzy of sales continued in May 1982 at the Cannes Film Market in France.

Since this event was an ocean away, Irvin Shapiro's budget could scarcely afford to send all of us, so Sam (as auteur) was chosen to go. Having learned a lesson or two from the American Film Market, we tweaked a few of our sales items—notably a brochure, which we translated into French. To do this, Sam and I enlisted our high school French teacher, the venerable Madame Tessem. In addition to a fine translation, she also coached Sam on local customs, maps, etc.

Here, on the French Riviera, we got our next break. At one of many screenings, Stephen King happened to see our film. He liked *Evil Dead* so much, he wrote a hearty endorsement in the magazine *Twilight Zone.*

In the article, he stated that *Evil Dead* was "the most ferociously original horror film of the year." You can't buy that type of promotion, so we begged him to let us put this phrase on all of our advertisements— he agreed, and it made a huge difference.

A plug from one of horror's legends sent up a protective force field around our little film. Suddenly, critics took a second or

There Goes the Neighborhood: Evil Dead *featured at the posh Carlton Hotel in Cannes.*

even first look at it and several good reviews rolled in. Among them was the *LA Times,* pronouncing *Evil Dead,* "an instant classic."

Eventually, with the invaluable assistance of Mr. King, our film began to sell, territory by territory, around the globe. England promoted *Evil Dead* like it was an A picture. I'm not sure how Prince Charles felt about the theater, named after him, displaying giant photos of possessed monsters, but it happened nonetheless.

Eventually, *Evil Dead* became the number one video seller in England for 1983. It was a treat to look *further down* the list and see Stanley Kubrick's *The Shining.*

THE DOWNSIDE OF THE UPSIDE   **26**

Eventually, with money coming in from overseas, New Line Cinema took renewed interest. I'd be a liar if I said the negotiation process was a love fest, but eventually we signed a distribution deal with them. January 6, 1983, we got our first domestic check.

That same day, we spent eight hours at the accountant's, sorting through four years of our shadowy past, trying to determine exactly who got what amount and when. We paid back thirty-three percent of our loans with that first New Line check. We were also able to keep that small town bank in the middle of Michigan from seizing my family's property and all three of us were able to pay off two months' worth of bills—it was a start.

February 4, 1983, *Evil Dead* had a sneak preview in New York. This was pre-Disney New York and the crowd on 42nd Street ate it up. Detroit was the same—May 6, I snuck into the Showcase Theaters and enjoyed a rowdy audience reaction.

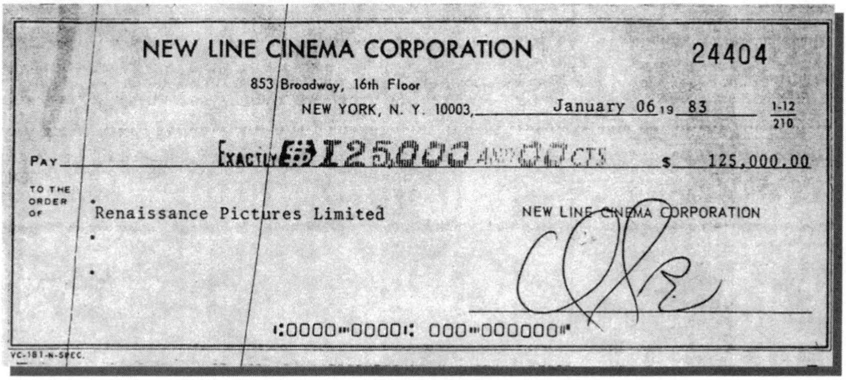

NEW LINE CINEMA CORPORATION   24404

853 Broadway, 16th Floor
NEW YORK, N. Y. 10003   January 06 19 83   1-12 / 210

PAY EXACTLY I25,000 AND 00 CTS $ 125,000.00

TO THE ORDER OF Renaissance Pictures Limited   NEW LINE CINEMA CORPORATION

⑈0000⑈0000⑈ 000⑈0000000⑈

VC-181-N-SPEC.

Cha-ching!

153

It was a thrill to see our film playing in the same theater I had patronized for years, but it was something of an anticlimax. *Evil Dead* had taken four years to make, but its theatrical run was only a couple of months—too short to get any sense of success.

Then there were the *other* reviews—the ones that made you want to crawl into a hole and die. I joined *Evil Dead* in Los Angeles for the *Filmex* festival. Fielding questions after the screening, the first inquiry put it all in perspective: "So, Bruce, are you going to use *real* actors next time?"

More pot shots came from various reviews around the country. "Sickest of the Sick" was Atlanta's description of the film. "Films that Stoop" headlined another entertainment review. After getting almost universal praise for *Evil Dead*, I suppose it was the balance we needed.

Evil Dead Footnote

All in all, our investors got their money back after six years. Nineteen years later, due to a built-up demand, we were back on the video charts at number three—right behind *Titanic* and *Lady and the Tramp*.

I fear for that buried time capsule—its days are numbered. I recently attended a film festival in Champagne/Urbana, Illinois. At a "meet and greet" session, a rock was plunked down in front of me—a craggy, toothlike rock similar to that used in the construction of . . . *the fireplace of our cabin!*

Bruce: Where the flyin' hell did you get this?

Fan: Your cabin was in Morristown, Tennessee, right?

Bruce: (warily) . . . Yeah . . .

Fan: Well, we went there and found it. The fireplace was the only thing that was standing.

He was right, the place burned down in late 1980. Over the years, this obscure cabin in the hills has become a mecca of sorts for the truly devoted. I did my best to dodge various e-mails and letters from Deadites (an affectionate term), asking where they might find this mythical cabin, but my efforts have come to naught. The word is out.

The time capsule: Its days are numbered.

WORKING IN THE INDUSTRY: 27
BC BECOMES AN ACTOR

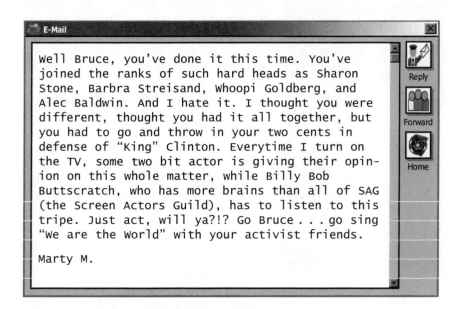

Well Bruce, you've done it this time. You've joined the ranks of such hard heads as Sharon Stone, Barbra Streisand, Whoopi Goldberg, and Alec Baldwin. And I hate it. I thought you were different, thought you had it all together, but you had to go and throw in your two cents in defense of "King" Clinton. Everytime I turn on the TV, some two bit actor is giving their opinion on this whole matter, while Billy Bob Buttscratch, who has more brains than all of SAG (the Screen Actors Guild), has to listen to this tripe. Just act, will ya?!? Go Bruce . . . go sing "We are the World" with your activist friends.

Marty M.

Reply

Forward

Home

I'm a little fuzzy on when I officially declared myself an actor. I had been exposed on film for ten years, with varying success, but I never made a living at it—and by Detroit standards, I couldn't say I was an actor until I could.

While *Evil Dead* was in post-production, there was a rushed trip to New York to audition for a romantic comedy. The project was hardly worth the plane fare, but try and tell that to a young actor with no perspective.

I cohosted a "pilot" for an automotive talk show. The Motor City seemed like a logical place to film such a thing, but nothing ever came of it.

During a sales trip to Los Angeles, I met with a manager for the first time and showed him some clips from the film.

"I think you could be a star, but you need to lose some weight," was his only assessment—the fact that I still lived in Detroit didn't help either.

What came of that meeting was the need for a head shot—an eight-by-ten black-and-white photograph that best represented what I was all about. This was an alien concept for me, since I had never "marketed" myself before. What kind of an actor *was* I? A *funny* actor? A *serious* actor? A *character* actor?

In Detroit, talent agencies solved that problem by insisting that clients create a composite photo that showcased your versatility. To prepare for this, I looked at other "comps." If you're ever in need of great entertainment, go to a talent agency and thumb through their stack of "Construction Workers," "On The Go Executives," and "Happy Home-makers."

Potato chip-eating geek.

A trip to Mike Ditz's photo studio put the pictures in motion. There, I'm embarrassed to admit, I allowed myself to be photographed as the "unshaven, shirtless stud," the "slick, James Bond–like dude," and the "bespectacled, potato chip-eating geek."

I'm not sure if these photos helped or hindered me, but at least I was ready to be submitted. One of my first bites from the outside world was a role in a promotional commercial for a Detroit TV station. Okay, it wasn't a *role*—I was hired to be an extra. Mind you, an extra in a ninety-minute feature film has a chance of being seen—an extra in a sixty-second commercial might as well do cartwheels naked for all the screen time they'll get. Still, I was happy for the 1.5 seconds of exposure.

After several auditions, I managed to land the role of teacher, Alan Stuart, in a homegrown soap opera called *Generations*. The basic scenario was no different than the average soap—a bunch of upscale people enduring never-ending personal problems. It wasn't exactly Harold Pinter, but they were paying thirty-five bucks a scene—thirty-five more than I had ever made before.

The only lasting benefit of doing this soap (other than paying off my Sunoco credit card) was learning to memorize lines of dialogue quickly and meeting an actress named Christine Deveau. She played my love interest on the show and, to perpetuate an old cliché, we became involved off screen as well.

I must admit, what attracted me most to Cris was her attraction to me. Simplistic, yes, but this was the first time a woman had openly expressed an interest, and I responded in kind.

Having been married before, Cris had first hand knowledge of things like "long-term commitment" and "co-habitation," but it was all Greek to me. Until Cris appeared on the scene, the film business was my only mistress, demanding full attention. Now, I had to divide my time more equally.

Waking up next to the same person each morning and coming home to them every night was an exciting dynamic and it felt very comfortable. Within six months, talk of the big "M" peppered our conversations.

Because marriage is such a personal affair, Cris and I felt that we alone should determine every aspect of the process—including when, where and how it should take place. As a result, we shocked the daylights out of Reverend Cowick at our first meeting at the Franklin Community Church.

Rev: It's so nice to have you two here. I am really looking forward to—

Bruce: Yeah, uh, Rev, could you marry us right now?

Rev: I beg your pardon?

Cris: We have everything with us.

Rev: Well, I...

Bruce: Could you? Right here?

Rev: But I don't even know you.

"I beg your pardon?"

Bruce: With all due respect, Reverend, you never will. This is between the two of us and the Big Guy upstairs.

Reverend Cowick remained unconvinced, however, and encouraged us to have a "proper" ceremony.

I had been in the Franklin Village Church many times, rehearsing with the Franklin Village Junior Players. While fine-tuning a talent show in 1973, the contestants took a short break to watch Richard Nixon resign. Ten years later, I was there for something far more important than politics—I was about to close the door on bachelorhood.

The ceremony on March 13, 1983, was as small as possible. We managed to pare participation down to a witness and a ring bearer. Rob and Sam made for dual Best Men/witnesses and Sam's mother, Celia, presented the ring because if she wasn't allowed to attend, she swore she'd never speak to me again. Having endured her loving wrath for years at the Raimi household, I knew she was dead serious. The wedding went off without a glitch, and the Michigan weather gods provided us with a warm, sunny day.

By the time Cris and I tied the knot, the soap opera, *Generations,* had been cancelled. In an ironic twist, years after my marriage collapsed, this tragically poor soap lived on. Watch closely to a scene in the Coen Brother's film *Fargo,* where a bad guy is glued to the TV in a cabin. There, in poor reception, you can see me arguing with my "girlfriend." Screen time in an Academy Award-winning film—what more could a guy from Detroit want?

My next gig came from an ex-employer. Ron Teachworth, a teacher for whom I taught film classes, decided to pony up his own money and make a film—what resulted was the independent feature, *Going Back.*

Up to this time, I had mastered the prolonged scream, the horrific recoil, the slam against a wall, but I never really had to do what would be considered *acting.*

A scene from Going Back: *"Look, Ma, no blood."*

Going Back was fun because there wasn't an ounce of blood anywhere in sight—just a strange thing called dialogue. Method acting and I are strange bedfellows, but it was refreshing to rehearse scenes, just like a play, and shoot them simply and efficiently.

The entire film was shot in two weeks in the middle part of Michigan. The beauty of having next to no budget is that the cast and crew remain small. By the time I was done filming, I knew each person by name and whether they snored or not, since most of us bunked in a single trailer home.

Okay, so I starred in a couple films, and bluffed my way through a go-nowhere soap opera. So what? I still wasn't a member of the Screen Actors Guild—the Holy Grail of "professional" validation.

The great wheel of Karma rolled back around as I attended an audition for a Chrysler Industrial film. The producer was a fellow I knew from my production assistant days. In fact, my 1973 Chevy Bel Air had been towed as an abandoned vehicle while under his employ, and I suppose he felt sorry for me.

"What are you doing here?" he asked. "Get me a cup of coffee."

"Get your own damn coffee," I shot back. "I've stepped in *front* of the camera, pal—I'm a movie star. You gonna hire me or not?"

He did, and my first union job was portraying a car salesman with an interesting twist. My character, suit and all, was in a boxing ring next to a Chrysler—the car of choice. When the bell rang, I'd leap out of the corner, weaving, bobbing and jabbing the opponent (a salesman for Ford in another ring) with sales-friendly praise for my car.

There is nothing harder than memorizing technical jargon—phrases like, "Let's not overlook the McPherson Strut Suspension" don't exactly roll off the tongue. Still, that first job filmed for twenty hours and the union overtime alone paid for all of my Screen Actors Guild dues. I was happy to be back in familiar territory, only with a new and improved status—I wasn't fetching coffee anymore, I was having it fetched for me.

Ring around the SAG card.

THE FIRST "HOLLYWOOD" FILM
"THE TERROR THAT ATE MOTOWN"

28

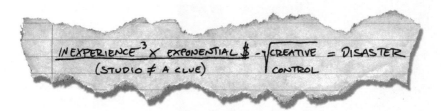

$$\frac{INEXPERIENCE^3 \times EXPONENTIAL\ \$}{(STUDIO \neq A\ CLUE)} - \sqrt{\frac{CREATIVE}{CONTROL}} = DISASTER$$

It was time for another flick. I was a card-carrying actor now, damn it all, and the boys and I were gonna go "Hollywood."

Sam had concocted an idea about two crazed killers several years prior to this, calling it *Relentless.* He recruited his new pals, the Coen Brothers, to assist him in fleshing out the script.

<u>Sam:</u> Edna, our editor, said, "You've gotta read the Coen boys' scripts—they're such good writers." I went, "Oh God."

<u>Bruce:</u> "Here goes another one."

<u>Sam:</u> You know, Joel's brother, Ethan, was just a statistical accountant at Macy's at the time, and I thought it's probably going to be awful, but I'll read it because I like Joel. And I read it and I thought, "This is really a great script. These guys know how to write scripts." I needed help, because ours was no good and they came in and helped me with it.

The plot became one that Hitchcock used often: a mild-mannered leading man (a security camera installer in this case) gets caught up in a web of fear, murder and mayhem.

Mentor Irvin Shapiro had a hand in devising a new title for the film. He figured that putting the letter "X" and the word "Murder" in the title would somehow draw the eye of moviegoers. Who were we to doubt this man?

The film became *The XYX Murders* and based on the strength of *Evil Dead,* financing fell into place.

At the time, we had no idea how good of an experience *Evil Dead* was. Sure, we burned off four years of our lives and didn't pocket a cent, but we had total creative control. Jumping into the big time meant dealing with the excruciatingly specific and alternately vague demands of a studio—unlike Michigan dentists, Hollywood executives took an interest in *everything.*

Embassy Pictures, our new boss, was the brainchild of TV guru Norman Lear. His Midas touch, it was assumed, would translate to full-length films.

Crimewave (the new title, complements of Embassy's marketing department) ended up being more like a master's degree in humility than a film. All along, it was assumed that I would play the lead role of Vic, but a particularly intransigent executive at Embassy Pictures saw things differently and insisted on a screen test.

Why do I have to test for this thing? I asked myself. *I didn't have to test for* Evil Dead.

My consolation prize: Renaldo the Heel.

So, in Mike Ditz's photo studio (where else?) we staged a scene on 16mm and presented it to the execs for consideration. An edict came down from on high: Bruce Campbell will *not* star in this film.

Up to this point, we had never heard the word "no" in the context of film-making. Graciously, Sam offered to beef up a secondary role for me—Renaldo "the Heel." As a coproducer of the film, less screen time allowed me to take a more active role behind-the-scenes; this was a good thing, because we needed all the production help we could get.

THE HOLLYWOOD ACTOR

Crimewave provided the first opportunity to deal with this odd breed of human. The studio insisted that "name" actors be cast in the lead roles because this would allow the film to be sold around the world. *That's odd,* I remember thinking, *didn't we just do that with a cast of no-name actors?*

With a starting budget of 2.5 million, the expectations were a little higher—the film *had* to sell well, so the main roles were cast out of Los Angeles.

As well as being expensive, each "Hollywood" actor we hired had, shall we say, "unique qualities." Because I was a coproducer and a part-time actor, I found myself dealing with the actors; or rather, with the actors' problems. By the time the shoot ended, I could have published a doctoral thesis on insanity.

One day, I got a call on the walkie-talkie.

<u>Claudia:</u> Bruce, you'd better come to the set. . . .

<u>Bruce:</u> What's going on?

<u>Claudia:</u> Louise is freaking out—she won't come out of her trailer.

<u>Bruce:</u> Why not?

<u>Claudia:</u> We don't know . . .

As I approached Louise's trailer, the makeup woman was leaving hastily. "She just threw her curlers at me. . . ."

I knocked on the door and asked if I could come in—tentatively, Louise agreed. As I entered, I got the shock of my life. Louise had covered her face with clown-white makeup and wore bright red lipstick.

"That makeup girl doesn't understand my makeup," she insisted, "so I've decided to do it myself."

There wasn't much point in debating the fine art of makeup because we were behind schedule already. The solution ended up being pretty simple—Louise could put whatever she wanted on her face first thing in the morning, then we'd lure her to the set, away from any mirrors, and completely redo her makeup under the guise of "touch-ups."

Brion, a talented character actor, took his role as a criminal a little too seriously and tore his Ramada hotel room to shreds. The explanation was a classic: the ghost of his girlfriend's ex-boyfriend was in the light fixtures, so they had to remove all of them.

And they say cocaine is a dangerous drug.

BAD COP, WORSE COP

Crimewave was a film about good guys and bad guys—as we negotiated for services within the city of Detroit, we ran into a few real-life characters.

The Hughes Brothers were a classic example.

This duo of lawyers owned a place called the Tuller Hotel. In the Roaring Twenties, this was *the* place to be. Situated in the heart of Detroit, it stood as a reminder of what the

"So, I'm a heel. What of it?"

Motor City used to be, boasting twelve hundred rooms, an elegant lobby and a ballroom of hand-carved oak.

In 1983 it was scheduled to become a retirement home for members of the AFL-CIO. To gain access, we had to get permission from the owners—

163

the Hughes Brothers. In a conversation worthy of a Coen Brothers film, we attempted to persuade these fellows to let us use their hotel as a location.

"How much do you have to pay?" began John, the "Good Cop" Brother.

Rob and I looked at each other.

"We've got ten *thousand* dollars," Rob announced.

With that, Mike, the "Bad Cop," jumped up blurting, "Hey, guys, I've got better things to do with my time," and disappeared from the office.

Wasn't $10,000 a boatload of money? I asked myself.

John, the "reasonable" one, countered with, "Guys, you'll have to forgive my brother Mike—he's a little testy. Tell you what, you think about what you *really* want to offer us and I'll see if I can get him back in the room."

Rob and I exchanged glances again.

"Shit, what do these guys want? How about if we double it?"

Mike sulked back into the office and Rob offered up the generous amount of twenty thousand dollars for two weeks in this dank, rotting palace.

With that, Mike sprang from his seat, as if electrocuted, and vanished without so much as a word. John threw up his hands with, "Sorry, guys, if I knew you were gonna come up that cheap, I never would have brought him back in."

"Okay, $30,000 and all the martinis you can drink..."

Rob and I were utterly stupefied. The entire *Evil Dead* location budget was something like $2,000. Rob bit the bullet and upped the price again—to an outrageous thirty thousand dollars. Eventually, Mike, "against his better judgement," agreed and the deal was made, but the contract also guaranteed the Hughes Brothers prime seats as extras.

Look closely to a scene filmed in their elegant ballroom and you'll see two gentlemen dressed in tuxedos, smiling triumphantly and ordering martinis.

CRASH AND BURN

To this day, the mere mention of *Crimewave* to a Detroit teamster elicits a shudder.

"Now that was a bitch, that one. . . ."

Rightly so—it was three months of swimming against the currents.

John Cameron was on board as a second assistant director and had his share of heartache.

<u>John:</u> I see *Crimewave* as a real turning point in a certain way, because if you survived that experience, nothing in the business could ever be as hard again.

<u>Bruce:</u> And how, brother.

<u>John:</u> It was the most difficult film ever in my life, and if I were a little older or hadn't been young and naïve I never would have survived. It was terrible—terrible. The unions and the work rules I knew nothing about and the production reports I knew nothing about. We had always been so independent it was like, "Who are you asking for this crap to send to Susan somebody in LA? I mean tell her to drop dead. We're dying out here. I don't have time to do this bullshit."

Josh Becker signed on as an extra, but he could smell trouble right from the start.

"I worked the first four days, but I thought, 'Like hell I'm going to continue on this mother as an extra,'" Josh explained. "It was so fucking cold out here, so awful. Sam is shooting so slowly. I'm gone man, gone."

I think Scott Spiegel was the only person who had any fun on the shoot.

"What? Me worry?" Shortly before my death in Crimewave.

<u>Scott:</u> You hired me and said, "Hey, you want to be extras wrangler?" and I go, "Crap, yeah, I can use some dough."

<u>Bruce:</u> But you also wound up getting in front of the camera a lot.

<u>Scott:</u> Yeah, it was great. I was a guy shivering in the cold in one shot, an old man at an elevator, a bum in an alley with you, a dinner guest—all kinds of things.

<u>Bruce:</u> You know what's funny about that—you were on camera so much, I got a call from Susan about you—she was the Embassy exec.

<u>Scott:</u> Really? How horrible. What did she say?

<u>Bruce:</u> She goes, "I saw that damn Spiegel kid in dailies again. Why does he have to be in every scene?"

I also got in trouble for "Shemping" too much. I put myself in a news segment as a goofy anchorman and Susan spotted it right away.

"Why were you in that scene, Bruce?"

"Well, you see, it's like this..." I stammered, groping for an answer. "That newscaster was the day job of my character, the Heel."

It was total bullshit, but she bought it.

Every motion picture budget has a buffer of ten percent. As overtime mounted, we exceeded that percentage by almost fifty percent. When this

IF CHINS COULD KILL

Trying to get a shot done in Crimewave.

happens, things start to change. Embassy Pictures' first order of business was to dismiss our production manager, Joe. Granted, he wasn't up to the task—his mind was on other projects. I should have gotten the hint when he insisted that a special "Bat Phone" be installed in his hotel suite—three stories above the production office.

Regardless of who was managing the crew, the shoot was moving too slowly and someone had to take the blame. Sam seemed prepared and was actively engaged at every level, so Rob and I figured that he wasn't the problem—it must be the cameraman, Bob. His work was good, but he wasn't exactly a speed-demon.

As producers, Rob and I felt obliged to "lean" on him. We drove him home after wrap one night, and led the conversation with an innocent question.

<u>Rob:</u> Hey, Bob, the pace of the shooting seems to be really slow. Anything we can do about that?

<u>Bob:</u> Well, in case you haven't noticed, Sam is attempting some very tricky stuff. He's an ambitious director.

Rob and I were well aware of Sam's embellishments and couldn't disagree.

<u>Bruce:</u> Well, sure Bob, we all know that, but why is it taking so long to light the shots?

<u>Bob:</u> If you're referring to the speed of my work, I can only go as fast as I go. If you want to let me go, that's fine, but I can't and *won't* be shooting any faster than I already am.

Bob's fearlessness put an end to our discussion and he stayed for the entire shoot.

Sam liked the look of wind on film. As a result, much of *Crimewave* was staged in the path of an impending storm. In order to achieve the type of gale force needed, several "Swamp Boats" had to be acquired from Florida. Just so we're clear here, I'm talking about the type of boat with a big fan behind it, powered by a 350-horse Chevrolet engine.

One such scene was filmed downtown at night, directly in front of a retirement home. As the wind machines raged incessantly, a bottle crashed to the street from high above. Inside the shattered glass, a pathetic note read: "The noise is keeping me awake all night long and I am getting sick. I am dying because of you. . . ."

My many jobs on *Crimewave,* aside from demoted actor, temporary assistant director, and actress cajoler (there should be a union local for this one) also included second unit director. In the case of *Crimewave,* it meant that I was responsible for getting shots of cars driving, wheels spinning, the odd foot on a brake pedal—the exciting stuff.

One of Sam's shots required a high angle looking past a car to the Detroit River below—the only problem was that at thirty below zero, the water had iced over completely. Because this wasn't part of the story, it became our responsibility to get rid of it.

We started by throwing things off the Belle Isle Bridge—rocks, tires, anything that would penetrate the frigid layer. I managed to find a cinder block and with great gusto I wiped out several yards of ice. Surveying the aftermath, I spotted a lone mitten floating on the water.

"Look at that," I shouted above the gale, "some poor bastard lost a glove!"

Seconds later, I realized that it belonged to me—I had to find warmth and fast. Fortunately, the mechanical effects guys always had a truckload of gear and I begged my way into a new pair of Gore-Tex gloves.

Eventually, having run out of debris to hurl, we laid primer cord (a powerful explosive) across the ice and blew the living crap out of it—as they say, "Anything to get the shot."

The bridge that ate my glove.

Hack and Slash

Shooting came to a halt some twelve weeks after it had begun and editing commenced within the confines of our dentist offices in Ferndale.

Unsatisfied with both the pace and the results of our Midwest approach, Embassy pictures eventually yanked the editing from us and unceremoniously relocated all postproduction to Los Angeles.

Sam: That was horrible. It was the worst time of my life. I realize now that they were a bunch of idiots, because if you're making a three-million-dollar movie, you should let the director have a preview, you know. Let him cut his movie. Let him put sound with it and watch it once—don't look at half a rough cut and before you've—

Bruce: They yanked that sucker before it was even cut.

Sam: It was really wrong. It was such a horrible, horrible, horrible, depressing scene.

This meant that Rob, Sam and I had to get our butts to the West Coast if we had any hopes of remaining involved in this film. It all led to a tense meeting in Century City—nerve center of Embassy Films. There, we were informed that the company would pay for *two* of us to stay in LA, but not all *three.*

Feeling like the third wheel, yet emboldened by months of hard work, I spoke for the group in an unforgiving tone.

"Hey, guys, there have always been three of us. We're all partners. This seems like nickel-and-dime bullshit . . ."

No sooner had the words left my mouth than Jeff, the production accountant responsible for tracking costs of *Crimewave,* leapt from his chair and pointed an accusing finger at me.

"Look, *ASSHOLE,*" he began, "do you have any idea how much you guys went over budget?"

Embassy Studios: Tower of Babble.

I'll spare you the rest of Jeff's tirade. At the receiving end of red-faced invectives, I replied with a resolute, "Look, do whatever you want, pay for whoever you want—the *three* of us made this film and we'll all be here in LA until it's done."

With that, I got up to leave the office, but Jeff stopped me with, "Hey, Bruce, it's just *business . . .*"

I didn't even know how to react to that statement. If this kind of treatment was representative of the film business, then the hell with it. I left the office and went down to the parking garage. Waiting in our Rent-a-Jalopy for Rob and Sam to return, it seemed like a good cry was long overdue. It felt good to rage against the absurdity of this studio system. *Hollywood sucks Grade A, Free Range, All-Natural eggs,* I told myself, wiping back a tear. *What a bunch of insensitive, money-grubbing pricks!*

Embassy, to their credit, eventually paid for all three of us to oversee the "new version." From an office in Los Angeles, we endured what has since become an almost mandatory function in Hollywood—reediting and reshooting. In the case of *Crimewave,* it meant reediting the film from almost the ground up with a "Hollywood" editor, and filming a set of "bookends"—a new beginning and ending that would help explain more clearly what audiences were about to see in the middle.

In the end, it didn't make any difference—"cross-genre" films like *Crimewave* send marketing people scurrying under a desk. A straightforward genre film is no problem. If it's action, you make sure someone is holding a gun in the poster. If it's a drama, you show a big close-up of the lead actor looking pensive. Comedy is a little trickier, but you might employ a conceptual artist to "Lampoon" the film. Combine the genres, however, and you're asking for congestion on Madison Avenue.

Crimewave, in its desire to please all viewers, test-marketed as *Broken Hearts and Noses* in San Diego. Foreign countries seemed to roll with the off-kilter tone of the film more easily. In France and Italy, it was called *Death on the Grill* and *The Two Craziest Killers in the World*, respectively.

Upon completion, we watched helplessly as the film went down in box-office flames. To meet a minimum HBO release requirement, the film opened only in Kansas and Alaska. To coin a phrase, "This film wasn't released, it escaped!"

There was only one good screening of *Crimewave* in its miserable existence and that was at the Seattle Film Festival. The host of the festival took the stage immediately before the show and proclaimed, wisely, that the film they were about to present was "silly."

"Put on your silly hat," he told the crowd of Pacific Northwest intellectuals. My mother happened to attend that night, and thanks to the properly warned audience, she maintains to this day that the film was "cute."

John Cameron has since come up with a term he calls "The *Crimewave* Meter"—a little alarm that goes off in his head when he knows he's about to work on a screwed-up film project.

Overall, *Crimewave* was a lesson about abject failure—no matter how you slice it, the film was a *dog,* and everyone involved can pretty much line up to take forty whacks. As filmmakers, we failed to execute a misguided concept and our studio refused us the benefit of any doubt.

One good thing came from this mess—my daughter Rebecca was conceived during production. While *Crimewave* was in post-production, she was born at the Henry Ford Hospital in downtown Detroit.

BACK TO BASICS

"THE SOUTH WILL RISE AGAIN!"

29

I have seen how a misstep like *Crimewave* could, and has, put filmmakers on studios' "don't bother" lists. Fortunately, we had a fallback position—doing the sequel to a successful film. *Evil Dead II* was all about licking our wounds.

$$\frac{EXPERIENCE^3}{\$ ADEQUATE \$} \times \frac{(\leq 1\% \ STUDIO \ INTERVENTION)}{r_x} = \frac{CREATIVE}{APEX}$$

Rob, Sam and I had been languishing in a slow-as-molasses financing deal, and because no green light had been granted yet, we couldn't give firm commitments to crew members, even though we had interviewed many. Then an interesting thing happened. One such woman headed south to Wilmington, where Stephen King was filming *Maximum Overdrive* for Dino De Laurentiis. For some inexplicable reason, she happened to take an audience with him and mentioned that she was interviewing for *Evil Dead II*, but we were having trouble getting the money.

With that, Stephen King called Dino, Dino called us, and we found ourselves in his gigantic office. Twenty minutes later, a deal was in place. We were urged to film as close to Dino's studio in Wilmington, North Carolina, as possible, but we were more interested in avoiding studio intervention, so we made a case for shooting in the rural town of Wadesboro. All in all, it made for a hands-free filming scenario, since executives either had to drive three hours from Wilmington, or fly to Charlotte and drive another hour and a half.

On the lookout for studio intervention.

Wadesboro was the same town where Steven Spielberg shot *The Color Purple.* We considered filming on the same piece of property since the owner, Harry, had experience with film crews.

The Color Purple was what Harry's face turned when I told him how much we had to spend on locations. I explained that it was unusual for a film company to install three-phase power, central air-conditioning and nine-inch irrigation pipes to "enhance" a location, as was the case with the Spielberg film.

"He was the Cadillac of motion pictures, Mr. H," I offered, "we're just the Chevy Nova." Eventually, Harry agreed to the deal as long as we funneled additional services through him.

The crumbling local high school was our command center: sets were built in the gymnasium, dailies were screened in the auditorium and the library made a fine production office—the school cafeteria didn't have to double for anything because we used it to cook our crew meals.

THE PAIN TRAIN

Filming in Wadesboro was a pleasant experience, with the exception of the weather. Ted Raimi would be happy to offer up a few words about temperature, both external and internal. Sam assumed that because his brother was both young and eager, he could get him to play the "heinous horror hag."

To accomplish the desired look, Ted was fitted with a foam body suit, complete with monster feet. It took a full five hours to get him ready for camera. Bear in mind, the temperature outside was at least 100 degrees, with eighty-five percent humidity. Inside the gymnasium, with poor ventilation and Tungsten lights, it hovered around 110 degrees.

The makeup effects crew carried a video camera everywhere they went and documented Ted's waking hours on and off the set. My favorite image was one of the guys pouring the sweat from Ted's monster booties into a series of Dixie cups.

At one point in the film, Ted's character had to spin in the air and cause general havoc. To do that, he was fitted for a flying harness. Depending on where they're attached to your body, these things will either dig into your groin, pinch your hips, or restrict your breathing—Ted's harness, I suspect, did a little of all three.

On top of that, Ted had to wear those damned white contact lenses. Technology had improved greatly since 1979, but these lenses were still oversized and could not be left in indefinitely.

Ted's biggest challenge, over and above everything else, was to deliver a high-energy performance. His big scene arrived, and he was spun in the air, take after take. Crew members standing nearby were spattered with flying sweat. In the finished film, look closely as Ted spots my character and bellows fiercely—you'll see a stream of sweat pouring out a slit in the makeup around his ear.

In-between takes, Ted was lowered to the floor and propped up on an apple box. When not gulping cups of Gatorade, an oxygen mask was clamped over his face until the next setup.

"It was worth it," Ted explained later. "It got me into the Screen Actors Guild."

Evil Dead II required my character, Ash, to grow from "cowardly wimp" to "leader of men." This was the first time I ever had to do any kind of long-term weight training. Bulk wasn't so much the issue—it was more about creating a sturdy physique that would work in harmony with the hero-in-a-torn-shirt concept.

To achieve that, I needed help.

Enter Mr. North Carolina—this beefy fellow helped me set up a mini-gym in an empty classroom and created a program that called for working out two hours a day, six days a week for twelve weeks.

Sam, in his inimitable style would wander past my door, mid-workout, and holler, "You call yourself a movie star? Get that lard-ass in gear!"

"Bruce, you're fat."

The other half of getting in shape dealt with food intake—or what *not* to intake. Gone were the morning Egg McMuffins, the banana cream pies at lunch and the buttered mashed potatoes at dinner. These were replaced with Diet Slice, fruit, fish and a protein supplement. The twelve weeks of working out during preproduction went well, but once shooting began, the two hours of working out after twelve hours of physical torment on the set became a real test of discipline.

As the program began to take hold and my system kicked into a faster metabolism, I began to shape-shift—parts of me began to shrink, like my stomach and butt, while my chest and arms began to expand.

The interesting thing about altering the way I looked was to observe the end result on film. Because it was shot out-of-sequence, you can actually watch the *before, during* and *after* versions of myself.

SAM RAIMI STRIKES AGAIN

Sam Raimi is an exponential filmmaker—his knowledge of film and its technique increase with each film. At the end of the grueling twelve-week shoot, Hamid, the focus-puller, remarked that he had to use every technical trick he had ever learned just for this one film. It was always amusing to catch Hamid out of the corner of my eye during a difficult shot, because he was sweating more than I was.

Sam is a technical animal—as well as knowing lenses, he dives specifically into exposures and shutter speeds—things that directors usually banter about in vague ways, like, "I want this film to look kinda moody." Sam would confound the camera department daily with his notions—and subsequently the mechanical effects department, since they had to build the rigs required to get his outrageous shots.

One such contraption was the "Ram-o-Cam"—a higher budget version of its *Evil Dead* counterpart. This consisted of a twenty-foot iron pole, attached to a rolling cart, with the camera mounted at the end of it. This device was designed to "puncture" the rear window of the "Classic," then proceed through the length of the car and burst out the front. Twenty-six takes and six windshields later, we got it in the can.

RAM-O-CAM II

COUNTER WEIGHT — METAL POLE — CAMERA POSITION "A" — CAMERA POSITION "B" — CRASH!

METAL CART — SAM'S DELTA

The mother of all rigs was the "Sam-o-Cam." This hellish device was a rotating, cast-iron "X" that was attached to the end of a crane arm. I was lashed to this "X" and spun around in either direction and at variable speeds. Verne, the mechanical effects coordinator, tried to make small talk as he strapped me in.

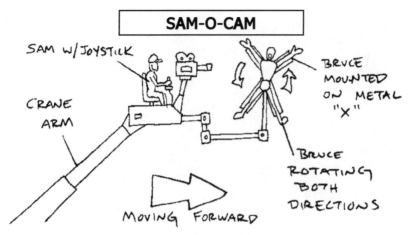

SAM-O-CAM

SAM w/ JOYSTICK

CRANE ARM

BRUCE MOUNTED ON METAL "X"

BRUCE ROTATING BOTH DIRECTIONS

MOVING FORWARD

"So, Bruce, what did you have for breakfast?"

"Why do you ask?"

"Because I'll be right below you—I want to know what's coming at me. . . ."

Sam was at the remote controls. I was his very own "Game Boy" for an entire day—and this was all to get *one* shot.

Another effect called for a "blood flood." To get the visual of liquid traveling horizontally at great speeds, trick photography was required. To do this, we built a portion of the set sideways. The camera was also tilted, thereby resulting in a "normal"-looking perspective. To understand this, tilt your head to the left. Now imagine that the room around you was tilted the same degree. Blood could then be poured from a rig in the ceiling and it would look horizontal.

This meant, however, that to assume a standing position, I would actually have to lie sideways, supported by a board. Above me, a fifty-five-gallon drum of fake blood was mounted—with a bathtub-sized plug. The idea was to pull the plug and I'd get hit full force.

<u>Sam:</u> Okay, now Bruce, if something goes wrong and you're drowning, wave your arms.

<u>Bruce:</u> But that's what I'm supposed to be doing anyway—how will you know the difference?

Sam looked at me blankly, then turned to the mechanical effects guy.

<u>Sam:</u> How long will the blood last?

<u>Effects Guy:</u> Long enough to empty fifty-five gallons.

<u>Sam:</u> Huh . . . good point . . . okay, let's shoot it!

I lived to tell the tale, but every time I blew my nose for the next two weeks, the snot was bright red.

Sam has never been one to stick to the industry standard of filming at twenty-four frames per second—twenty-four frames to Sam is slow motion. Many sequences in the film were photographed at varying speeds to achieve different effects. One scene was filmed much as an animated scene would be done—one frame at a time. This made it interesting for the actors,

175

"I'm gonna be fly-free in Number Three!"

as we were forced to slow our motion down by twenty-four times. . . .

Then there was the issue of reverse motion—this effect can be used to inexpensively achieve strange and otherwise unattainable movements from actors. Watching dailies one night, during a scene in which I was assaulted by my former girlfriend's tongue (a scene deleted from the film), Sam pointed at the screen and shouted, "That's the worst reverse-motion acting I've ever seen!"—something you would only hear on a Sam Raimi film.

The remaining weeks were spent spinning, getting doused with perhaps the highest volume of fake blood ever recorded on film and napping with a fly swatter. Out of sheer bullheadedness, I had insisted on using the original, time-tested Karo syrup formula from the first *Evil Dead* film. The visual effect was nice, but I became the object of desire for every fly in Wadesboro.

Go West, Young Man 30

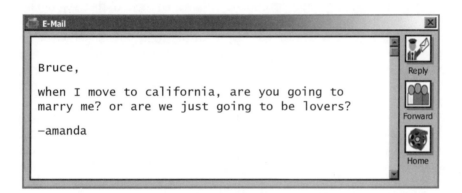

Now that *Evil Dead II* was in the can, it dawned on us that we should get our butts out to Los Angeles, permanently, and have a go at it.

One of the tools of an actor's trade is the demo reel—a collection of scenes that highlight whatever it is you think you can do best. Fortunately, I had the footage from three films available and put together a serviceable presentation.

Armed with this, and a new batch of head shots, I reconnected with the manager I met years before and he took me under his wing. His first duty, aside from masterminding my career, was to help me get an agent.

The process starts by meeting with any agency your manager can get you into—those that find you "marketable" will invite you back. These "callbacks" usually take place in the agency boardroom and the goal is to charm the pants off every agent in the room because, in many cases, they won't take you on unless they all agree. The questions come fast and furious:

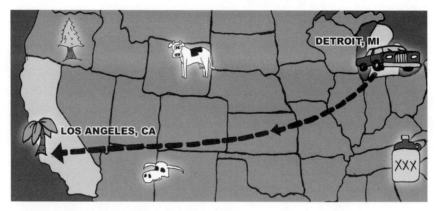

"How do you feel about TV, Bruce?"

"I never thought about it."

"You should. It's a great way for a mass audience to become familiar with you, and it makes it easier for us to place you in bigger features."

"Oh, okay, I . . ."

"What do you see yourself doing, Bruce?"

"Well, I've been doing independent features, so more of those would be fine . . ."

That's the point where all the agents in the room exchanged nervous glances, because I had just signaled to them that I might not be the cash cow they were hoping for.

"Sure, independent features are a great place to start Bruce," an agent offered, "but where do you see yourself going eventually?"

That was a great question, but I didn't have the answer. The idea of chasing the Holy Grail of fame and fortune never crossed my mind. I had moved my young family to California because it seemed like a logical progression, but to assume that I would immediately skyrocket to fame seemed absurd.

"I'm a working stiff actor," I told them. "I just want to work."

"So, you *will* do television?"

"Sure, I guess so. . . ."

Apparently, that was the right answer, because the agency hired me.

Flush with cash from the sequel, I promptly bought what was most likely the last house in Southern California priced under one hundred thousand dollars—a "great starter home" on Delight street in the outlying community of Canyon Country.

Getting accustomed to the insanity of California real estate was the biggest adjustment I had to make in moving west. Back home, I gave up a two-story home on a tree-lined street, in a good location that had cost thirty-five thousand dollars—now I had a single-story home on the edge of the desert with a dirt backyard for three times that much.

Well, I'm here, I thought to myself. *I'll give it a go and see what happens.*

To my amazement, I got the first acting job I auditioned for—a supporting role on the waning television show, *Knot's Landing.*

As the makeup man surveyed my face, I sensed that something was very wrong.

"I think we should pluck between your eyebrows," he said, with the bedside manner of a field nurse.

"Really, why would you do that?"

"Because you'll look far more intelligent."

Foolishly, I let him do this, but he had other ideas and rummaged in his bag for a small container called Mellow Yellow.

"This gets rid of all the red blotches," he explained. "Errol Flynn would have had no career without it. . . ."

With that, he proceeded to cover up every wrinkle, blotch and inconsistency on my entire face. It didn't really matter to him what type of character I was playing, he was more concerned with fulfilling the TV mantra—make everyone look perfect.

That episode, filmed on the old MGM lot, was an eye-opener—the *speed* and clinical nature of it boggled my mind. Michelle Lee, the leading lady, ran the set like a drill sergeant and laid out all the blocking. *Isn't that the director's job?* I asked myself.

After the first take, the director looked to his camera crew.

"Okay with you guys?"

"Yep. Good for us."

"Cool. Print it—let's move on . . ."

One take? Are these people out of their minds? I was used to ten, fifteen or twenty takes to get a shot right. This wasn't filmmaking, this was posing in front of the camera.

When I got home after that first day, my wife, Cris, chuckled at me.

"You look prettier than I do."

I didn't have another TV job for six years. . . .

Revelation #19: The Hollywood term "Dream Factory" is true—or at least the *Factory* part.

Meanwhile, cash was running out—the *Knot's Landing* gig plugged a tiny hole in my financial dike, but I had to find another job fast. My son, Andy, was born not long after arriving in Los Angeles. Aside from the elation that comes with being a father the second time around, I was struck by the realization that my financial obligations were mounting.

Before things got ugly, I got a call from a director, Bill Lustig, whom I had met during our *Evil Dead* sales days. He had just seen the release of *Evil Dead II* in a theater and was convinced that I was perfect for his next film, *Maniac Cop.*

"You're a cop, see, and you're mistaken for another cop who comes back from the dead to get revenge on all the bad cops who set him up. Sound good?"

It was a ludicrous idea, but Mr. Bank Account convinced me to take the job. Next thing I knew, I was weaving through a massive crowd on the streets of New York City during the St. Patrick's Day parade, shooting my first "non-boys" movie. Despite myself, I felt like an adult. *Maniac Cop* was the perfect job at that time, but I was so in debt that I wound up flat broke by the time the shoot ended.

At the cast party, I said my good-byes and slipped out about 11:30 that evening. This was early for a Hollywood party, but my security guard uniform was in the car and I had to report for work at midnight.

On Guard

Back in Michigan, I filled income gaps with the occasional odd job. Broke once again, I considered the options and decided that being a security guard at night would fit the bill just fine—if I had an audition during the day, I could always drag my butt out of bed and make it happen. Aside from that, I got to wear a costume. . . .

This bud was for me . . . for a month.

In the office of Desert Patrol Security Services, an employment officer reviewed my application with confusion.

"It says here, Mr. Campbell, that you made $125,000 last year. Is that true?"

"Yes, sir."

"Then what are you doing *here*?"

"That was last year."

I'm sure he figured me for a closet alcoholic, but I got my assignment: the midnight to 8 A.M. shift, Gate 2 at the Anheuser-Busch plant in the San Fernando Valley—effective immediately.

So, there I was—guarding beer. Frankly, I was hoping to snag a boring assignment at some obscure part of the facility, but that's not my lot in life—Gate 2 was the trucking gate and all vehicles coming in or out of the plant had to pass by us. Each night, for eight hours, we had to tag and weigh a never-ending stream of trucks hauling Beechwood ("Beechwood

Aged," just like the ads say), grain and beer. My gate partner and I got along pretty well until he recognized me.

"Holy shit—you're that guy in them *Evil Death* films. Say that *groovy* line."

Eventually, the Detex assignment spared me from the hell of Gate 2. This entailed walking the entire complex, an eleven-mile route, key-punching a handheld clock at specific locations and at specific times. This was all fine by me—I'd rather walk for four hours in solitude than listen to the ramblings of Carnie Boy or our dope-smoking C.O., Sergeant Know Nothing.

Some mornings, after the shift, the bleary-eyed guards were gathered to attended "Terrorist Prevention" classes—God forbid that beer should fall into enemy hands. Being a security guard was great for character studies, but it was time to move on.

Fortunately, the studio behind *Evil Dead II* was in search of a television version of the film, and we managed to weasel ourselves onto the payroll. I hung up my guard uniform the day I got the news.

Editing *Evil Dead II* for television was an absurd endeavor. The film, in its uncut state, races on through carnage and mayhem without so much as a second glance from my character and it all seems like a twisted Warner Bros. cartoon. Cutting the violence down, and lingering on my horrified expression, made the violence seem far more real and disturbing. Whatever the case, the film has never seen the light of network TV and most likely never will.

Evil Dead II: *A twisted Warner Bros. cartoon.*

CA$HING IN ON THE CULT   31

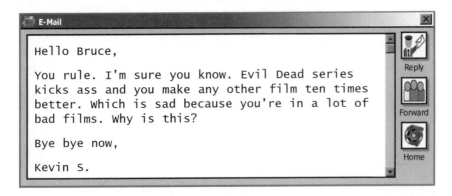

Hello Bruce,

You rule. I'm sure you know. Evil Dead series kicks ass and you make any other film ten times better. Which is sad because you're in a lot of bad films. Why is this?

Bye bye now,

Kevin S.

Everyone's got to start somewhere—Jack Nicholson, one of the most respected contemporary actors, got his start in a B movie, *The Terror,* in 1958. Steve McQueen, a personal favorite, hit the big screen in *The Blob,* and lest we forget, James Cameron, the man who brought you *Titanic,* the most successful film of all time, also made P*irhana II.* I was happy to be in such good company as I began a run of B films following *Evil Dead II.*

Scott Spiegel, now also living in LA, got his director's wings and shot a horror flick called *Intruder,* based on a Super-8 film we shot years before. I played a small role as a cop who surveys the aftermath of a night of carnage, and the actor who played my partner was Lawrence Bender, who went on to produce *Reservoir Dogs* and P*ulp Fiction*—further supporting my theory that all roads lead to B movies.

Another project, this one in Michigan, was a science fiction film called *Moontrap,* and I was commissioned to play second fiddle to *Star Trek*'s

... *s ideology, only be ...ie to locate it in *American mainstream"* (Charles Krauthammer).

main·stream film (mân'strêm' film) *n.* 100,000 people seeing a single film ten times.

...er ... ...ce of an authoritarian, charism...c leader. **n.** ... followers of such a religion or sect.

main·tain (mân-tân') *v.* 1. To ke... *good relations* ... 2. To keep it...

cult film (kùlt film) *n.* Ten people seeing a single film 100,000 times.

...**l·ti·gen** (kùl'te-jen) *n.* An organism, especially a cultivated plant, ...as a banana, not known to have a wild or uncultivated ...part.

Walter Koenig. John Cameron was coproducing the film, so it was a great homecoming.

This job brought to mind an old adage I'd heard as a Detroit actor—"If you want to work in Detroit, you have to leave." The idea behind it was simple: If you lived in Michigan, you weren't considered a *serious* actor—I guess now that I lived in LA (for all of six months) I was "legit."

The challenge of *Moontrap* was to present a convincing tale which took place largely on the moon—all within the confines of a Michigan warehouse. After much testing, Readi-Mix concrete powder was chosen as the best substitute for moon dirt. My favorite image of this film was a hand-crafted sign, posted at the edge of the set proclaiming: "No liquids!"

Later that year, an offer came through, in the nick of bank-balance time, to join the cast of a "horror/comedy" called *Sundown: A Vampire in Retreat*—destination: Utah.

As a kid, I used to pore over maps of the western states. The "lack" of humanity in Wyoming and Utah astounded me. *Is the Wild West still alive?* I'd ask myself. As I looked around the isolated town of Moab, Utah, the answer was, *Hell yes, it is.* Moab has since become the "mountain bike capital of the world," but in 1988, there wasn't an ATM machine in sight.

Having come to the attention of director Tony Hickox in the *Evil Dead* films, I was hired to play a descendant of Van Helsing, the legendary vampire hunter. Actors love to spin tales of long hours and backbreaking work on film sets, and I could bore you with that too, but this shoot was different—I was paid to explore the howling wilderness of Utah.

Plagued with a character who appeared intermittently throughout the film, the production company didn't know what to do with me. There weren't enough days between shooting my scenes to let me go home, and it didn't make economic sense to shift scenes around to accommodate me, so they just kept me in Moab. On average, I worked two days a week for six blissful weeks.

B movies are a great crossroads where actors on their way up meet and work with actors on their way down—*Sundown* was a textbook case. David Carradine played the lead vampire and had starred in his own TV show, *Kung Fu,* back in the seventies, but since then, he has been in his share of exploitation films. I shared a van ride with David to the set one night. The driver was all excited, because he was a big fan.

Driver: Mr. Carradine, I just got to tell you this—I still have my *Kung Fu* lunch box.

David: So do I—the second season, I used to bring my lunch in it. . . .

John Ireland, who played a puritanical vampire, had been in a number of A pictures, including the best picture of 1949, *All the King's Men.* I'll always regret not capitalizing on a chance meeting with him at

Van Helsing raises the stakes.

a local restaurant. John was sitting at a table right next to me, but I was too shy to go over and introduce myself.

GET JOHN TRAVOLTA ON THE PHONE

Ironically, this immersion into cheesy genre flicks rekindled my interest in independent filmmaking. *If these morons can get money for their films,* I thought, *so can we.*

The following three months led partner David Goodman and I on a trip down Nightmare Lane trying to finance *Man with the Screaming Brain*—a sci-fi/horror flick that's basically *Body Heat* with a brain transplant.

During the *Evil Dead* experience, we met honest businessmen who were willing to gamble on hard work and ingenuity and it gave us a fair shot at success. This time around, our project became a magnet for every schmuck, loser, and blowhard in the Midwest.

Along the way, we pitched the project to anyone who would hear us— and maybe that was the problem. Our search led us down some strange roads, and I'm not just talking metaphorically—a pitch meeting with the scrap metal king of Detroit almost resulted in our untimely death.

Pulling into an industrial compound worthy of *Blade Runner,* we were met by a Doberman and an unstable security guard.

"Who are you and what do you want?" he demanded, as if we had ridden to the outskirts of his Western town, looking for trouble. With that, I reached into my briefcase to get a business card and I suddenly heard Goodman gasp.

Bruce: You said, "Bruce, put the briefcase down."

Dave: Right—"Calm down. Put it down."

Bruce: But, see, I didn't know what you were talking about. I thought, "What is Goodman's problem, I was just getting a card?"

Dave: That's because you couldn't see his gun. I was staring down the barrel.

Unbeknownst to me, on Goodman's side of the car, the security guard pulled his piece and had it trained on us—his twisted mind must have assumed that I was reaching for my six-shooter.

Our most absurd attempt to raise money was in the presence of a self-proclaimed venture capitalist. Goodman, upon laying eyes on this 350-pound character, nicknamed him "Jabba the Hut." The guy, for some reason, had a fixation with John Travolta.

Jabba: Do you think you could use John Travolta in it?

Bruce: Why do ask that?

Jabba: Because I know him. I can get John Travolta.

Goodman and I shared a look—if this putz was so damned smart, why was he working above a pizza parlor in an office that looked like it was decorated by an agoraphobic?

Bruce: Hey, Dave, you know what? I think John Travolta could nail *Man with the Screaming Brain*.

Dave: I think you're right. In fact, he's perfect.

Bruce: (to *Jabba*) Get John Travolta on the phone.

Jabba: What?

Bruce: Get him on the phone. He's a friend of yours, right?

Jabba: Well, I would need some advance notice.

Dave: Come on, let's close this deal.

Jabba: It's a time zone thing, really, I don't think . . .

Bruce: Hey, look—tell you what. When you can deliver John Travolta, you give us a call.

Goodman's tragic flaw.

Our frustration came to a head with a meeting that Goodman set up. The prospective investor was a widow, flush with cash. Dave insisted on running this pitch and it was fine by me, I was happy to take a breather.

During his spirited banter, I could see that the investor, Karen, was losing interest. Her eyes began to wander. I followed her gaze down toward Goodman's feet. What we both saw at the same time, was Goodman's calf-high basketball socks under his shorter, black dress socks.

In the middle of Goodman's spiel, Karen pointed at his ankles.

"You have white socks on!"

The blood drained from Goodman's face and his pitch ground to a halt. On our way back down to the lobby, via the world's slowest elevator, Goodman had a strangely determined look on his face.

"What's the matter, Dave?" I asked. "You did fine. It wasn't you. She was never gonna invest in the first place."

"That's what pisses me off," he said through clenched teeth. "That *bitch* . . ."

And with that, he hunched over like a sumo wrestler and squeezed out the most prolonged fart I had ever witnessed. Raising money for *Man with the Screaming Brain* was a little bit like being trapped in a slow-moving elevator after someone farted—the ride took too long and the atmosphere was foul.

Storyboards from Man with the Screaming Brain. *Scenes you'll never see.*

When I finally straggled back to Los Angeles, three months of "iffy" income had taken their toll—I had no prospects for work and a mortgage that had to be paid.

Wait a minute, I thought. Mortgage . . . that's the key word—maybe it was time to pass our mortgage to someone else.

In the late eighties, Los Angeles real estate was out of control. My wife and I sold our first generic house in ten days and pocketed $15,000 in the process. Our current house was closer to town, and had more to offer—if we sold it, we could live off the profits. That's exactly what Cris and I did, and five days later, we walked away with about $45,000 in profit. Listen to me, I'm sounding like that infomercial joker— "I made millions, from my *one-bedroom apartment*!"

THE DARK SIDE OF AMBITION   32

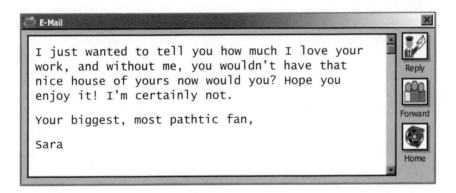

I just wanted to tell you how much I love your work, and without me, you wouldn't have that nice house of yours now would you? Hope you enjoy it! I'm certainly not.

Your biggest, most pathtic fan,

Sara

Cris decided to go back to school, so we relocated to the inland city of Chino—known for two things: cows and convicts. With a new mortgage on my back, the only vague opportunity for work seemed to demand a return to Michigan—again. . . .

This time, it was to assume the role of producer. Sam Raimi and Robert Tapert managed to get their hands on some cash for a film Josh Becker wanted to do called *Lunatics—A Love Story.*

<u>Josh:</u> I remember sitting there on the back porch of my Hollywood apartment. I had no money and I hadn't paid any rent and I had no food and I thought, well this is pretty much the lowest point of my life. I have to think of an idea. This is the moment. I'm not getting up off this friggin' stoop here until I've got an idea that someone will buy, 'cause I don't have anything else. So, I just started to think about titles—psycho and other words for craziness and crazies and lunatics.

<u>Bruce:</u> Was there some reason you were thinking about that type of—?

Josh: Well, I wasn't even thinking of any type of movie.

Bruce: I see.

Josh: I mean maybe I was thinking about horror movies, I don't know, and I hit on the word lunatics and I thought well what if it's not a horror film—what if it's a love story? So I went over to Renaissance Pictures and pitched it to Sam and Rob.

The boys got behind the idea and convinced several *Evil Dead* investors to put up some cash—*some* being roughly half the budget. In order to start filming, a lot more had to be raised.

I recruited David Goodman to help—we were both still stinging from the *Brain* failure, and were determined to prove that raising money for an independent film could be done.

As we began the process of pounding the pavement again, I became grateful for all of those hours as a kid, glued to the TV watching *The Little Rascals.* Those kids put on a show of some sort nearly every episode and their fearlessness amazed me.

Darla: We need a stage curtain.

Spanky: No problem, my sister can sew.

Alfalfa: What about refreshments?

Froggy: I'll make lemonade!

I decided to adopt this hopelessly romantic attitude—if we couldn't find cash, we'll just do without.

I fished out a Yellow Pages directory and began to make a series of palm-sweating cold calls. All I can say is: *God bless America.* The fact that merchants of every ilk actually bothered to hear our rambling sales pitches impressed me. Here we were, in a large metropolitan area during the cynical eighties, and folks were still willing to listen to a dreamer's tale.

𝕽𝖊𝖛𝖊𝖑𝖆𝖙𝖎𝖔𝖓 #28e: The secret to raising money is that there is no secret.

"Hello, sir, my name is Bruce Campbell, and I'm producing a film in this area. I was wondering if you'd be interested in a business opportunity. . . ."

"Bruce. Look, I'm a busy guy. What do you mean? *Specifically.*"

"Uh, well, sir, we're wondering if you'd like to invest in the project."

"Why in the devil did you call me—of all companies?"

"Well, sir, you have what we need," I said, my confidence building, "gasoline."

"Gas? For what?"

"For our cars and trucks, sir. We need to move our film crew around for about a month."

"All right, come on in and we'll talk about it. . . ."

What followed was equally amazing: a deal for office supplies, catering, printing, film processing, lighting equipment, construction equipment, lumber, hardware, and paint. To the credit of these fellow entrepreneurs, all of these deals were made with a simple agreement of not more than a page and a half.

Goodman was busy hustling in his own right. He knew a wealthy crowd, and he knew where to find them.

Dave: I was pals with a lot of the parents who sent their kids to Camp Tamakwa, so I showed up on the day when all the kids got sent off. I was taking their luggage out of the trunks of the Cadillacs and Jaguars. I was schmoozing and throwing business cards into the trunks. I got two or three calls and eventually got one investment. You do what you have to do to get your movies made.

It was always a treat to watch Goodman race into my office and perform an impromptu victory dance. Whenever he did this, I knew he had snagged another investor.

Still, by the time shooting began, we were extremely cash poor—the in-kind deals left us with very little hard currency in the bank. Ironically, it made negotiating very easy. When I told a crew member or agent or supplier that I didn't have that kind of money, I wasn't blowing smoke up their butt—I really didn't have it.

The same principle even applied to director Josh Becker.

Josh: I just remember the first night of shooting where I had spent forty-five minutes setting up a shot, was just about to shoot it, and you walked out and went, "That's a wrap." I was like, "Oh but we just—" and you go, "No, no—twelve hours is twelve hours. That's a wrap." I go, "Okay, I see how this works." You laid down the law.

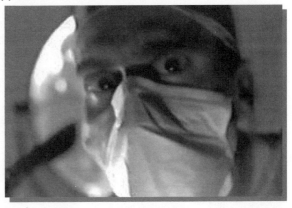

Menace, anyone?

Bruce: I did feel kind of cruel.

Josh: Look, you'd given your word to the crew. Once I realized that was the way it worked, that's the way it worked. But I was like, "You can't really mean this."

Fortunately, our ragged plan worked well enough to complete the film over the next year and a half and the investors got their money back—plus a tiny morsel of profit.

'TIL DIVORCE DO US PART

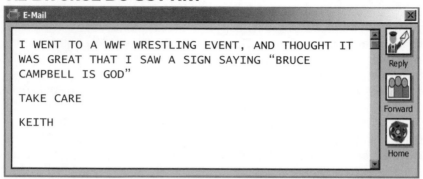

I WENT TO A WWF WRESTLING EVENT, AND THOUGHT IT
WAS GREAT THAT I SAW A SIGN SAYING "BRUCE
CAMPBELL IS GOD"

TAKE CARE

KEITH

The euphoric feeling that comes with true independence also has a price. All those months of making magic in Michigan were having another effect on the California home front—a cold wind of alienation was blowing. Fueled by other follies over the years, *Lunatics* wound up being the straw that broke my wife's back.

My daughter Rebecca flew out to Michigan so she could drive back across the country with me. We had a great time taking pictures and writing a book about the experience, but when we got home, Halloween day, something was different about the place. Margarita, a woman who helped around the house, was there, but Cris wasn't.

I took Rebecca and my young son Andy trick-or-treating—his dinosaur costume was a big hit with the neighbors. When we got home, Cris was still nowhere to be seen. I put the kids to bed and killed time by unpacking and watching television for a couple hours, but with each passing minute, my sense of dread intensified. It wasn't women's intuition, but I knew something was up—Cris was never one to stay out late.

About 11:00 that night, she came home, but there were no hugs and kisses. Instead, Cris stayed on the other side of dark kitchen.

"Hey, how you doing? Great to see you . . ."

Marital Symbolism.

"I've been thinking a lot about things and I'm not sure we want you back."

"Excuse me?"

Cris wasn't mean, but there was a resolve in her that I had only seen one other time, when she was giving birth to Rebecca, and I knew she wasn't bluffing.

"Is this open for discussion?"

Silently, she shook her head *no.* "How soon can you find a place to stay?"

Initially, this seemed out of the blue, but a year or so later I flashed upon an incident that should have sent up warning flares. I was taking a walk with Cris during a Fourth of July vacation—she was weary of my excessive traveling and the inconsistency of our lives. I had no solution and could only offer, "I don't know what to tell you, kiddo. This is my life—I'm not sure if it's ever gonna change. You may have to trade me in for a better model." I said it with a smile on my face, but Cris wasn't laughing.

There wasn't anything else I could say to change Cris's mind, but in the course of the next week, I certainly tried. With all sincerity, I offered to get out of the business entirely if it would keep things together, but it was too late—Cris had truly lost all interest. In our six years of marriage, I was away from home for two of them and she saw no end in sight.

I'm happy to say that we managed to avoid damaging arguments in front of the kids, and those nasty custody battles—we settled our divorce through the same lawyer. Cris wasn't after revenge, just a change of life.

There was one moment in the lawyer's office when I gave it a last stab. The lawyer had excused himself to get some documents and I looked over at Cris across the table.

"You know, this is all just a stack of paper right now. Nothing is signed—we don't have to go through with this."

"I understand how you feel," Cris explained, "but I think it's the right thing."

THE CAR GAG

An interesting event transpired during the course of filming *Lunatics* that lightened the heavy load of a broken home life. In preparation for the road trip from Los Angeles to Detroit, David Goodman bought himself a 1981 Renault. He was proud of the $500 he spent on this car, really proud—smug actually. For days before the trip, he'd carry on about his great new car.

Finally, the day arrived to depart for the homeland. John Cameron, whom I enlisted/begged to line produce the film, rode in my car while Goodman, loaded down with his entire world, traveled solo.

Communication between cars was by way of a Radio Shack CB—that way, we could keep each other informed about the need for food, gas, bad jokes, etc.

The trip was a smooth one until we got into the wilder portions of the West—specifically, Green River, Wyoming, off the I-80 freeway. As John and I rose over the crest of a hill, we passed Dave's car on the side of the road. Inside, Dave was barking into his CB radio that no longer had power to transmit.

"Fuckin' car. It just died on me."

John and I exchanged a knowing look.

"Gee, Dave, what a shock."

My cell phone wasn't getting any reception way out here, so John and I skipped into Green River to get AAA in action. Within a short while, the driver, Dale, pulled up in his tow rig—he was missing several teeth, and had hair in all the wrong places.

As he hooked up Dave's car, he regaled us with tales of shooting grizzly bears that wandered beyond the boundaries of Yellowstone Park, further to the north. He punctuated his story with the occasional spit through a gap in his remaining teeth.

At a Green River garage, the prognosis for Dave's car was iffy.

"Might be the battery," the mechanic said.

"Fine," said Dave confidently. "Pop in a new one."

The Green River Trio: Flanked by John on the left and Goodman on the right.

Eighty dollars later, the car would still not start—it wouldn't turn over, it wouldn't make a sound.

"This is gonna take some time to sort this shit out," the mechanic figured. "You boys ain't in a hurry, are you?"

Fortunately for us, the Flaming Gorge National Recreation Area was just around the corner. History buffs will be excited to know that John Wesley Powell launched his famous Colorado River exploration from this area. We launched ourselves into the man-made reservoir created in the sixties and cooled off. It was a beautiful place and left a lasting impression—which is important to note, as you will soon see.

Back in town, the news came back and it was not good—the car's electrical system was completely on the fritz.

"Maybe I could get parts in a couple days, but there ain't no guarantee of success. Know what I mean?"

These are the times that try men's souls, as the saying goes, and Goodman stood trial for about four seconds.

"No. You know what? Fuck it. Take the car," he said with a rare finality.

"Really?" the mechanic wondered. "You sure?"

"Yep."

In a historical context, I shouldn't have been surprised by Goodman's irrational behavior—this is a man with bad car karma. His loyal Datsun pickup truck had been taken by the New York City police department because Dave simply refused to pay any parking tickets.

<u>Dave:</u> I was walking down the street where I lived in Manhattan and I saw the cops in front of it with a tow truck and they go, "Who's got this

Michigan license?" I just turned around and walked the other way and then the car was gone and I figured, well I had it for five years and—

Bruce: And so you never tried to get your car back?

Dave: No, because the car wasn't worth what the tickets were going to be to pay.

Bruce: Which was how much?

Dave: Like eight grand.

Bruce: But why didn't you just pay your tickets?

Dave: Because I was busy—I was fuckin' busy. I went, "Well the car's not worth it. Just let them take it."

Lest we forget, he's also the guy who delivered the death blow to my Opal Isuzu.

Dave and the mechanic negotiated a $150 sale. The only glitch was that Dave didn't have the title of his car. The mechanic wasn't worried and forked over the money.

There was no room for Dave in our car, and we could only take some of his stuff. Fortunately for him, Green River was a Greyhound stop and we bought him a one-way ticket to Detroit.

On the last leg to the Midwest, John and I chuckled about Goodman's dilemma. We enjoyed knowing that he was about to endure the longest ride of his life. Busses stop in every backwater town and the trip was bound to add at least a day to his travel schedule. Still, we plotted how we could rub his nose in it all—automotive smugness must be punished at all costs.

En route, we talked about Dale, the oily mechanic, and how memorable Flaming Gorge was. Eventually a gag evolved—what if we concocted a false scenario whereby

Seconds before I knock Goodman's ass to the ground with a full-court-press.

the mechanic and Dale stripped his car, set it on fire and dumped it into the gorge? It sounded great, but how would we pull that off? We'd have to create an airtight chain of events and some convincing paperwork.

Unpacking one of Goodman's boxes in Detroit several days later, we found the first piece of the puzzle—the title to his car. This was an omen that the gag had to proceed.

During the production of *Lunatics,* I had several dealings with the Pontiac police department. Casually, I asked a representative if they had paperwork for things like theft, etc. Naturally, they did—it was called an Incident Report, and they gave one to me.

After laborious days of filming, John and I (who were office mates) wound down by working on "the gag." A little bit of white-out removed the

Pontiac police logo and an old typewriter provided just the right font. To get that "official" look, we stamped a "received" date on it and copied the whole affair several times over in order to blend the rough edges.

One thing we lacked was imposing stationary upon which to write a nasty letter outlining the "irreversible" damage Goodman had done. This came by way of John's girlfriend, Maureen, who worked at a law firm in Detroit. She got her hands on stationery from the Office of the Inspector General, U.S. Treasury Department—it wasn't ideal, but it was close enough for Goodman.

By the time the shoot ended, our package was ready to go. I had a long drive back to California, and I routed my trip through Cheyenne, Wyoming, so that even the postmark would look authentic. The letter was addressed to David, c/o my brother Don's address in Michigan, which Goodman still claimed as his official address. One quick call to Don put him on alert for the letter and everything was in motion.

Upon returning to Los Angeles, I was promptly kicked out of the house. All seriousness aside, this provided me with the perfect vantage point to watch the car gag unfold—from Goodman's couch.

A few days later, Goodman got the letter in question, but he tossed the heap of mail on his desk and ignored them for another day. I casually suggested that he get organized, and that meant *answering his mail.*

Early the next morning, while cradling a cup of coffee and sucking on a Marlboro Light, Goodman opened the fateful envelope. He's one of these guys who moves his lips when he reads, so it was easy to tell where he was in the text. His expression darkened with each paragraph.

"Flaming Gorge? What the fu . . . ?" he mumbled incredulously. "Those bastards. Those goddamn, redneck bastards!"

"What's the matter?" I asked, playing dumb.

This set Goodman off into a tirade about those rat bastard hicks and how they screwed him over with the car and how he was wanted in the state of Wyoming and that a warrant was issued for his arrest.

"Wow," I said, nonplussed. "Sounds like a mess . . ."

Knowing that Goodman relied on a close circle of friends, John and I had alerted them all that this gag was in the works and not to offer any advice, other than the fact that he was screwed. Sure enough, each person he called was someone we had already contacted. The color in Dave's face drained as he heard, call after call, that he was screwed.

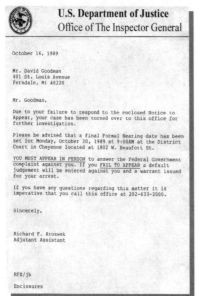
The opening round.

A wedding was scheduled that weekend in San Diego. Dave's good lawyer friend, Vic, was going to be there.

"I'll take the letter there," Dave said confidently. "Vic will know what to do."

Vic *did* know what to do all right—we had already called him and urged him to repeat the same response to Dave: "You're screwed."

Dave returned from San Diego a broken man. He began to rub his fingers together—something he only did when he was tormented. I related this information to John and we were left with only one option—turn up the heat.

Mike Ditz's photography partner in Detroit, Paul Price, had a menacing voice. We enlisted Paul to leave a series of messages for Dave regarding the best time for U.S. marshals to come and arrest him.

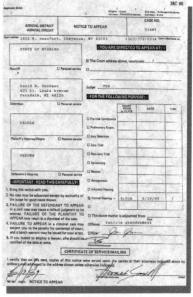

Turning up the heat.

The timing of each call was easily coordinated since, as his new roommate, I knew when Dave was home or away.

The secret of a successful gag is to match the right gag for the right person. With Goodman, panic was the key element—if you got him to panic, all reason would be thrown to the wind. This particular joke would not have worked with any of the other boys, since logic would have prevailed. With one or two calls to law enforcement agencies in Wyoming, the whole thing could have been excused as a hoax.

Dave endured another anguished day or two, circling his apartment, smoking and rubbing his fingers together. As much as it bothered Dave, I was getting tired of watching him act like an insane person, so I suggested to John that we throw in the towel.

We arranged a final call from Paul Price, this time while Goodman was home. After a final legal scare, Paul explained to Goodman that this was all just a gag. Goodman got the color back in his face, but this time it was red and he slammed down the phone.

"You guys are assholes, you know that?"

"Look, I'm sorry Dave," I explained through laughter. "It was just a *gag . . .*"

"Making fun of the tough situation I'm in . . ."

"What do you mean?"

"What do you mean, what do I mean? The car thing, the fucking car . . ."

I realized at this point that Goodman wasn't aware of the full scope of the joke—he thought we were simply making fun of his legal dilemma. I had to explain to him, in great detail, that it was *all* fake—the stripped car, the Flaming Gorge scenario, the warrant—*everything.*

"Oh," Dave said as his eyes rolled back in his head.

From his reaction, I couldn't tell if he was going to stab me with a butcher knife or hug me.

"Oh, man . . . what a shrek! What a *great* shrek!"

Shrek is an old term for "gag" and Goodman knew it well—he had delighted in many a shrek. Now, he started laughing—hard. I'll say this for the poor bastard, he knew a good gag when he saw one. He commended John and I for the elaborate preparation and grilled me for the next hour about how we pulled it off.

I'm still waiting for Goodman's payback. Waiting and trembling . . .

GOING SOUTH IN NORTH HOLLYWOOD

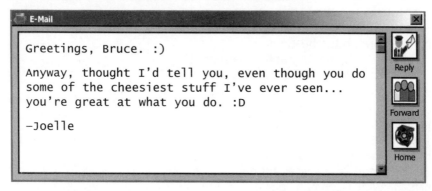

After dodging the affiliation for as many years as I possibly could, I now found myself an official member of the "down-and-out actor, living in a crappy apartment in Hollywood" club. It had been a while since I had to worry about stereo noise or "deposits" and all the rest of that "single guy" stuff.

From my apartment, I could hear the muffled thump of music emanating from an actor's bar, Residuals. Good lord, what was next: bussing tables, a subscription to *Dramalogue*? I had done an end run around the system for ten years, but now I was warming the bench. The concept of being an actor was one thing, but *feeling* like one gave me the willies . . .

Having been a poster child for *Fangoria* magazine, it made sense that I wound up in their first film production, *Mindwarp*.

Eagle River, Wisconsin, is the snowmobile capital of the world, though apparently this wasn't enough because some enterprising fool decided that a film studio in the frozen north would supply a great need.

I was pleased that at least part of this "apocalyptic" *Jeremiah Johnson* was filmed in Michigan—Gay, Michigan, to be exact. Local entrepreneurs at the town's bar printed up T-shirts proclaiming, "Go *straight* . . . to the *Gay* bar." In a town of thirty-four, you've got to fill the time any way you can.

At a cast and crew brunch, I spotted a cute woman across the room, sitting with a bunch of stuntmen. She was attractive, but a leather biker's cap pulled low across her eyes made her look tough. I had actually talked with her on the phone before the shoot. Ida Gearon was the costume designer and she needed my sizes to prep the costumes.

The Residuals Bar. What's next, bussing tables?

Ida: So, you're playing the lead guy—are you really tall or something?

Bruce: No, not really—about six feet one inch with boots.

Ida: Well, then, are you really buff or anything?

Bruce: No, not really . . .

Ida: Then why did they cast you?

Bruce: What do you care? Look, do you want my sizes or not?

Eventually, we warmed up to each other and it was a good thing—the location was an abandoned copper factory on the shores of Lake Superior, and the shoreline was still clogged with ice flows. My character had to wear "nonseasonal" clothing, so filming would churn along until I could no longer feel my hands, then I'd pile into a waiting van, "defrost" them on the heating vents, and get back at it.

Shooting in the warehouse/studio wasn't much better. My character is captured at one point and tossed down a labyrinth of landfill tunnels. This effect was accomplished by a "Mazola" slide—it wasn't that some guy named Mazola invented it, the slide was lubricated *with* Mazola cooking oil—gallons of it. The oil had been used by stunt men for several days before the actors were brought in, and by the end of the day, I smelled like a bucket of "extra crispy" KFC.

My character is then forced to dig as a laborer in the tunnels, under the supervision of "crawlers." The art director, hoping to save money, brainstormed that they could just get the tunnel dirt from a real landfill.

It became a daily challenge among my fellow actors to find the most heinous substance lurking within the dirt. Motor oil was one of them, so our wardrobes turned a slightly darker shade every day. Broken glass was not uncommon, as well as rusty nails and scrap metal. I won the prize with an archaeological find of asbestos, removed from an Eagle River school years before.

It really wasn't a surprise when I got a nasty cut in the "dirt" one day. The immediate concern wasn't whether I would be all right, it was more about whether shooting could continue. Since the same makeup effects guys from the *Evil Dead* days were supervising this film, I knew what items they carried in their set bags and immediately asked for some "355."

"Hey, Stan, what do you think of the costume chick? Do you think she'd go out with me?"

This stuff, now discontinued because of its questionable manufacturing process, was surgical adhesive, developed in the rice paddies of the Vietnam War—in the heat of battle, it could be poured directly into wounds for a quick fix. This was as close to war as I'd ever been, so I glued my finger shut, covered it with dirt, and went back to digging. . . .

SECOND TIME IS THE CHARM   33

I wasn't sure whether the "trench affair" Ida Gearon and I just experienced would translate to Los Angeles. Often on a film set, cast and crew members become unusually close, but many of these "relationships" crash and burn once people return to their former lives—or should I say *wives*? Fortunately, Ida and I flourished in neutral territory and it was a huge relief to see first hand that life actually continued after divorce.

Well aware of pop-psychology terms like "rebound relationships," I was determined to follow my gut. From the moment I spotted Ida in Eagle River, Wisconsin, I knew I had to find out what her deal was, so I enlisted my co-star, Marta, to dig up the dirt. After a day of shooting, she reported back, but the news was mixed: Ida was in a relationship with a production manager in Los Angeles, but it was "on the rocks."

Okay, I plotted to myself, *at least there's a window of opportunity . . .*

The first step was getting to know Ida better. I could do this by hanging around the wardrobe room, but I'd have to have a decent excuse. Aside from the fact that their department was the only place with a decent heating system, I argued that my postapocalyptic character had to know primitive survival skills.

Ida: (a little peeved) You want to do what?

Bruce: I want to learn how to sew.

Ida: Well, look, as you can see, we're a little busy here. They didn't give us much time to prep.

Bruce: Yeah, but I don't need one of your sewing machines. My character would maintain his clothes by hand. (vamping now) He'd . . . he'd sew like Fred Flintstone would—with leather thread and . . . and stuff like that . . . yeah . . .

Ida: But, why bother? I didn't see any sewing scenes in the script.

"Lulabelle."

Bruce: (in ad-lib over-drive) Well, true, but in scene thirty-two, I have that long chat with Marta. My character wouldn't just sit there, he'd be doing something . . . like . . . sewing.

Ida: (rolling her eyes) Okay, big guy, whatever floats your boat. I'll set you up.

At least I got a foot in the door. For the remainder of the short shoot, I spent every opportunity refining my pioneer skills.

Ida got the hint pretty quickly that it was all a ploy to hang around her, but she didn't seem to mind. By the second week of shooting, we began to spend time together off the film set.

It's an individual thing, but eventually I get to the point in a relationship where it either intensifies (as in consummates) or comes to an end. Personally, I was eager to apply the lessons I had learned from my first go around. Ida had never been married before, but she seemed interested enough to give it a whack. Within a year of meeting, we decided to go for it.

This time around, our wedding ceremony was exponentially larger—all of twenty people were invited. We chose another non-denominational church in North Hollywood known simply as "The Little Brown Church." Ronald Reagan married Nancy in the same building, and I'm not sure if that's good or bad, but it seemed to work for them.

Now that I had two small children, the dynamics of the ceremony were quite different, so I gave the kids designated jobs. Rebecca, who was seven, made a lovely flower girl, and she preceded Ida down the aisle, tossing petals in every direction. Andy, all of four, took the place of Celia Raimi as the ring-bearer. Because we weren't sure how he was going to perform under pressure, we pinned the ring to his miniature cardigan.

The actual service went faster than any of us could have anticipated. Ida raced down the short aisle (I assumed this was a good thing), and we churned through the vows in record time.

Following the reception, you might assume that Ida and I immediately jumped on a plane to some far-flung tropical island for a week of bliss. For two people in the entertainment industry, this was not to be. Back home in North Hollywood, we shared a laugh then looked at each other with a nod.

"Okay, back to work!"

A FLY ON THE DARKMAN WALL   **34**

Revelation #8: The lowest common denominator is not only alive in Hollywood—it is revered.

Mindwarp paid off some debts, but I needed another source of income. Out of nowhere, a behind-the-scenes job bailed me out—my official job description was "temp sound guy" for Sam Raimi's *Darkman.*

Sam: I wanted to produce a movie, but I didn't think it was a good enough story to direct it.

Bruce: It was your story.

Sam: Yeah. I really wanted to make *The Shadow*. But Universal Studios wouldn't give me the rights to that. I met with them, but they didn't like my views at all, so I went, "I'm just gonna write my own superhero."

Bruce: You had a decent budget this time.

Sam: Yeah, that was a whole new experience for me. It was giant. I had cranes and dollies and a crew of hundreds, makeup effects, helicopter battles over the city of Los Angeles, big stunts, explosions and miniatures. It was a great movie experience, but it was slightly more removed than our *Evil Dead* experiences, so it wasn't quite as fulfilling in many ways.

Bruce: How was it creatively? Did you get hassled?

Sam: Well it took just forever for them to green-light the script—I went years. Finally, I said, "If I don't get a call saying that the movie's finally going to go, because I've spent three years of my life on this thing and it's not like I'm trying to make an art picture, I'm selling out to you—if you don't call me by ten o'clock, I'm out." Ten o'clock came and went and I had a bottle of champagne and I went, "Fine, at least I'm free of it." They called around eleven: "All right we'll make your movie." They really make sure they've messed with ya.

Little did Sam know, that was just the beginning.

With nothing to lose, it was a great "fly on the wall" experience for me. Sam had his hands full with an extensive amount of optical effects for the film, so he turned much of the early sound work over to me. Sam and I had worked closely on the sound for all of our previous films, so he felt comfortable with my input.

"Doing the sound" meant sitting in with actors as they replaced any missing or unusable dialogue, creating a temporary (temp) music track from CDs, overseeing sound effects editing, and supervising the mixing of all these elements.

One of the first dividends for Sam was my ability to scream. You'd think a scream is a scream is a scream, right? Not true—there are infinite variations, from a nervous whimper to the pedal-to-the-metal wail of agony. At Sam's encouragement and often insistence, my screams wound up filling in for almost every criminal who was shot, run over or tossed off a high object.

A rendition of my beleaguered cry.

My voice filled in for star Liam Neeson in the early stages, when he wasn't available to loop. Ironically, one dub of mine, a distant call of "Juuulieee!" made its way into the final version.

Darkman allowed me to see, firsthand, how a film can literally change genres under studio leadership. There was much discussion about whether the film was a *Beauty and the Beast* story, or a darker P*hantom of the Opera* tale. As a result, I saw versions of the film that were almost all romance, immediately followed by versions that were mostly action—in the end, it wound up being a hybrid of both.

I also had the unpleasant task of supervising a looping session with Frances McDormand in New York (Liam's love interest in the film), where she witnessed, reel by reel, the wholesale butchery of her most dramatic scenes.

Fran: Wait a minute. Where's the scene in the apartment?

Bruce: Oh, that. They're working with a version that doesn't have it right now. . . .

Fran: What about the scene in the lab—my big speech?

Bruce: Well, Fran, you might say the film is in a state of flux right now. For all I know, the scene could be put back in tomorrow. . . .

That was true, because the "test screening" process had not yet begun. Let me give you an example of how it works: Acme Test Marketing company approaches would-be audience members in local malls, asking them if they want to see a free, "new and exciting film" from the guy who made the *Evil Dead* films. Once they get enough participants, they hold a screening at a real movie theater in, say, Glendale, California.

The film is then shown to this "test" audience, and they are asked to remain afterward to fill out a questionnaire, answering queries like: *Would you recommend the film to your friends? What scene did you like the most, and why?* etc.

Around twenty audience members also volunteer to stay after the screening, to participate in a "focus group." Here, one of the marketing gurus will, à la Jerry Springer, encourage audience members to voice general and sometimes outrageously specific opinions about the film.

Afterward, the cards are collected and the film is scored for its approval rating. If any particular scene bothered the audience, chances are good that it will be cut out—a good example of this came when they butchered my favorite scene. Allow me to explain:

In *Darkman,* a wealthy developer attempts to woo Darkman's girlfriend after he is supposedly killed during a lab experiment. The man is charming and magnetic, but he's also a creep and should be avoided.

This point is very convincingly made in a scene where the same developer, alone in his apartment, stands at the foot of his bed wearing nothing but a bath towel. He picks up an ornate box and lifts the lid, sending a shimmering reflection across his face. He spreads the contents of the box across his bed, revealing gold coins. The developer then drops his towel and dives, buck-ass naked on the coins, writhing in ecstasy—he is clearly a man with a problem.

The next day, he appears in his office, charming as ever, but the audience, now knowing his terrible secret, will never look at him the same way again. I found this scene to be extremely effective for what it was supposed to accomplish: make us loathe this man and fear for Darkman's girlfriend when he makes advances.

However (and herein lies the rub), many of the questionnaires returned with that scene mentioned as the one the audience liked the least, reasoning that it "made them uncomfortable."

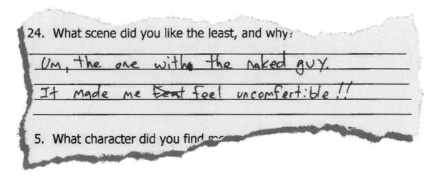

24. What scene did you like the least, and why?

Um, the one with the naked guy.

It made me feel uncomfertible!!

5. What character did you find m

Hello! That was the idea! Instead of applauding the filmmaker's success to this end, the studio insisted that the scene be cut from the film.

After all was said and done, *Darkman* finally opened in theaters and went to number one. Sam and I used to joke about that back in Ferndale—if any of us ever got to the top of the *Variety* movie chart, we'd call each other and engage in phony mogul dialogue.

"Who's on top? Who's on top?" Sam would ask.

"You are, Sam, you are . . ."

<u>Sam:</u> I couldn't believe that we had the number one movie.

<u>Bruce:</u> In its first week, right?

<u>Sam:</u> Yeah, then it was number two after *Ghost*. It was great to be number one in the country.

Well-Crafted Dialogue...
Shoe-String Budget
Emphasis on Story...
...Thought-Provoking Drama
APPROPRIATE CASTING...

HOLLYWOOD HOMOGENIZER

absurd casting...snappy one-liners...mean-spirited violence...emphasis on effects...$20 salaries...

The "Hollywood Homogenizer": Every studio executive should have one!

Evil Dead Goes Hollywood　35

Riding on the heels of a successful *Darkman,* Sam and Rob were able to set up the financing for another *Evil Dead* sequel relatively easily through a combination of Dino DeLaurentiis (foreign money) and Universal Studios (domestic money).

With a shooting schedule of 111 days, the new film, *Army of Darkness,* far outreached any challenge the three of us had faced thus far.

Army of Darkness became the awkward challenge of reconciling high school with Hollywood. With a *starting* budget of eight million, we had outdone our *Evil Dead* budget by 22.8 times, yet because it was directly linked with our past, there was a yearning to do things like the old days.

On the production side of things, we had to hire a number of people we had never worked with before because this film called for large sets, horses, extras, and a complicated special effects process called "Introvision." But, when it made sense, we did our best to get familiar faces in front and behind the camera. John Cameron was brought in as first assistant director.

<u>John:</u> It was a real movie in that kind of nonunion world; the crews were competent and good, but the shoot was too long. Typical of Sam, and I think it's a good thing, every shot becomes an epic in and of itself—if there's one torch, you've got to have a hundred standing by because he's going to keep building it through each rehearsal until it's bigger and bigger.

<u>Bruce:</u> Plus, the other theory would be if he had thirty extras, he was gonna put them in every shot.

<u>John:</u> He really wanted armies of thousands and of course that was out of the question.

Casting was another way to keep familiar faces around us. A Super-8 regular for years, Tim Quill, was new to the California scene. He was eager

Tim Quill, shaven head and all.

to give this professional thing a whack, yet we had to prove to the Screen Actors Guild that he was experienced enough to qualify for membership. It was difficult for them to accept the fact that he had been "really funny" in our 1974 classic, *No Doughboys.* Tim was eventually let off the hook because he was willing to shave his head for the role.

Sam's brother Ted also showed up—not to play just one role, but four. He was a panic-stricken villager, a doubting warrior, a loyal follower, and a stockboy at S-Mart. At least the art of Shemping was still alive in *Army of Darkness.*

Josh Becker also stopped by for a couple days as an extra.

Josh: I was a villager when you were thrown down in the pit. Sam put me next to Embeth (the lead actress), because he needed someone he could trust next to the starlet. Then I came out for a couple different nights as a skeleton.

Bruce: Oh really? Did you wear one of those monster suits?

Josh: Yeah, it was horrible—there was no fly in them. Really good thinking . . .

YOU'RE IN THE "ARMY" NOW . . .

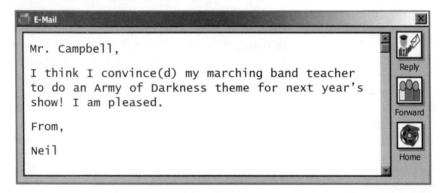

After years of making it up as I went along, I had to learn new skills. Since the film took place largely in the 1300s, the main mode of transportation was by horse. I couldn't ride to save my life, so lessons were arranged.

To me, horses were just big, dumb animals to be feared and left alone. I'm sure my horse Buster could sense this right from the start, and he launched me off his back the first day in the corral. From then on, we agreed to hate each other and I never really did learn how to ride.

Unfortunately, Sam wanted numerous shots of me racing across the wasteland like Roy Rogers and even wrote a horse chase sequence—it's a good thing we were doing a horror film, because the fear in my eyes was real.

The character Ash, now elevated to full-blown hero, also had to know his way around medieval combat. This required fighting lessons, which included hand-to-hand techniques as well as staffs and swords. The main reason for this was because Sam wanted the climactic sword fight to play out as elegantly as a Fred Astaire movie and he wanted it all in one crane shot.

I must have rehearsed the routine for three weeks, but when it came time to shoot, the rigors of running up and down steps, fighting with both hands, and flipping skeletons over my head was too much to pull off without cuts. After ten takes, I knew Sam was pissed off, because he yanked the bullhorn from John Cameron.

"Okay, obviously, this is *not working*, and it's *not going to work*, so we're going to break it up into *a thousand little pieces*."

When Sam gets upset, he lets you know it, and he'll torture you for days afterward because he's one of those guys who never forgets. The first "little piece" of the sequence was a shot of me ducking as a sword glances off the stone wall behind me.

"Dance lessons?"

"So, you think you can do this, Bruce?" he'd say, loud enough for the entire crew to hear. "Or should I break this *one* shot into *three more shots*?"

Sam also threatened to put Ash in a chorus line with skeletons.

"Okay, mister, we're gonna do a number like they do at Radio City Music Hall—only the Rockettes are skeletons."

"Are you serious?"

"Of course I am—you have to be able to dance like Gene Kelly."

I took jazz dance lessons for weeks, but thankfully, the budget put an end to that absurd idea.

EXTRAS, EXTRAS, READ ALL ABOUT THEM!

We filmed primarily on a private ranch in the desert, north of Los Angeles. In the city, things like police sirens, airplanes and traffic can plague a production—out in the desert, it's another story. With nothing to block the sound . . . it *carries.*

Actress Tippi Hedron maintained a lion sanctuary near our location, and whenever feeding time came around, the hungry roars of the big cats would carry across the broad valley and freak the living daylights out of the horses.

Night shooting also made it harder to keep track of another animal—"the Hollywood Extra." Most of these folks come well-prepared for the long day ahead of them—any extra worth their salt shows up ready for any kind of weather, provides their own chair and the thickest book they can find.

Some of the less motivated folks snuck out of the available light, which was easy to do, and passed the night sleeping or, in one scandalous case, making love inside the castle set. Mating in a skeleton suit was quite an accomplishment because, as a monster myself (I also played "Evil Ash"), I couldn't even get the hang of urinating—and it wasn't exactly a task you asked for help with.

> *glamorizes police work.*
>
> **glam·or·ous** also **glam·our·ous** (glàm'er-es) *adj.* Full of or character... by glamour.
>
> **glam·our** also **glam·or** (glàm'er) *n.* Fumbling around in Yucca-laden prairie grass, blinded by white contact lenses, attempting to unzip your fly with two-inch "monster" finger nails.
>
> **glam·or·ize** also **glam·our·ize** (glàm'e-rīz') *verb, transitive.* **1.** To make

I usually get along well with extras. In many cases, they are instructed not to talk to the actors, but I have no problem interacting with them as long as it's not distracting from the job at hand.

Most background artists get a feel for the film they are working on within a day or two—where their "characters" fit in the scheme of things and the general tone, but like any profession, some folks just don't get it.

One guy learned the trick of "finding the lens"—he knew just enough to be dangerous. It wasn't until viewing rushes that we saw what a gigantic camera hog he was. God bless the man for his enthusiasm, but damn him all the same for his lack of discretion.

Another man, a Mr. Ryan, managed to fall into the opposite category—that of immovable object. During a scene where my character is led in chains back to the castle, I was surrounded by a column of soldiers. Sam gave these men rigid instructions to keep pace and to conduct themselves in a soldierly fashion, and he made them maintain a unified marching cadence.

Geographically, Mr. Ryan was at the back of the line, far from Sam's discerning eye. He was, however, about four paces in front of me and I witnessed his refusal to cooperate with any such thing. Sam seemed satisfied and headed off to prep the shot.

"Hey, pal," I asked, as friendly as a chained man in the scorching heat could. "You gonna do what the director asked?"

He turned back to me. "I'm not in the army. I don't have to do this if I don't want to."

"True," I agreed, "but you also don't have to get paid either."

With that, Mr. Ryan threw down his spear and stomped off into the desert, never to be seen again. The production report documented the incident as follows:

Necrophilia Hollywood-style: Two of these skeletal extras were found "boning" each other.

6/6/91

P. Ryan (b.g. foot soldier) removed himself from a shooting set-up. While doing so, he removed his wig and beard. The beard fell to the ground and when it was found, it was unusable and will need to be replaced. It was priced at $29.95 by the Hair/Makeup department.

And people wonder why movies cost millions of dollars. . . .

"BRUISE" CAMPBELL

On a stunt-laden film like this, something was bound to go amiss. One night, while flipping a stuntman down the castle stairs, I gouged my face on a protruding piece of armor. I didn't even know what had happened until someone pointed out my bloody breastplate. It appeared as though I needed stitches, but of course, I was a messy mixture of real blood and Karo syrup, so who could tell? I was taken to the local emergency room anyway. And because I was an actor, Rob Tapert summoned a plastic surgeon, in case an extra nip or tuck was needed to maintain my looks.

This is a good time to explain what the character, Ash, looked like. Because of the abuse heaped on our hero, the makeup woman had to devise a plastic template that fit over my face so she could keep track of the cuts I had inherited from the other two films, as well as the new wounds inflicted.

At this point in our shooting schedule, my face was in full disarray—I already had eight to ten cuts, along with slashes, welts and dirt. As the surgeon leaned toward my face, I had to assure him that I had only *really* been cut once.

"Which one is it?" he asked.

I pointed out the real one and two nips and a tuck later, I was in the van, zooming back toward the castle. Because of the amount of damage my face already displayed, we had no need to shoot around my injury— nobody could tell the difference.

Army shaped up to be one of *those* productions—because it was a long and challenging shoot, few people were spared some form of indignity, as notes from the production reports will attest:

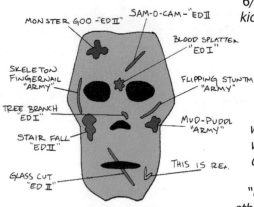

MONSTER GOO "EDⅡ"
SAM-O-CAM-"EDⅡ"
BLOOD SPLATTER "EDI"
SKELETON FINGERNAIL "ARMY"
FLIPPING STUNT™ "ARMY"
TREE BRANCH "EDI"
MUD-PUDDL "ARMY"
STAIR FALL "EDⅡ"
THIS IS REA.
GLASS CUT "EDⅡ"

An actor's template.

6/3/91: *Wrangler (D. York) kicked by a horse. He refused medical assistance.*

6/12/91: *L. Lawrence (extra) had possible allergic reaction to sting of unknown insect.*

6/27/91: *R. Betancourt who was working as a mounted warrior fell from his horse during a scene which involved a mounted charge of the "castle" with approximately 50 other riders.*

6/28/91: *M. Faba, mechanical effects technician, ingested diesel fuel while attempting to siphon fuel for special effects torches.*

7/5/91: *R. Leclair, extra, crushed tip of middle finger on left hand while attempting to free his car, which had become stuck on a large rock in the Polsa Rosa parking lot.*

7/15/91: *Three trenches uphill of castle were left unmarked at night. R. Jacobson, mechanical effects, stumbled into a trench. He was treated by the Set Medic, rested briefly in his car, and returned to the set.*

7/22/91: *C. Garnell, assistant props, injured nose when she ran into another person on set.*

7/29/91: *At 11:50 a.m. a small fire ignited the interior walls of the Blacksmith's furnace.*

7/30/91: *E. Davidtz, principal actress, bumped her lip on the Evil Ash armor during scene 107.*

8/8/91: *A. Rizzo, Sound Mixer, went to visit Dr. D. Evangelatos for treatment for overexertion.*

By the time August rolled around, those of us who weren't already incapacitated wished we were.

LIFE IMITATES ART

We also had one disaster of spectacular proportions. The opening of the film finds Ash dumped out of the sky into a barren wasteland—in this case, a gravel pit in Southern California. The desired effect was for Ash to fall from the sky as his car crashes down behind him, and the solution was simple enough: just do it.

My part was easy—I had to jump off a ladder and crumple when I hit the ground. Behind me, Sam's crappy Delta 88 was suspended via aircraft cable from a large crane on an access road. On cue, I would jump and the car would be released. We knew that this was within the realm of possibility, because we had already done it once back in 1986 for Part II. Why didn't we just use that footage, you ask? It was a rights issue—don't ask . . .

Everyone was in place, waiting for their cue, but without warning, Sam's car crashed to the ground.

What was the deal? No signal had been given.

As we looked up toward the crane, it was evident that something was wrong. About this time, everything went into slow motion and Steven Spielberg took over as director of the scene.

The extended arm on the crane was wobbling more than it should—this was for good reason, because the support legs holding the crane in place had given out and it was slowly falling off the cliff.

The crew watched help-lessly as this gigantic ma-chine crashed to the bottom of the gravel pit. Unbe-knownst to us, a man was on the cliff side of the rig as it gave way. With reflexes born of adversity, he ducked under the truck as it tipped over and was spared a horrific fate.

These are the times when "make believe" and reality meet head-on—the rest of the day was a wash.

The Classic jumping its cue.

Ironically, after all the hassle, we wound up using the footage from 1986.

Events like this and the effort to make the film we wanted to make took their toll on our budget. To get our funding from $8 million to $11 million, Rob, Sam and I agreed to personally put up the contingency (totaling about a million dollars) in case we went over budget.

By the time we finished principal photography, the money had trickled through our fingers like a fine desert sand. Something was terribly wrong with this scenario: this was part three of a successful string of films—weren't we supposed to *make* money off this film?

ACTING BY THE NUMBERS

After six weeks in the desert, we settled in for months of studio work. Sam Raimi continued his undisputed reign as master of the technical nightmare—this time, he reduced me to acting by numbers, literally, through a process called Introvision. It was one of the few instances where the old cliché, "It's all done with mirrors," really applied—mirrors were part of this front-screen projection process.

"34! . . . 35! . . . 36! . . . 37! . . . 38!"

"Thirty-four, thirty-five, thirty-six, thirty-seven, thirty-eight . . ." Those numbers barked out via megaphone by an effects assistant all correlated with specific movements of an animated skeleton that I had to interact with—in this case, during a sword fight.

At #34, I had to arrive at a critical mark on the floor. At #35, I'd turn toward a specific spot on the rear screen since I couldn't actually see the skeleton. At #36, I'd duck a swipe from the skeleton, and as I rose, a live-action puppet skeleton attacked me from behind. I'd have about 2.5 seconds to fend him off before #40, when I'd take a swing at the animated skeleton. By #42, the beast would be defeated and I'd be off to the next fight. Notes from a director for scenes like this take on a bizarre twist.

Sam: Bruce, thirty-eight wasn't right. It was late.

Bruce: I know, I was still thinking about thirty-six. But, I think I nailed forty.

Sam: Yeah, that was better—and you've got more time before forty-two . . . maybe a second.

Bruce: Okay . . . no sweat.

SLICE AND DICE

Shooting came to a halt in the fall of 1991 and the process of editing several hundred thousand feet of film began. During this, I began to witness the negative effects of making, for lack of a better description, a "dumbbell" film.

A film like *Army* is very hard to defend—the plot is simple-minded and the narrative drive is wrapped around a series of action sequences. Witness, if you will, an editing room conversation:

Dino: Six skeletons blowing up is too much. Three is all you need.

Rob: No, Dino, we've got to have six!

Dino: Why?

Bruce: Because we . . . because . . . we *need* them?

Dino: I'll send the footage to you. Cut them out. . . .

This haggling went on through the test screening process. According to test audiences, *Army* was too long, and the end, where Ash wakes up in a postapocalyptic world, was too "depressing."

214

I'm sure by now, you can guess the outcome. Sam's original director's cut was ninety-six minutes long. Fifteen minutes of battle footage, most of it financed by us, was removed. The new studio version with a "happy" ending was eighty-one minutes.

Evil Ash: Definitely not my good side.

The only saving grace of shooting a new beginning and ending was that Bridget Fonda was involved. She had been a fan of the series and asked for a small role. What were we gonna say, "No"?

Anatomy of a Paycheck 36

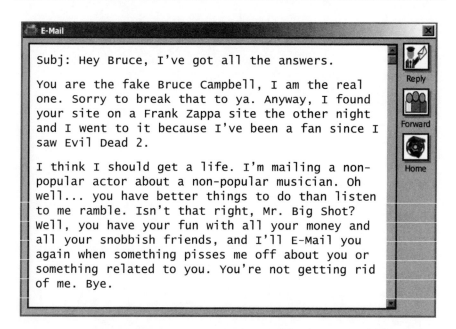

We all hear about how much money actors make. Admittedly, some earn more for a single job than the gross national product of small countries, but I would like to offer a little perspective.

Let's say that you starred in and coproduced *Army of Darkness*. This was a second sequel, and by all accounts, you're entitled to earn a little moola for your efforts.

Just to pick a figure out of the air, let's start with $500,000—a king's ransom. Now get your calculators out and stay with me. First thing you do is subtract twenty-five percent of that amount to cover agents and managers—$125,000. That leaves you with a whopping $375,000.

Okay, before you buy that big house, slice that figure in half—between federal and state taxes, all at the highest rate, and someone to prepare a more complex tax return, you're left with $187,500. That was fast, wasn't it?

But wait, there's more—if you had been divorced just prior to *Army,* your ex would be entitled to half of the take from that film. After taxes that's $93,750, and it leaves you with the same amount.

You're thinking, "That's still some serious coin!" I couldn't agree more, but between a long production schedule and studio squabbling, *Army* took two years to complete, so crunch those numbers again and divide by two— that leaves you with $46,875 a year. You, too, can become a rich movie star.

LONG LIVE THE "HUD" 37

Near the end of *Army*, I announced to Sam Raimi, "I hope that's all you have to shoot, pal, because I'm off to work on a *real* film!" Of course, Sam knew what I was talking about—he had cowritten the Coen Brothers' industrial fantasy, *The Hudsucker Proxy.* In theory, the film wasn't all that different than our dud *Crimewave,* except for the fact that the Coen Brothers had ten times the money and big-shot actors in their pocket.

I was contacted to audition for the part of the wisecracking newsroom reporter, Smitty. For the first time in a long while, I had to stop and think about it. I auditioned for a bit part in *Barton Fink*, but didn't get the role, and I had just finished *Army of Darkness* for a major studio. Granted, *Army* was a genre flick, destined to become a college drinking game, but a line in the sand had to be drawn—my history with the Coens spanned more than a decade.

> Revelation #48: "No" is the most powerful word in the Hollywood dictionary.

I decided to say no. I would gladly and willingly accept the role, but these fellows knew my work well enough to spare me the audition. *No.* Use the word wisely, and it can be liberating—use it a lot and you'll starve. In this case, it worked because I was offered the role, minus an audition. This may seem trivial, but to an actor it means *everything*—it is the difference between crawling through glass and being carried on pillows.

That said, I was thrilled to be a part of this classy production. John Cameron was the assistant director of the film, so it was a comfortable setup. The Coens asked me to join their two-week rehearsal process, reading the miscellaneous roles that needed a voice. I jumped at the

chance because it was a return to "fly-on-the-wall" status.

That first rehearsal was a heady experience—one by one, they came through the door: Jennifer Jason Leigh, Tim Robbins, and eventually, P-P-*Paul* N-N-*Newman*.

No more low-budget stuff for me, I thought. *Time to cross* Maniac Cop off the resumé!

Another of my duties during this time was to run lines with the actors any time they wanted. When Paul Newman took me up on the offer one day, I wasn't sure whether to jump for joy or barf, because I was both elated and terrified.

As we sat in his trailer preparing to read a scene, my first goal was to make sure not to piss him off by doing something stupid.

Bruce: So, uh, Mr. Newman—

Paul: Call me Paul.

Bruce: Okay, sure. So, uh, *Paul*, when we run these lines, how picky do you want me to be?

Paul: What do you mean?

Bruce: Well, do you want me to correct you a lot, a little, or not at all?

Paul: Tell you what, I just need to stumble through this first—how about if I call out for the line if I need it?

Bruce: Okay—you got it . . .

Paul: It's funny, I used to have a mind like a steel trap. Then, one summer a long time ago, I did eighteen different plays in twenty-four weeks and it all turned to mush. . . .

The two weeks of rehearsals were also a good time to get fitted for my costume. Normally, on the low-budget stuff I had done, I'd give my sizes to the costume designer over the phone and hope for the best. Not so on *Hudsucker*—Richard Hornung was a designer who really did it right.

I only had a small role, but when I showed up for the fitting, I never saw more clothes in my life. Richard and I began with a discussion about colors—he felt that my character should start in lighter colors, then go a little darker when my character gets creepier. I hadn't even thought of that, but it sounded good to me.

Next, we talked about hats, since we both agreed that Smitty was "a hat guy." Richard brought out a stack of hats and I tried on each one until we found several that were perfect. I didn't say much during these sessions, because he knew what was right. By the time we were done, I had three outfits that fit both my body and my character.

When filming began, all of my scenes were with Jennifer Jason Leigh. I knew my way around a film set and had performed some difficult tasks, but nothing was as challenging as keeping up with her. Jennifer was an acting machine—she knew every one of her voluminous lines from day one of rehearsal and never tripped up, not even once. I hadn't been nervous like that in a long time and I liked it.

Jennifer Jason Leigh: Acting Machine.

Whether you like the Coen Brothers' films or not, you've got to hand it to them—*Hudsucker* was a long way from Joel's beginning in the *Evil Dead* editing room. I've always been impressed by how ballsy the brothers are, and I think it's allowed them to get where they are today. *Hudsucker* was a good example of this: they had turned down numerous offers to make the film at other studios, but declined in each case because the budget wasn't enough for them to make the type of film they had envisioned. They would rather not make the film if it couldn't be done right—how many filmmakers can say the same?

THE FOX WHO ATE MY HAT

While shooting *Hudsucker,* I filled my free time by peddling around Wilmington—it's a flat city, just right for two-wheeling. I rode my bike to rehearsals every day, carrying my script in a blue vinyl backpack.

One Sunday afternoon, I rode away from town on my single-gear dork bike. In a half hour, I got to the city limits where the industrial areas on the outskirts of town began to decline.

Scrub was on my right. In the low, level woods to my left, I caught a glimpse of what looked like a fox. I was familiar with the lanky gait of a coyote, and I knew it was some sort of wild creature, so I stopped the bike. Sure enough, it was a fox, with a pointy nose and red tail.

I figured I might as well watch for as long as I could until it ran away, but to my surprise, it did nothing of the sort—in fact, the fox seemed positively relaxed as it rooted in the ground for something. When it spotted me, I figured that was game over, but the fuzzy creature approached and then stopped at the opposite side of the road.

I was surprised when, without hesitation, it crossed the road and approached the back end of my bike! I lowered it slowly to the ground and the fox began to chew delicately on the knobby rubber.

Eventually, the fox worked its way toward me, but stopped within about five feet, sniffing the air. I had worked up a sweat riding on this hot day,

That darn fox loved to chew my "Crew."

and I'm sure I put off a pretty good scent. I removed my J. Crew hat and tossed it gently to the ground in front of me and the fox surprised me again.

He came right up to the hat and started rooting inside the sweaty rim, then grabbed it in his teeth and sprinted off about fifteen feet, thrashing it side to side like a rag doll before dropping it—he was playing just like a dog would.

I slowly moved toward the hat, talking calmly the whole time, and picked it up. The fox circled around behind me, so I turned and tossed the hat again. The fox grabbed it again, but this time he took off across the road and entered the fringe of forest on the other side.

Oh, great, I thought, *there goes my new J. Crew hat,* but the fox stopped about ten feet inside the forest and dropped my hat again. I figured if this game was going to continue, the little bugger needed a name. I worked for the Fox network once, run by a guy named Sandy, so thereafter he became "Sandy."

I walked over and picked up the hat, but this time I hung it from a branch about three feet off the ground to see how interested he really was. Apparently, Sandy was still game, because he rose on his haunches and snatched the thing off the branch. This time, Sandy began to chew on the adjustable strap and before I could do anything, he snapped the back band off.

I was a little surprised and pissed, but I didn't think there was any point in saying "No, Sandy, *bad* fox!" Sandy then felt compelled to mark my hat, and as he hunkered down into a squatting position, I stepped in and shooed it away—this was cute, but enough was enough.

Even though he no longer had a hat to chew on, Sandy didn't feel the need to leave, so he stretched his legs and relaxed in a patch of grass. That looked like a good idea, so I sat down and we hung out for about twenty minutes.

When I got back to civilization, I was surprised at the reactions of people—most didn't believe me and those who did scolded me.

"That thing probably had rabies—you shouldn't have gone near it. I wouldn't have. . . ."

All the more fox for me, I thought.

LIFE IN THE FAST LANE: 38
THE RISE AND FALL OF BRISCO COUNTY, JR.

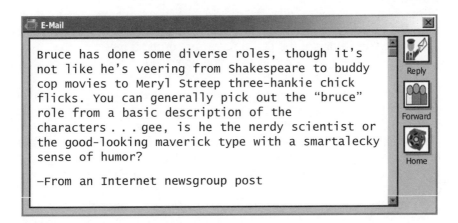

E-Mail

Bruce has done some diverse roles, though it's not like he's veering from Shakespeare to buddy cop movies to Meryl Streep three-hankie chick flicks. You can generally pick out the "bruce" role from a basic description of the characters . . . gee, is he the nerdy scientist or the good-looking maverick type with a smartalecky sense of humor?

—From an Internet newsgroup post

Reply

Forward

Home

"*Hud*" was in the can, *Army* was about to hit the theaters, and I had just landed a new talent agent—things were looking up. My first audition as their client was for the lead in a new Western TV show.

With a television series, you don't just "get" the lead part, you've got to "earn" it, and landing the title role in *The Adventures of Brisco County, Jr.* was a journey of its own.

Audition #1 was for the casting director. Their job, among other things, is to separate the chaff from the wheat and send only the best actors to the next level. Actors all look for a way to leave an impression on casting directors to avoid being lost in the shuffle. One audition piece for the show involved some fighting—there wasn't much I could do in this small office, so I fell back on an old "Bonzoid Sisters" routine and flipped myself, head over heels.

"Oh, my God!" the casting director screamed, as he lurched back in his chair.

TELEVISION

INTO TV / BY JOHN PETERSON

GOOD IMPRESSION: Some stars jump through hoops to make a mark at this time of year, as TV critics gather in Los Angeles to preview the fall season. Going the tradition one step further, **Bruce Campbell**, star of Fox's new *Adventures of Brisco County Jr.* He did a bone-crushing back flip fall in the middle of a press conference, and got a round of applause. He was ~~ing off his prowess~~ at~~~~

Fortunately, this left a favorable impression and I was able to audition for the producers. They carry a large amount of weight when it comes to who gets cast for what, but in this high-stakes chess game, producers are not the final word—not by a long shot. With a reading and another flip, I cleared that hurdle. . . .

Audition #3 was with the producers again. More of a work session than anything, it was to prepare me for the Warner Bros. TV execs.

Audition #4 was in a room full of attentive, quiet people—among them were the one or two individuals who could send me up to the next level. Just before the audition, the casting director cornered me.

"Bruce, you're gonna do that flip thing again, aren't you?"

"Yeah, sure," I said. "As long as the back holds out . . ."

Audition #5 was the big one—this was for an even larger group of quiet people. The freaky thing about network auditions is that you have to prenegotiate your deal—you have to hammer out every detail, down to plane tickets and per diem, with agents, lawyers and business affairs people, and you still might not get the part. Networks had obviously been in the awkward position of approving someone and then failing to close a deal.

After the audition, which I could do in my sleep by that point, I decided to give the network brass a little speech. Actors aren't encouraged to interact with them, but I thought, *The hell with it, they should know who they're getting into business with.*

"Look, uh, I just wanted you folks to know that if you cast me in this part, I won't stab you in the back. I'm a hard worker and I'll do everything I can to help you make this show a success. Okay, well, I guess that's it. Thanks for your time. . ."

Driving home that night, I got "the call." I'll spare you the descriptions of how I whooped and hollered—it's far too embarrassing.

THEY "SHOOT" HORSES, DON'T THEY?

This old dog was about to learn some new tricks—I had to become a cowboy.

"Can you ride, son?" asked head wrangler, Gordon Spencer.

"Heck yeah, I rode a lot in the last film I did."

"Good, why don't you hop up on that horse there and take him for a spin."

I cantered around the corral a few times and when I stopped, I noticed a big smile on Gordon's face.

"Not bad, eh?" I asked.

"Son, you look like a monkey humpin' a football."

What followed was a month of trying to conquer what cowboys call the "ass/saddle battle," and learning how to ride for real.

The proving grounds.

Horses are large animals that aren't as dumb as people think. They know when a rider doesn't know what he's doing and they'll take full advantage of it. Early on, I had a great deal of trouble with control—I couldn't get my horse to go, and when I did, I couldn't get him to stop.

"Hey, Gordon, this horse is being a pain in the ass. What's wrong with him?"

"I don't know, let me get on him and take a look."

The instant Gordon got on the horse, he would behave beautifully, following every command.

"Yep . . . must be the horse," Gordon said as he dismounted.

Eventually, I learned that with riding, "pilot error" was the problem ninety-nine percent of the time. In the show, Brisco and his horse had a close relationship—almost like siblings at times. In order to pull this off, I had to develop a decent relationship with the main trick horse, Strip.

Strip did all of the head nods, hoof steps and lip quivers for scenes where we had to interact. Like actors, Strip worked on the reward system—only he liked grain. I had a special pocket sewn into the inside of my leather jacket just for that purpose, so we got along fine.

Strip was a great horse, but you wouldn't want to ride him—trick horses are too fidgety. The bulk of my riding was on a horse called Copper, otherwise known as Lead Belly—he had a very smooth gait and never got overly excited about anything.

Copper was a trustworthy horse, but he knew just when to step on my foot—it was always early in the morning when it was cold outside. This only happened a couple of times, but it felt like someone had backed a 747 over my instep. The only thing I could do when this happened was punch him in the shoulder as hard as I could until he moved.

WARNER WAS MY BROTHER

The show was staged on the Warner Bros. back lot, in their remaining vestige of a Western town—Laramie Street. I didn't care what was left of what, because I was working at the same place that once employed Humphrey Bogart, Bette Davis and Errol Flynn.

Driving on the Warner lot for the first time was a thrill, because I was now a contract player for a film studio—a notion that I always found very romantic within the world of acting.

An assistant director showed me to my trailer and I dumped my stuff inside.

My own trailer, I thought. *This is all right.*

I looked around and marveled at the comforts of home—air conditioning, a gas stove, microwave, stereo, TV, dining table, bedroom and even a reclining chair.

The irony there, of course, was that I never had time to enjoy my trailer. Because television is known for speed, I spent almost the entire workday on the set.

Veterans on our crew scoffed at "the feature guys." Their reasoning was simple: TV crews could always move slower like feature crews, but feature crews couldn't necessarily speed up.

As soon as one episode was in the can, another script was right behind it—if "Brisco in Jalisco" ended on Tuesday, "Bad Luck Betty" began Wednesday morning, complete with a new bad guy and, inevitably, a new love interest. All too often, I'd find myself in the middle of an intimate scene with a guest star and have to ask, "I'm sorry, what was your name again?"

To shoot forty-five minutes of screen time, a feature might take as long as forty-five days—for *Brisco* we had to do it in seven. There was only one way to achieve this—by using time-tested TV filming methods.

-footed refusal. **3.** Unable to react quickly; unprepared.

flat·foot·footed mas·ter (flăt'fŏŏt'ĭd măs'ter) *n.* The concept of walking actors into position and permanently rooting them there for an entire dialogue scene. ...t burdensome. **2.** *Law.* Entailing obligati...

...(flăt' out')a... exceed advantages.

...t out.

on·er with a cou·ple of pops (wŭn'er wĭth ă kŭp'el ôv pôps) *n.* A scene which can be filmed essentially in one shot with exception of one of two quick cutaways to another character.

one·self (wŭn-sĕlf') *pron.* **1.** One's own self:. **a.** Used reflexively as the direct or ...

It didn't mean that the show was a bore to do—far from it. During the course of twenty-six episodes, my partner, Julius Carry, and I found ourselves in the damnedest predicaments—from struggling in quicksand and fighting underwater to running from burning buildings and being lashed on a railroad track. There is no question that my stunt double, Clint

Lilly, performed the most dangerous stuff, but Julius and I did our fair share.

One particular stunt involved hanging from the third-story window of an old building. The thrill of the shot was to show the danger without the aid of cuts or stunt people. It's amazing how high three stories is, once you actually get up there and look down, but the scariest part was when the video camera came out. Stunt coordinators use them these days to document approval from all integral parties—that way, if anything went wrong, they wouldn't be liable.

Stunt Coord.: So, Bruce, you understand what's going on here?

Bruce: Yeah, I have to hang from that ledge up there.

Stunt Coord.: You're comfortable with how the gag is laid out?

Clint Lilly with his "dialogue double."

Bruce: Comfortable? Well, this harness isn't exactly comfortable . . .

Stunt Coord.: But you're satisfied that all precautions have been taken to insure your safety?

Bruce: Sure, for not having done it before and not knowing what to expect . . .

I'm happy to say that on *Brisco,* nobody sustained any life-threatening injuries. All stunts were meticulously planned and performed, but there was occasionally what I called the "X" factor.

One scene called for me to be lashed in the middle of the street with the heroine of the week. As the action unfolded, the idea was for us to narrowly escape a stampede of cattle by rolling under the safety of a nearby wagon.

As the actress and I rolled under the wagon, the cattle were supposed to be herded around in a safe manner—but as the cameras rolled, a logjam formed, and the cattle began to panic. Dozens of them began piling up behind the wagon and it lurched forward—everyone involved had to think fast. The actress wrapped her body around the front axle of the wagon. I spun around on my back and jammed my boots against the back axle—I figured if I was going to be trampled, I wanted to see it coming.

Fortunately, with the aid of the wranglers, the herd was soon dispersed and the danger was over. Interestingly, even though the cameraman abandoned his post, his camera stayed straight enough to capture the shot in all of its raw glory, and the footage appears in the episode.

RON WEBBER

Have you ever noticed in classic television Westerns like *Bonanza* or *Gunsmoke* that there are never any horse droppings in sight? That's because of fellows like Ron Webber.

Ron was the craft service guy on *Brisco*—this meant he had to show up before everyone else, fix the coffee and lay out foodstuffs for the crew all day long. It also meant that Ron had the unpleasant task of cleaning up after the horses. The union negotiation that joined the jobs of food preparation and horse manure removal is beyond my comprehension, but that's the way it was.

One of Ron's favorite sayings was, "It may be horse shit to you, but it's bread and butter to me." Such was the nature of this man—each time he'd scoop up another "road apple," he'd proclaim, "another shingle on my roof!"

Chatting with Ron between shots, I learned about his journey through the film business. Eons ago, he found himself painting studio boss Darryl Zanuck's home in the Hollywood hills. Ron did such a fine job that Zanuck moved him over to the Twentieth Century Fox lot, where he continued as a painter.

As the story went, Ron was painting one day, when veteran TV producer Irwin Allen strolled by and caught a glimpse of his bodybuilder physique. Irwin was apparently looking for someone to do a bit in his TV show, *Lost in Space.*

<u>Irwin Allen:</u> Hey, buddy, can you pick up a guy over your head?
<u>Ron:</u> Hell yes, I can. . . .

Guy Williams up in arms—Ron's to be exact.

Ron turned to the nearest painter and hoisted him over his head. Irwin Allen hired him on the spot.

"Next thing I know," said Ron, "I'm in the damn show."

I was skeptical of Ron's story, so I asked my archivist pal, Scott Spiegel, to check through his extensive *Lost in Space* video collection and see if there was such an episode. In about two minutes, Scott popped a tape in his machine and sure enough—there was a younger Ron Webber, deftly hoisting Guy Williams over his head. I'm not sure why, but I was flabbergasted.

I came to the *Brisco* set the next day with a copy of the episode in hand and got the crew members to gather around the VCR—Ron included. When the big moment arrived, Ron just about had a heart attack, and when I told him to keep the copy, he almost cried.

"Gonna show this to the grandkids," he beamed.

It turned out that Ron had had a few brushes with fame. He later worked on the crew of the awful cult classic, *Myra Breckinridge*, with an aging Mae West. One day, Mae called Ron to her trailer and slapped a hand on his thigh—apparently, she was fond of bodybuilders. Her advances continued, and Ron soon found himself in a dilemma. Not knowing how to avoid a scene, he leaped up and exclaimed, "Ms. West, you're my *favorite* movie star!" and ran out of her trailer.

Ron worked on many films and television shows as a craft service guy. One was the Warren Beatty hit, *Shampoo*.

"I was workin' on that damn *Shampoo*, see, and they was shootin' a scene where Warren was on his motorcycle. He was supposed to come around a corner one way and Jack Warden was in a Mercedes, comin' the other way. Well, ol' Jack, he come around too far, see, and Warren had to lay his bike down to avoid hitting the car. So, there was Warren Beatty, stuck under his motorcycle.

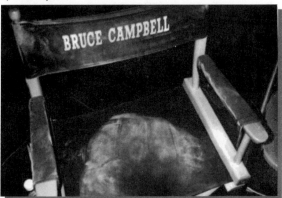

Brisco had one dusty ass.

Now the crew, they didn't like him too much, but you know what? I says, 'Hey, that ain't right,' and I pulled the darn thing off him. As I was doin' it, he was kickin' so hard to get away from the bike, he kicked the damn tail pipe into my arm and burned me but good."

At this point, Ron rolled up his tight, worn T-shirt revealing a substantial scar.

"Went clean through my navy tattoo."

The next day, Warren Beatty walked past Ron and noticed his arm.

Warren: What happened to your arm?

Ron: Hey, man, you kicked that damn bike into me and burnt my arm.

Warren: What's your name?

Ron: Ron Webber.

Warren: Ron, from now on, you're on all my films.

Ron looked at me with a big smile as he finished this story.

"And you know what? I was . . ."

On average, Ron worked fourteen-hour days, five days a week—dutifully, cheerfully, and with no thanks. It bothers me to think that so much of the film business is comprised of hard-working grunts like Ron, but all we ever hear about are the people in front of the camera.

By the time *Brisco* was done, Ron had almost enough union hours to retire. I hope he's home in Oregon right now, swinging in a hammock,

with BRUCE
"THE ADVENTURES O

TIME		MARKET	STATION/AF
8:00		HOUSTON	KRIV/FOX/NE
8:08		WASHINGTON DC	WTTG/FOX/N
8:16		MINNEAPOLIS	KITN/FOX/"10
8:24	L	LOS ANGELES	KTTV/FOX/"GC
8:32		GREENSBORO	WNRW/FOX/IN
8:40	L	SAN FRANCISCO	KTVU/FOX/"MOI
8:48		TAMPA	WFTS/FOX/INTE
8:56		NATIONAL	"E" ENTERTAIN
9:04		BOSTON	WFXT/FOX/INT
9:12		ST LOUIS	KDNL/FOX/W
9:20		OKLAHOMA CITY	KOCO/ABC/"C
9:28		BALTIMORE	WBFF/FOX/N
9:36		MIAMI	WSVN/FOX/NE
9:44		SALT LAKE CITY	KSTU/FOX/NEW
9:52		GENERIC INTERVIEW AVAILABLE	

Saturday, October 23rd

5:00 p.m.	Depart Peabody Hotel for Universa
5:15 p.m.	Arrive USF
5:30 p.m.	Shoot promos at "Back To Th
6:00 p.m.	Go to the "Slaughter Haunted
6:45 p.m.	Shoot promos at "Jaws" Ride
7:30 p.m.	Publicity Interviews
8:20 p.m.	Introduction on Main Stage
8:35 p.m.	Shoot promos at "Robosaurus"
9:15 p.m.	**BREAK**
10:00 p.m.	Promo Party at Lombard's
10:20 p.m.	Second introduction on stage/Part
12:30 a.m.	Depart USF for Peabody Hotel

Sunday, October 24th

telling his grandchildren how he saved Warren Beatty's life.

WAGGING THE DOG

To get a TV show on the air was one thing, but to *keep* it on was a horse of a different color. The impressive thing about the efforts behind *Brisco* was that promotion crossed the typical barriers. Coming attractions for the new show ran not only on the Fox network, but in conventional movie theaters as well—"Event television" became the mantra.

On several occasions, we were summoned before call time to hawk the show to global markets as well as national—try saying something clever to Israel at 6:27 in the morning.

More grassroots events came in the form of mall appearances, fairs, haunted houses and, of course, rodeos.

The week of shooting usually wrapped up late on Friday night, sometimes 3:00 in the morning. A car would come to pick me up at 6:00 A.M. that same morning and whisk me off to the airport so I could promote the show in some far-flung region.

Getting home Sunday night, I'd learn my lines, and be on set the next morning at 7:00 A.M. The saying, "Be careful what you wish for . . ." began to echo in my head.

Going to rodeos were particularly fascinating, since I'm not a cowboy. Growing up in suburban Detroit, my idea of horsepower was to look under the hood of my dad's Chevy Impala.

The persona of "hero cowboy" was taken a little too seriously at these functions. I turned down all "team roping" events, since three cameras and half a day of clever filmmaking were the only things that would allow me to bring down a single calf. I usually wound up parading around the ring on a horse provided by the rodeo, giving away free tickets to something, and even that wasn't always a good idea.

At a rodeo in Chicago, the ring leader introduced me to "a nice, quiet horse." I later dubbed him "Widow Maker," since he did his best to kill me at every turn.

It was a kick to meet real cowboys who rode the bulls and roped, but they weren't as impressed with me. After a brief introduction, the conversation generally took a nose-dive—my phony-ass pretend world was so far removed from these legitimately tough guys that we had nothing to say. I'm not usually one to come up on the short end of a conversation, but I'll be darned if I could get these cowboys to even *look* at me, let alone discuss the finer points of securing a flank strap.

RIDING INTO THE SUNSET

You shouldn't miss bottom-dwelling Fox entries

Sassy sagebrush saga deserves wider audience

'Brisco County' rides high with fans, low in ratings

Will 'Brisco' ride into the sunset?

Try as we did to let the entire world know about *Brisco,* the inevitable happened—the ratings started to slip. When a show is a hit, everyone is a genius. When a show drops in the ratings, the analysis begins:

Exec #1: Should the scripts be funnier?

Exec #2: Maybe they're too funny.

Exec #1: We need more action!

Exec #2: But the show is already too damn expensive!

Exec #1: Maybe the actors aren't making the emotional connection they need to.

Exec #2: Friday is the wrong night for the show—people still go bowling, you know. . . .

To explain why a TV show is canceled is almost impossible. Ironically *Brisco,* with its off-kilter humor, wouldn't have been developed on any other network, yet the appeal of "Westerns" was still rural—not the side Fox's urban bread was buttered on.

Weekend promotions continued, but the quality of the venues became more suspect. The end of the line came when I found myself signing autographs in a Reno pawnshop. There are many times when actors can kid themselves about their glamorous life, but this was downright embarrassing.

I got the news of our cancellation while recuperating at a remote bed and breakfast in Texas. I could lace this part of the story with all the bittersweet emotions that race through an actor's head, but frankly, after I hung the phone up, I danced a jig. The gilded cage had been flung wide open—my life had been handed back. It was a time to reflect, sure, but it was also a time to *sleeeep*.

Oddly enough, my *Brisco* days weren't over yet—months prior, I had been booked to host a local Emmy award show in Cleveland. I contacted them, assuming the engagement was off.

"Hell, no, we'd love to have you!"

"Yeah, but the show is canceled," I reasoned. "Seems kind of anticlimactic, doesn't it?"

"No, here's the gag. We just dumped *Fox*! Our station is ABC now—let's all have a night of fun at their expense!"

The check had already cleared, so I dusted off my spurs and headed to Cleveland. Upon arrival, they informed me of a particularly grand scheme.

"Get this . . . we'll cue the music, hit the spotlight and you'll ride into the ballroom on a horse!"

"A . . . horse?"

"Sure. Piece of cake, Bruce. We've got this nice, quiet horse for you. . . ."

Images of "Widow Maker" flickered before my eyes. I'm not one for premonitions, but I was doing an untested horse gag for a show that was no longer on the air, for a station that was no longer part of Fox.

I could see the headline . . .

I'm relieved to say the event came off very well and actually helped put a little humor into the cancellation of the show. *Brisco* was a wild and woolly ride—without a doubt, the longest and most exciting year of my life.

BE QUICK, OR YOU'RE DEAD 39

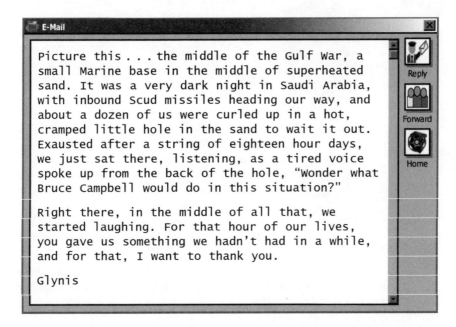

Picture this . . . the middle of the Gulf War, a
small Marine base in the middle of superheated
sand. It was a very dark night in Saudi Arabia,
with inbound Scud missiles heading our way, and
about a dozen of us were curled up in a hot,
cramped little hole in the sand to wait it out.
Exausted after a string of eighteen hour days,
we just sat there, listening, as a tired voice
spoke up from the back of the hole, "Wonder what
Bruce Campbell would do in this situation?"

Right there, in the middle of all that, we
started laughing. For that hour of our lives,
you gave us something we hadn't had in a while,
and for that, I want to thank you.

Glynis

During *Brisco*'s run, Sam Raimi landed his first A picture. With a cast like Gene Hackman, Sharon Stone, Russell Crowe, and Leonardo DiCaprio, *The Quick and the Dead* couldn't have been much bigger.

In this world, however, Sam found himself dealing with elements that were out of his control—elements like Movie Stars.

Gene Hackman was an actor who insisted on respect. The first day of shooting, Sam explained what he had in mind.

Sam: Okay, Gene, when you come out that door, I'd like you to tip your hat to the guy across the street, then come over here and sit in this chair. Now, I know this isn't scripted, but I'd like you to lean over to this guy and whisper, "What are the odds on the kid?"

Gene looked at Sam in silence for a beat.

Gene: I'm not doing any of that.

Cut to Sam, turning white—fortunately, he is extremely prepared.

Sam: Well, you don't have to tip your hat, but I already got a shot of Pat Hingle across the street reacting to you. You signal the gunfight, so it can be whatever you want, a wave or a nod—

Gene: All right, I'll tip my hat, but I won't sit in that chair.

Sam: Hmmm—well, the reason I thought you might want to sit, is because you're the king of this town—the king sits. I've got the extras all standing like peasants.

Sam, *giving Hackman hell on* The Quick and the Dead.

Gene: All right, I'll tip my hat and sit in the chair, but I'm not gonna say that line.

Sam: That's fine—you don't have to, but later on, when the audience realizes that you are the kid's father, they'll think back and say, "Cool, he really did care about his son."

Gene looked at Sam in silence again.

Sam smiled at me as he popped a VHS tape of dailies into his machine. I watched Gene Hackman walk outside, tip his hat, sit down, and whisper the new line.

"Huh? Who's the boss?" Sam asked, jerking a thumb at himself.

John Cameron was Sam's assistant director, and his personal cross to bear was Sharon Stone. His challenge came in trying to get her on her mark.

Bruce: So, you couldn't boss her around, eh?

John: I'd get irritated—we'd have rehearsed it, she's all ready, she's touched up, she'd be on the mark. I'd say, "Stand by." She'd step off the mark, "Oh Sally, you know for tomorrow the dinner with Frank . . ."—you know, that kind of thing—talky, talky, talk.

Bruce: So what did you do?

John: So you would just roll, and she'd be like, "You rolling?" I said, "Yeah, we're rolling. Ready when you are." She goes, "Goddamn it, stop rolling without me being ready and when I'm ready, then you can roll." So I said, "How in the hell am I supposed to know you're ready? You're on your mark, we're ready to go and you know we're ready." I was, like, mad and she goes, "Oh, when you need me on that mark, I'll be there." You know it was calling on the professionalism thing. We got along just okay.

The Quick and the Dead even managed to torment me. I came to visit Sam on the set when I had just a few days off the *Brisco* shoot—all I wanted to do was hang out behind the monitor with Sam and crack jokes, but he had other ideas.

The minute he saw me arrive on set, his face lit up—it wasn't that he was glad to see me, it's just that I represented a solution to his current problem.

<u>Sam:</u> Come here, you, I'm gonna put you in this film.

Sam, John and I on the set of The Quick and the Dead.

<u>Bruce:</u> No, really, Sam—I just want to—

<u>Sam:</u> Shut up and come with me.

Sam dragged me to the wardrobe trailer and shoved me in.

<u>Sam:</u> Hey, gals, I'd like you to make this guy look like a loser—like he used to be rich, but now he's a nobody. Make the clothes dirty and rotting a little bit.

When I was done with the impromptu fitting, Sam pushed me into the makeup trailer.

<u>Bruce:</u> Sam, this is great, but—

<u>Sam:</u> Shut up. Mike, make this guy look like a bum—like he's got some horrible disease. Give him a sore on his lip and everything.

<u>Bruce:</u> Oh, Sam, I don't—

<u>Sam:</u> Shut up, it'll be great. See you out there. . . .

About a half hour later, an assistant director came to find me.

"They're ready to shoot with you now, Bruce."

"Shoot? Shoot what?"

Only Sam knew for sure—it turned out that he didn't need me to help plug some hole in his plot, he needed me to help him shut an actor up. Pat Hingle, a great character actor for forty years, had been pestering Sam about why his character never got revenge on the pimp who sold his daughter. Sam never had an answer for him—until I showed up.

<u>Sam:</u> Okay now Pat, this guy here is going to come up to your daughter and say "Come on, girlie girl, you and me are gonna do the devil's dance."

<u>Bruce:</u> I am?

<u>Sam:</u> Quiet, mister. So Pat, you see this happening, and before this horrible guy can do anything else, you jump in there and save your daughter.

<u>Pat:</u> So, I should rough him up a little?

Sam: A little? Hell, you'd be *pissed*. Don't worry about this guy, he's like a stuntman, you can do anything you want. I think you should choke him, actually.

Pat: Maybe I could throw an arm around his neck from behind.

Sam: Yeah, that's great! Then you throw him down the street and kick him one last time in the ass.

Pat: Okay, sounds good, Sam.

Bruce: Hey, Sam, could I ask a question? Where is my character coming from? Should I come from over there?

Sam took this opportunity to humiliate me in front of the entire crew.

Sam: Oh, so Bruce has questions. Well, maybe we should all just wait while we answer every one to your satisfaction.

Bruce: Well, Sam all I—

Sam: You'll stand where I tell you to stand, mister—you'll say what I tell you to say—you'll do what I tell you to do.

Bruce: Okay, Sam, whatever. . . .

After numerous takes of this rough encounter, Pat Hingle seemed pleased. As he walked away a happy camper, Sam approached me.

Sam: Thanks for your help, buddy—that scene will never see the light of day. . . .

Scott Spiegel was bullied into a role as a scavenger. He too suffered the public wrath of Sam.

Scott: Sam was so funny as the director. He goes, "Okay. Let me hear how you're gonna sound." It was, like, in front of everybody. I mean can't he just pull me off to the side or something? But it was cool—

Bruce: Didn't you hang out with the guy that nobody knew?

Scott: Yeah. Russell Crowe. I met him on a van ride to set. It's seven in the morning. I'm next to Woody Strode and all these character actors—

Bruce: And he fires up a cigarette?

Scott: Yeah. We're in a closed van. And he's listening to like the worst Australian rap music, and I'm like, "What are you doing?"

Bruce: Did you bug Leonardo?

Scott: Well, he was really into what he was doing—but he and that little blond kid were playing the most childish games. They were playing tag. I'm like, "Will you get out of here?" But I saved a call sheet. It was so cool—Leonardo DiCaprio, Gene Hackman, Sharon Stone . . . Scott Spiegel. I'm like, "Oh my God."

Sharon Stone, Gene Hackman and . . . Scott Spiegel?

A Madness to My Method 40

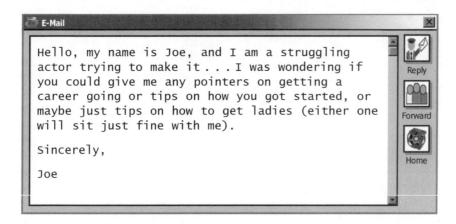

Hello, my name is Joe, and I am a struggling actor trying to make it . . . I was wondering if you could give me any pointers on getting a career going or tips on how you got started, or maybe just tips on how to get ladies (either one will sit just fine with me).

Sincerely,

Joe

Reply

Forward

Home

I once heard that Robert DeNiro lived with a steel-working family for six weeks in order to prepare for his role in *The Deer Hunter*. I've watched interviews with actors who tell wrenching stories of how hard it was to "shake" a character after filming was complete. That's all well and good, but ninety-nine percent of the time an actor is lucky to know what scene is being shot.

Of course, some films have rehearsals where you can work out blocking and discuss every nuance of your character ad nauseum. Since my first film in 1979, I've rehearsed like this maybe two times. Most film projects, and certainly all of TV, simply don't have the time for it.

In this more realistic world of acting, you have to think fast or you'll get buried. My first TV gig, *Knots Landing,* left me speechless. The director introduced himself to me in the morning and never said another word to me for the rest of the shoot. As they were setting up my first shot, I realized that I had no props. Here I was, playing a businessman at a meeting, and I didn't have a watch, a briefcase, or documents of any kind. I quickly wrangled the prop man and got what I needed.

Welcome to TV, I figured.

On any given day, projects other than big A pictures are gonna shoot between five and eight pages with or without you, so acting can't always be about "method." Often, big dramatic scenes are filmed at inopportune times under the *least* dramatic circumstances. The concept of "intimate" doesn't really apply when there are thirty crew members standing around, and you're the only reason they haven't gone to lunch yet.

What happens when you have to break down in tears and the sun is about to dip below the horizon? I can guarantee you, that big yellow ball doesn't give a hoot about motivation. What if your big scene falls at the end of a twelve-hour day, which always seems to be the case, and you can't even think straight, let alone hit your marks? In situations like that, I say, "Bring on the fake tears. How soon can I get them?"

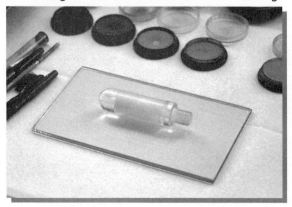

I have often opted for saline drops or, in more extreme cases, menthol crystals, to bring on the waterworks. Menthol crystals work best—they're packed into a small plastic tube and just before you film, the makeup person blows menthol gas directly into your eye. The results are almost immediate, as your eyes frantically attempt to ward off this semitoxic substance.

Menthol Crystals: A TV actor's best friend.

Every time I think of it, I laugh at the notion that Charlie Chaplin, in his heyday, would let shooting grind to a halt for days on end until he came up with a clever idea. In today's environment, he'd be strung up by his thumbs.

Actors are renowned for changing dialogue, and I'm sure writers love to hang them in effigy, but sometimes there are good reasons for this. Actors bring a fresh eye to the material after a writer has sometimes lost valuable perspective. No matter what writers say to the contrary, I can tell you that any actor worth their salt will analyze their character just as much as the writer has done. During the rewrite process, an actor's input becomes even more crucial. In many cases, a writer will make changes in plot, tone, and dialogue, usually to suit their employer and will fail to "track" the ripple effect on characters throughout the piece.

Granted, actors can also be major bullshit artists—demands to make dialogue more "organic" should be ignored because it means that the actor doesn't know what they're talking about. More forgiving are demands to make the dialogue suit their personality. I don't buy this a hundred percent either because the actor is, after all, hired to play someone who is *not* them.

Sometimes, an actor will simply do what they can to reduce the *amount* of dialogue. I can tell you, expository dialogue is the hardest to memorize, because it always includes new names of places and people.

"Okay, people, listen up. Willy, you and Jenkins take the Ridgeback Road to Blanding Field by twelve o'clock. George, you and Eddy take the X-11 and make sure those simulators get to White City in one piece, or Captain Murdock will have our asses."

"Let's see, how can I make this dialogue more organic?"

In *McHale's Navy*, Tom Arnold played the leader of a motley crew. It was his job as a character to explain what was going on in almost every scene. To combat this, Tom reassigned lines almost every day.

"Hey, Bruce, you haven't said anything in a couple days, why don't you take this line?"

"Whatever you say, big guy. . . ."

In some cases, an actor can't change a line of dialogue even if he wanted to. This would be common in either the arena of theater, where a playwright's words are more precious, or, in the case of *Congo,* where the writer obviously had enough clout to enforce it.

John Patrick Shanley won an Academy Award for *Moonstruck* and has written a number of plays. I'd be willing to bet my salary on the film that he had a no-changes clause in his contract, because after the first take of my first scene, the script supervisor came up to me with a worried look.

"Excuse me, Bruce—that last take you added an 'umm,' and a 'well,' and a 'huh.'"

"Oh, did I? Okay—what's your point?"

"We really need to keep to this script."

"Exactly?"

She nodded gravely.

I have to tell you, that really pissed me off because when take two came along, all I could think of was, *Am I getting these lines exactly right?* instead of how to best present the idea of the scene. Good lord, I was just trying to smooth out lumpy transitions—I had no desire to change the *intent.*

Aside from all that, let's not kid ourselves—*Congo* was *adapted* from

Moments after being lectured by the script supervisor on Congo.

another author's novel, so it wasn't even an original screenplay, let alone some play that opened on Broadway to rave reviews—this was a big, schlock, summer film.

Once you get past the script stuff, you've got to lay out your scene in the form of blocking. I enjoy getting the overall sense of a scene before it's broken down into a million shots. Many directors, particularly those suckled on MTV, lean more toward the technical side and don't really know how to talk to actors. One poor sap, thinking he was laying out the blocking, came over to explain a scene.

"Okay, the first shot is here. We see you in the doorway, Bruce. Then, the second shot comes swooping around to reveal Claire at the window. After that, I've got this great shot of you over at the table. You sit and we track in to this movie-star close-up. Sound good?"

"Yeah, if I was the cameraman," I countered. "How did I get to the table and why was I in the doorway? Maybe we should back up a second."

In rehearsing a scene, I like to block first—just like a play. It sounds so basic and elementary, but it's becoming a lost art. In my first half dozen films, the concept of blocking wasn't foremost in my mind—it was more like, *Cool, I'm working on a film.* After the goose bumps wore down and I got a better sense of what was going on, it seemed like the basics were being ignored seventy-five percent of the time.

Any film set, regardless of how fast it's moving, can spare the time to let the actors go through the scene, line by line, so everyone gets a sense of the movement. Once that's done, I frankly don't give a rat's ass how the director wants to shoot it, or in what order.

Now that the actor is happy, what does he bring to the party in exchange? This leads me to the topic of memorization. An actor must decide how well he or she wants to learn the material at hand. *The Hudsucker Proxy* was a study in contrasting acting styles. Jennifer Jason Leigh showed up at the first day of rehearsal and knew every one of her many lines *cold.* She also made an early decision, right or wrong, to play the role in a very specific way—speech patterns and all—and it was now just a matter of committing it to film.

Tim Robbins, on the other hand, liked to "warm up." He held the script in his hands through most of the rehearsal process and enjoyed six or seven takes on film to get where he needed to be.

I'm not suggesting that either method is best, but they are very different. Becoming intimately familiar with the script can allow an actor to explore other aspects of perform-ance—like tone, pacing, etc. Actors who show up on a film set not knowing their lines (and you'd be astounded at the high ratio) have only one hope for the day: get through it the best they can.

"Get this camera out of my face!"

I was determined to know my lines for the pilot episode of *The Adventures of Brisco County, Jr.* as well as I possibly could. Aside from a great respect for the writing, I wanted to be ready for anything. Deke Anderson, an actor buddy of mine, put me through the paces of memorizing to the point where he could toss out any cue line in the script and I knew the response. We called this little game, "Stump the Actor."

This preparation allowed me to be more accommodating to other actors because I wasn't solely concerned with the lines. The downside of over-prepping is that you run the risk of losing quirky elements that make some performances very appealing. On the other hand, a loosey-goosey approach can throw off the rhythm of the other actors and increase the likelihood of forcing the director to film more angles to cover themselves in editing.

Some actors play the dirty little game of screwing up their lines in every take except their close-up. It's funny how an actor can bumble about during wide shots and medium shots, then become super-focused, alert and competent when that fat 135-mm lens comes out. That's when, as an actor or director, I just want to slap them silly. I don't really live or die for close-ups—I find them too restrictive and technically oriented. By delivering a consistent performance, regardless of the shot, it allows the director to edit freely, and assemble the best possible scene.

Aside from basic disciplines, there are intangible qualities that actors can embrace or reject. For example, they must ask themselves, *Should I eat lunch with the crew?* This may seem snobbish, but it's an important decision whether to acknowledge the people who support what you do, or whether to keep them at arm's length.

You'd be surprised how many actors eat by themselves. I have never had a problem mingling "below the line." I figure we're all on the same sinking ship together, and particularly if the shoot is long and hard, I'll take all the friends I can get.

Actors must also decide how much they want to know. Should they make the effort to become acutely aware of what every other crew member does and their relationship to it, or should they just act? Personally, I feel that all actors should attend a filmmaking workshop because it would give them a far greater appreciation for all of the hard work done around them.

"I don't care about your shot! What's my motivation!?"

To me, it works this way: You could give the performance of a lifetime, but if the shot is out of focus because you didn't take the effort to mark out your movements with the focus puller, then you've boned yourself because the take can't be used under any circumstance. I like to get very familiar with the camera crew and what their needs are. I have on many occasions made "deals" with the camera operator.

"Okay, look, I promise not to go any closer than this (and I'd demonstrate), and I won't go any further away than this . . ."

If an actor really wanted to, he could also make himself familiar with camera lenses and their many uses. Most establishing shots, for example, use a wider angle lens, in order to capture the full view of a building or landscape. If the actor is involved in the shot, his range of motion is almost unlimited, like it would be in a play.

When it's time for the big close-up, a "longer" (or telephoto) lens is often used. It makes the actor look cool and powerful, but it also makes focus and movement far more critical. On top of that, if there is less light available, the depth-of-field is reduced and the focus puller is more likely to have difficulty keeping the shot sharp. Knowing this, an actor can be a great help to that department.

Unwittingly, actors can be their own worst enemies. My wife, Ida, worked with an actor, Eric, who mumbled all of his lines because he loved to redo his performance in post-production. This is problematic on several fronts—aside from making the sound man your instant enemy (he almost got in fistfights with Eric daily), you are forcing the other actors to guess when you're done talking.

I make it a point to warn the sound team if I'm going to do something unexpected that would either blow their headphones off or cause them to dive for the gain knob. It's really just common sense—if I bone them, I'm gonna find myself replacing the dialogue later, dialogue that I might not want to do over again.

On a film shoot, an actor spends most of his day waiting around. To pass the time, I've seen them read, run lines, make whoopee in their trailer, smoke crack, sleep, or simply hang out with the other actors, smoking cigarettes and complaining about their agents.

In the case of *McHale's Navy*, it was Tom Arnold's mission to see how *little* time he could spend on the set every day. Granted, the temperatures were blistering, but you didn't see Ernest Borgnine racing back to his trailer after *every take.* Here was a guy, an Academy Award winner, in his late seventies if he were a day, in full dress uniform, and he never left the set. Ernest would find a piece of shade, remove his hat, and wait patiently until he was needed. Production assistants, concerned for his well-being, constantly hovered about.

"Can I get you some water, Mr. Borgnine?"

"No thanks, son," he'd reply politely. "I'm just fine."

Ernest represented the old-school mentality of, "Let's quit crapping around and get this sucker in the can," and I really admired it. I think many actors today have learned some awful habits that have nothing to do with their craft—they have studied too long at Pain in the Ass University and graduated with honors. How does this start and where will it end?

"Anyone seen Tom?"

I worked with a sea- soned actor, John Mahoney, who once played the father of a big action star. For a particularly dramatic scene, they naturally filmed the star first. When the time came to turn the camera around and film the supporting actor, Mr. Big-Shot was nowhere to be found and this poor fellow had to perform opposite the script supervisor—now that's class.

John, who is one of the nicest guys you'll ever meet, also played the part of an evil hospital administrator. The good-guy star, Ray, felt that he had to "hate" John on and off the set. Every time John came into the makeup trailer, Ray would bolt out the other end and all efforts at making small talk were rebuffed. Much to John's shock, Ray approached him at the end of the shoot.

"John, it was really great working with you," he said—all smiles.

"I really wish I could say the same, Ray."

In my opinion, there's method acting and there's just being an asshole—some actors clearly can't make the distinction.

FANALYSIS   41

...art to celebrate . . . the offenses of another" (William Pritchard).

ce·leb·ri·ty (se-lèb'rî-tê) *n.* 1. The state of being celebrated. 2. A celebrated person. *Date: 14ᵗʰ century.*

ce·le·ri·ac (se-lîr'ê-àk', -lèr'-) *n.* An edible variety of celery *(Apium graveolens* var. *rapaceum)* cultivated for its swollen knobby

Why does celebrity fascinate us? What makes us care whether a princess divorces a prince, or what the inside of Kevin Costner's home looks like? Personally, I think the answer lies in the perception that celebrities have something we don't, whether it's money, fame, or a seemingly charmed life.

I wrote a fan letter to Steve McQueen because I thought he was the coolest guy on earth—he could race cars, put out burning buildings and get all the beautiful babes effortlessly. Typically, my letter to him was addressed, "Steve McQueen—Hollywood," and I never got a response.

In the case of Princess Diana, I think we found ourselves glued to her divorce proceedings because, deep down, we still wanted to believe that fairy tales were real. Her death united us in shock and horror because it was a tragedy of Greek proportions.

I was in Paris when Princess Di was killed. I was, in fact, out for a leisurely stroll with my agent, Jeff Goldberg, about a mile from the scene of the crash and close to the time of her death. It wasn't until the next day that I found out what had happened, ironically, from my wife in the States. Bad news travels fast I guess.

Personally, Diana's death haunted me far more than other celebrities that have recently passed. When Versace was gunned down in Florida, for example, I remember commenting about how cold-blooded it was, but were it not for the manhunt and ensuing media frenzy, I'm not sure how much more I would have thought about it.

But Princess Diana was different—her death gave me the willies because of the way she died. Maybe it's because, as an actor, I've had cameras jammed in my face by dozens of photographers yelling "Bruce! Bruce over here . . . hey, Bruce!" I've walked the gauntlet at various functions, and even in these controlled environments, it was unnerving—desperation seemed to permeate the air.

After Diana's death, "experts" debated the topic, in every form of media, and we tried to make sense of it all. Many folks blamed the photographers for her death. I'm sure they contributed in their own annoying way, but in the end they were merely errand boys attempting to satisfy demands placed on them by unimaginably callous employers.

Why would their editors encourage such behavior? The simplistic answer, they're quick to present again and again, is: "We are merely supplying the demand for stories like this."

Okay, so are these evil men and women, scheming in dark tabloid offices about how to cater to the lowest common denominator? Perhaps—but not so obviously, I suspect—they are simply doing nothing to rise above the "bad news is good news" syndrome.

We are a culture fascinated by the rise, and even more so with the decline, of famous people. Di's royal wedding was a big deal, sure, but the divorce was even better, and the only thing that could possibly top that was a horrible death—now *that's* news!

I got an e-mail from a fan recently that cuts to the core of the issue:

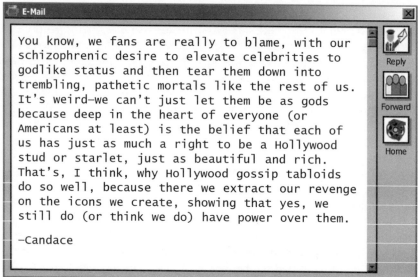

You know, we fans are really to blame, with our schizophrenic desire to elevate celebrities to godlike status and then tear them down into trembling, pathetic mortals like the rest of us. It's weird—we can't just let them be as gods because deep in the heart of everyone (or Americans at least) is the belief that each of us has just as much a right to be a Hollywood stud or starlet, just as beautiful and rich. That's, I think, why Hollywood gossip tabloids do so well, because there we extract our revenge on the icons we create, showing that yes, we still do (or think we do) have power over them.

—Candace

As a seventeen-year-old kid, fresh out of high school, I had my first brush with celebrity as a theater apprentice. There, I met a number of "famous" people and worked among them for three months.

Meeting actors in person whom I idolized as a kid was both a thrilling and horrifying experience. More than anything, I was shocked to see that celebrities aged just like normal people. Doug McClure wasn't the strapping man I remembered from his 1960s TV show, *The Virginian*—never mind the fact that the show was fourteen years earlier—and Abe Vigoda didn't look anything like his character on *Barney Miller.*

Apart from the disappointment, I was ultimately glad that they were human. The actors I met that summer were talented, for the most part, but they also got irritable, forgot their lines, and occasionally farted—all the normal stuff.

Turnabout is fair play, as the old saying goes, and I got to experience this recently at a public appearance. As a fan got close to shake my hand, she got a funny look on her face.

"Geez, you look like someone's dad," she said.

"Well, that's because *I am someone's dad.* . . ."

Evil Dead put me at the receiving end of fandom. Six months after its release, a Ferndale, Michigan, cashier squinted at me.

"You look a hell of a lot like Bruce Campbell's brother," he said.

"Yeah, that would make a hell of a lot of sense," I replied.

Not long after that, I got my first fan letter. I can't recall what it said, or how they even found me, but I was thrilled nonetheless, and responded with a handwritten note, thanking them for their patronage. As the years passed, and I became more identifiable as a genre actor, a steady trickle of letters found their way to me, but *The Adventures of Brisco County, Jr.* opened up the world of mass-market fan mail.

The increase in mail wasn't a result of some new acting ability, it was merely because there were more regular viewers. When I looked at the numbers it all made sense—even a low-rated TV show like *Brisco* snagged more viewers in a single night than all of the *Evil Dead* films combined.

I have found that the best place to interact with fans is at conventions—my first being a Fangoria Weekend of Horrors event in 1988. In a jammed Los Angeles hotel, I spent two days interacting with folks that assumed I was just like the characters I portrayed in films. This resulted in gifts of home-grown poetry that would make your hair curl, requests to sign

A gaggle of fans waiting for an autograph in Columbus.

pierced breasts, and offers to attend all-night *Evil Dead* drinking parties.

The same type of thing happened during the run of *Brisco*. Because I played a "cowboy," letters arrived with offers to buy or sell horses or to grand Marshal parades in rural Western towns.

The real fun began when the two types of fans converged at some of the larger *Brisco* events. A "kids fair" in Seattle drew more than kids, and it was amusing to scan the autograph line to see some ten-year-old kid in a cowboy outfit standing in front of a spiked, pierced, leather-clad "deadite."

Television wins the war of saturation, hands down. A motion picture can be shown around the world, but unless it's a blockbuster, it'll be gone from theaters within a month or two. The TV viewer can watch their favorite program week after week, sometimes for a decade or more, and the resulting impact, I feel, is far more indelible.

One day, I got a high school graduation tassel in the mail. The young man who sent it explained, quite matter-of-factly, that the tassel was a gift for me because, were it not for the show *Brisco,* he would have killed himself and never graduated.

Another note, sent from a despondent fellow, explained that he was about to commit suicide in his crappy Hollywood apartment, but he happened to catch an episode of *Brisco*. The positive image of life portrayed by the show caused him to reconsider.

Things like this can drive an actor crazy. On the one hand, I'm extremely grateful that a "positive" message helped someone in need, but on the other hand, what's to keep some kid, after watching *Evil Dead,* from slicing up Grandma with a chainsaw? The answer, I suppose, is "nothing," and that's the frustrating part. Filmmakers and actors all wish to have an impact on the world at large, yet at the same time, we're the first ones to shout, "Hey folks, it's all *fake*!"

As the information age blossomed, my fan mail morphed into e-mail. I have found this a much more manageable forum in which to communicate with fans, since no matter where I am in the world, my "mailbox" is always with me.

In case you've ever wondered what fans say to actors, I'll share a few notes, just to demonstrate the variety of sentiments floating around in the great cyber void.

Note: I have made no attempt to alter or aid spelling or punctuation.

This first example represents the sincere fans who send pleasant, upbeat letters—about fifty percent of what I get falls into this category. At the opposite end of the spectrum, there are fans who need twenty-four-hour observation. This next communiqué is one that I could not stop reading, regardless of how much I wanted to throttle the smug bastard.

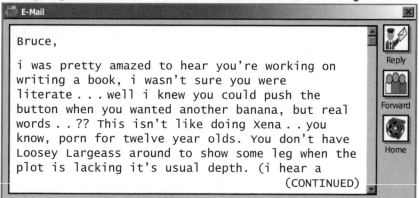

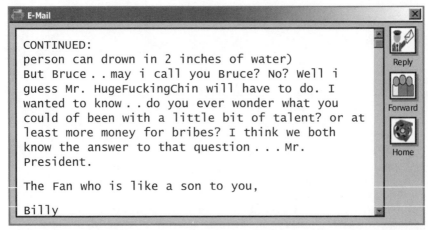

CONTINUED:
person can drown in 2 inches of water)
But Bruce . . may i call you Bruce? No? Well i
guess Mr. HugeFuckingChin will have to do. I
wanted to know . . do you ever wonder what you
could of been with a little bit of talent? or at
least more money for bribes? I think we both
know the answer to that question . . . Mr.
President.

The Fan who is like a son to you,

Billy

That e-mail is, of course, an extreme example and only represents about 1.7 percent of my total fan mail—*thank God.* E-mails that fall into remaining categories run the gamut from mildly amusing, to quirky, to utterly incomprehensible.

Regardless of the format, I can speak for most of the actors out there that we are genuinely grateful to anyone who takes the time, not only to faithfully follow our work, but to write something that is inherently designed to brighten our day.

Doing the TV Shuffle   42

When you've starred in a TV show, even one that's low rated, an odd chain of events are set in motion. After *Brisco* was canceled, I found myself able to travel freely within the realm of television because the credibility checks, once routine, became almost nonexistent. Suddenly, roles were simply "offered."

The first show to welcome me like this was *Lois and Clark: The New Adventures of Superman*. A certain logic prevailed here—this show was also produced by Warner Bros., and a writer/producer from *Brisco* had since defected to this camp. It was a good match of sensibilities, and I managed to slink in and out of three episodes as suave bad guy, Bill Church, Jr.

On the show, Peter Boyle played my evil father. As a character actor in a number of memorable films such as *Taxi Driver* and *Young Frankenstein*, he was no hack but, like so many other actors in his position, Peter was lured to television.

The medium can do odd things to actors—like beat them into submission. Not every actor can spit out lines at the drop of a hat and nail it in one take. Film actors, in particular, don't always enjoy a smooth transition.

Peter did a take that would never have been printed on any film set, low budget or not—he stumbled, fumbled, and groped his way through it. I was sure they would have another go at it, but the director glanced at his watch.

"Great, Peter," he announced. "Okay, moving on . . ."

Peter looked at me with an incredulous expression.

"It just doesn't matter, does it?"

Still, it was fun to work on the familiar Warner back lot, this time dressed in modern garb. As I stood behind the facade of a doorway, waiting for my cue, I glanced at the unpainted plywood. There, written in a black marker, was a note I had scribbled late one night while shooting *Brisco.*

Brisco was here—2/22/94, it stated simply.

Sam Raimi got a decidedly twisted TV show of his own up and running called *American Gothic.* My agent spotted a good guest-starring role, but Sam was hesitant to cast me because the show was "serious." Eventually, it led to a very strange phone call with the Grand Poobah himself.

<u>Sam:</u> Listen, mister, if I give you this role, you have to be serious.

<u>Bruce:</u> What did you think I was going to do, wink at the camera the whole time?

<u>Sam:</u> Well, this isn't like *Brisco,* you know. . . .

<u>Bruce:</u> Sam, *Brisco* was its own beast. For Christ's sake, I'm an *actor.* I think I can reach deep into the bowels of my soul and somehow manage to keep a straight face. Besides that, what other actor is gonna lie in a coffin and let you pour a box of live cockroaches on their face?

<u>Sam:</u> Hmmm, good point. . . .

The "serious" vs. "funny" issue rattled me. *My God,* I reasoned with myself, *I'm not a buffoon. As an actor, I should be able to do anything they throw at me . . . right?*

Getting hassled by "The Man" on Homicide.

As a result, I vowed to jump at anything dramatic that came my way. One such project was *Homicide: Life on the Streets.* The first phone call with producer Tom Fontana came as a complete surprise.

"So, is there anything you'd like to do?" he asked, casually.

"What do you mean? Like, what role would I like to play?"

"Yeah."

"Uh, gee . . . can I think about that for a couple days and get back to you?"

"Sure, just give me a call."

I was really turned around by this—actors are usually in the position of begging producers to let them play a certain role. Here was an offer I most certainly could not refuse. In fact, I did have a notion about loopholes in our justice system and pitched Tom a very loose idea several days later. His response further confounded me.

"Yeah, cool. We'll do a two-parter," he said as if it happened every day.

Within a month, I found myself in Baltimore shooting a strikingly similar story. The writers created a fine character—a police officer faced with the moral dilemma of whether or not to take justice into his own hands. Creatively, the experience was as close to perfection as I could have hoped for.

Other TV gigs materialized out of thin air. I got a call one morning to see if I could drop by the Disney lot and meet with Ellen DeGeneres and her producers about a role during their lunch break.

The meeting was only a few minutes long, and after a quick, closed-door huddle, I was invited to read a few scenes with Ellen and the director, Gil. The thrust of this session was really to make sure I could handle the snappy pace of sitcoms, something I had not yet done.

I guess now it was an issue of whether I could be funny *enough*.

After another closed-door meeting, the casting agent approached me with an almost apologetic look on her face.

"Bruce, um . . . what are you doing for the rest of the day?"

"Nothing in particular, why?"

"Well, we need you to go into rehearsals, right *now*. . . ."

I walked over to the stage, hastily introduced myself to the other cast members, and got to work. This was a Wednesday afternoon—the show was taped two days later, and voila, I was a sitcom actor. The undefined commitment on *Ellen* eventually blossomed into eight episodes, and it was a pleasure to learn a new side to my craft.

"So, Ellen, you wanna go for coffee after the taping? Oh, you are? I had no idea . . ."

Sitcoms are a freaky atmosphere—the entire week of rehearsal is spent trying to maximize the humor in every scene. To do this, the writing staff engaged in the most extensive script changes I had ever witnessed. The script from Monday's read-through would almost invariably be completely rewritten overnight, and Tuesday's rewrite wound up on my doorstep Wednesday morning.

When do these poor bastards sleep? I'd ask myself.

By Thursday, the script was usually beaten into shape and the technical stuff would take control. Friday night, a studio audience was recruited, as well as a comedian to keep them "up" during scene changes.

It was a lot of fun to watch Ellen, by this time an expert at the medium, work her way through a show. If the first take went well, she'd riff on the second take, tossing in a few curves, to the delight of both the cast and the viewing audience.

I was glad to be a part of the last "Out" episode. My character, Ed Billik, a right-wing kind of guy, was the dissenting voice in Ellen's journey to an openly gay network character. Much to her credit, this was Ellen's idea, and it made for some good drama in the middle of an otherwise funny show.

Another abstract notion sprang from my new TV status: the development deal. This is a relationship formed between an actor (or writer, etc.) and a production company and/or TV network whereby they pay you not to work for anyone else while a mutually agreeable concept for a new show is developed. Following *Brisco,* I engaged in several such deals.

Meetings were first on the agenda—dozens of meetings. Notions were kicked around with executives to make sure we were all on the same page, and we'd try like hell to define the type of show, its format and a rough time slot. Once this was hashed out, I spent the next several months meeting with what seemed to be every TV writer in Southern California to hear their pitches:

Joe Writer: It's kind of like *The Rockford Files* meets *Land of the Giants* . . .

Bruce: Gee, an incomprehensible blend of two shows from twenty years ago . . . that ought to knock 'em dead. . . .

Jeff Writer: See, you're an ambulance-chasing lawyer, and it's all about your private life . . .

Bruce: Let me get this straight—we're supposed to *like* this guy?

Jane Writer: Get this: You're a gym teacher by day and an international spy by night . . .

Bruce: Excuse me, I think I'm double parked . . .

This pilot missed, all right.

Eventually, the ideas all blended into a mishmash of baloney. More times than not, a show never gets on the air, but sometimes you get close. A development deal with ABC led to a sitcom pilot called *Missing Links.* The concept was based on a successful book and it operated in a milieu that I enjoyed. If I were pitching it to myself, I'd explain it as *Cheers* at a low-rent, public golf course.

The pilot went over well with our "live" audience and was one of the highest-rated sitcoms in their testing process that year, but ABC "didn't have a slot for it." This was a heartbreaker, and I'd be a liar if I said this experience didn't take a bit of the wind out of my sails.

Christ, am I just killing myself for no reason?

People often wonder why some actors fall off the face of the earth for no apparent reason. I've got news for you—there is *always* a reason, and frustration with the business is a huge factor.

"X" Marks the Spot:
The Great Wheel Turns

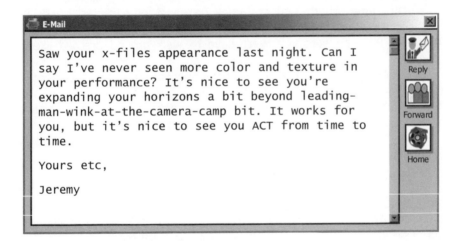

When most people think of *The X-Files,* they think of paranoia, mystery, and science fiction. I think of farts.

David Duchovny, known for his sober performances on screen, was actually a funny guy. One night on set, he got his hands on a fart cup—you know, those plastic cups, filled with a gooey substance, and he couldn't put it down. Eventually, we got into something of a farting contest, to see who could simulate the best potato chip fart (fast and dry), or the raunchiest Taco fart (slow and wet). We called it a draw when the crew couldn't handle it anymore.

Appearing on *The X-Files* was an interesting experience for several reasons—it marked not only a return to the Fox network, but a chance to join up with the show that *Brisco* preceded, seemingly a hundred years ago.

"Okay, Duchovny, did you just fart?"

Several *Brisco* directors went on to get involved with *The X-Files* and my former makeup man, Kevin Westmore, was on board, so it had the feel of coming home again.

I had met David Duchovny and Gillian Anderson doing promotion for our respective shows years before. David and I shared a plane flight to a sales event in Chicago. At that point, he wasn't the TV veteran he is today, and he leaned over to me during the flight.

David: What the hell are we supposed to do at these promo things?

Bruce: What do you mean?

David: Like, are we supposed to be funny, or charming, or what?

Bruce: A little of both, I guess. I think we're just there to press the flesh.

David: I feel like such a jerk.

Bruce: Hey, be glad you don't have to walk around dressed like a cowboy. . . .

Gillian Anderson and I met copresenting an award to some TV sales guy. I didn't take the event too seriously and wore a cowboy hat with my tux. The script they wrote for us was awful, like they usually are at award shows, so I tried to con her into doing some old routines.

Bruce: Hey, Gillian, let's do some of those ten-gallon hat gags, what do you say?

Gillian: Why would we want to do that?

Bruce: Well, this isn't exactly the Oscars. I thought we could have some fun with it.

Gillian: You can do what you'd like. I'm going to read my copy and get out of here. . . .

She must have thought I was an alien.

Quest for the Holy Grail:

Grabbing at "Phantoms"

...an Sea. Famagusta was a refugee center fo...
after Acre fell to the Saracens (1291). Population, 50,000.
fame (fâm) *n.* 1 **a**: public estimation: reputation **b**: popular acclaim: renown. *Date: 13th century*
a·mil·ial (fe-mîl'yel) *adj.* **1.** Of or relating to a family. **2.** Occurring...

Recently, while responding to e-mail on-line, I got an instant message from a fan.

<u>Fan:</u> Bruce, how do I become a famous actor?

<u>Bruce:</u> When I'm famous, I'll let you know. . . .

<u>Fan:</u> Seriously, how can I?

<u>Bruce:</u> Shoot a president.

<u>Fan:</u> What?!!

<u>Bruce:</u> Do you want to be famous, or do you want to be an actor? They are two completely different things.

Technically, to qualify as an actor, you could stand in your living room and recite the phone book to your cat. If you want to be a movie star, that's a whole new game with its own set of rules.

A movie star can't *just* be an actor, because in the truest sense of the word, an actor can be a man or woman, old or young, overweight, balding and unremarkable and it wouldn't really matter—as long as they could act.

A movie star, conversely, doesn't have to be that good of an actor, or even master the English language, as long as they possess qualities that separate them from the herd.

Some movie stars, and I'm using this obnoxious term only because it's so familiar, get by on sheer charisma, that great indefinable thing, or an astounding physique, but more often, it is a combination of pleasing physical characteristics, a basic acting ability, and a hell of a lot of drive. Actors who aspire to rise above the level of community theater, local commercials, or a syndicated TV show must apply themselves on a multitude of levels.

The first thing they must do is "look" like a movie star. If you're out of shape, you'd better renew that lapsed gym membership. Teeth too yellow, or crooked? No sweat, a trip to the local cosmetic dentist can fix that. If you wear glasses, just run down to the optometrist and get those contacts, or better still, get laser surgery to "permanently" solve the defect. While you're on the laser kick, maybe it's time to clean up some of those scars, warts and blemishes that have been haunting you for years—God forbid that movie stars should look like the rest of us.

Personally, I've always been amused by the fact that some of Hollywood's most renowned tough guys such as Bogart, John Wayne, and Burt Reynolds all wore toupees. Alan Ladd, a leading man in the forties and fifties, was cast opposite short starlets to mask his own diminutive stature. Ronald Reagan wore glasses. Clark Gable had smelly dentures and pinned his large ears back. I'll tell you, all actors should be grateful for the day when Sean Connery, one of the manliest men of the silver screen, removed his toupee for all the world to see.

Even with all the effort actors go through to perfect their bodies, it's nothing compared to what they do to be "discovered." When not at the gym, or the tanning salon, actors are networking, and Hollywood parties are an obvious starting point.

I saved a phone message from an ex-Michigan friend after he had been in Los Angeles for a couple years.

Bruce, hey, this is Nathan. Listen, I'm having a party this weekend and I'd like you to come. . . .

In Michigan, the message would have ended there, but not in Sporeville, USA—it continued:

. . . We got some great people coming . . . some really great people. . .

Nathan proceeded to name the luminaries he had "confirmed," as if I had to be "sold" on the concept. I didn't go, and it wasn't because his party wasn't good enough, it was because he never once mentioned that it might actually be fun.

By the time I tried to be a movie star, I had already been an actor in about fifteen films. More than anything, I was curious to find out how hard it would be to punch through the glass ceiling of film grades and exchange my B-grade status for a big, shiny A.

Jeffery Boam was one of the executive producers of *The Adventures of Brisco County, Jr.* He also had a day job as a big-shot Hollywood writer who participated in the *Indiana Jones* and *Lethal Weapon* series, among others.

His latest project, for Paramount Pictures, was a film adaptation of the pulp fiction hero, the Phantom, and he contacted me about the possibility of playing the lead role. With the help of my clever manager, Robert Stein, we began the journey on foot to see what we could see.

Our first meeting was with the designated director, Joe Dante. He was bright and pleasant enough, and we enjoyed a spirited conversation, but Joe wasn't where the buck stopped to get this role—not by a country mile. This was evidenced by the fact that he didn't even wind up directing the film.

Next on the list were the Paramount executives in charge of the film. These meetings are always short and produce little in the way of substantive conversation, largely since actors and executives don't have much to say to each other.

<u>Executive:</u> So, Bruce, you like the project?

<u>Bruce:</u> Yep. Sure do. It looks like a lot of fun.

<u>Executive:</u> We're really excited about it.

<u>Bruce:</u> I can understand that. It . . . looks like a lot of fun. . . . (*Didn't I already say that?*)

Meetings like that are more about the executives looking you over to make sure you have all your limbs and can string a full sentence together.

The real test was to make an impression on the film's legendary producer, Robert Evans. A fixture at Paramount since the seventies, this once-powerful man was behind classics like *Chinatown* and *Marathon Man.* To catch his interest, I had to come up with an "icebreaker," some sort of conversation starter.

I dug through a *Who's Who in Hollywood* book and found out that he was

The guy in purple tights.

once, like me, an actor. Rumor had it, he had been hand-picked by actress Norma Shearer to play legendary producer Irving Thalberg in the Lon Chaney biography, *Man of a Thousand Faces.*

That's obscure enough, I figured.

Robert Evan's face lit up the moment I mentioned this film from forty years ago. He waxed nostalgic for a brief moment, and it seemed to relax the atmosphere in an otherwise tense room.

Ironically, the last person I met with was the casting director—someone who, under normal circumstances, I would have met with first. As an actor, the ability to do an end-run around someone who has the power to stop your forward momentum is a huge victory. I must admit, I was undeniably cocky by the time I sat with her.

A still from my screen test.

The next and last phase of this campaign was the screen test. My manager got his hands on the number of the actress who would play opposite me. Normally, I wasn't expected or even advised to contact her, but nothing about this was normal, so I gave her a ring and weaseled my way into rehearsing with her.

No studio in their right mind would screen test just one actor so, in my case, it boiled down to two people—me and Billy Zane. Since the desire was to create a franchise out of this character, the project must have gone out to every "bankable" hero type in town but for whatever reason, Billy and I wound up on the ticket.

Like the network test I had to do for *Brisco,* a contract had to be negotiated in advance. This grueling phase didn't take long, but the trick was to dig up every contract I had ever signed and find every "perk" I had ever received. Negotiating with the studio's business affairs department (AKA, lawyers) wasn't that big of a deal as long as you could prove that you had already gotten everything you were asking for at some point in your career.

Finally, the schmoozing and strategy ended, and I found myself on the Paramount lot. I signed my contract in a makeup bungalow and walked into stage #21 to face the one-eyed monster. The shoot itself only took a couple hours and I left without fanfare.

Waiting for that big call is where you second-guess yourself to death and play all of the "would have/should have/could have" games over and over. I had two choices: wait by the phone and be tormented by every ring, or get as far away from it as I could. I chose the latter, and wandered the hills behind my house in southern California until the big verdict came down about thirty-six hours later. Paramount had found their man and it was. . . Billy Zane.

Do not pass Go. Do not collect $100.

I was surprised at how well I took the news. It was more of a relief than anything, because I was tired of all the games I had to play to get that far. To quote Rocky, I "went the distance," and it was good enough for me.

THE HIGHER THE BUDGET, THE LOWER THE PART   45

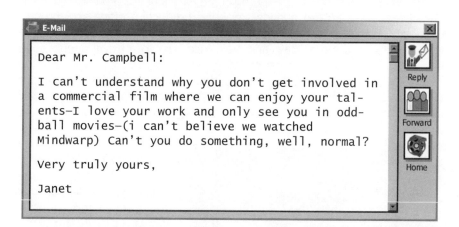

The Phantom proved indelibly that I was not in a position to barge into Acme Studios and insist that they offer up a fat role in their next summer blockbuster. It seemed that my lot in life was to either have big parts in small films or small parts in big films. I do work in the realm of fantasy, but I haven't lost touch with reality.

This became evident with the film *Congo.* I met with director Frank Marshall to con him into giving me the lead role, ultimately played by Dylan Walsh. I did my best to sell Frank on the fact that I was the guy for the job, the right one to sweat with him in the jungle. Frank was unconvinced, but kindly offered up the small, dead-in-five-minutes role of Charles.

Sometimes Hollywood is like a game show—if you don't win the brand-new car, you get a toaster. Who was I to argue with the man who used to produce all of Steven Spielberg's films? Where do I sign?

There was a distinct advantage to being a small cog in a very big wheel, and *Congo* was one of those situations where it was almost impossible to complain about being an actor. The amount of days it took to film my character was of little concern to a company that had to deal with issues like airlifting tons of film equipment to the base of one of the most active volcanoes in the world.

Standing at the base of the Arenal volcano with Frank Marshall, I joked that, maybe next time, he could find a place a little more remote.

"This is nothing," he stated plainly. "Try and get catering in the Sahara Desert." He was referring to a Spielberg epic he produced and I could tell that he wasn't joking.

In the film, my character leads an ill-fated expedition deep into the bowels of the Congo. A *second* expedition, with the principle actors, passed through the same areas, but had to stop and confront some challenge every step along the way.

On a practical level, this meant that shooting the first expedition required only a couple of shots in each location, while the second team invariably filmed for days on end.

For the actors in this first expedition, an excellent scam presented itself. Call sheets were posted outside the hotel production office at 5:00 P.M. every day. If the world "hold" appeared next to our name, it meant that we weren't needed the next day, and we'd race over to a travel agent, open until 7:00, and book an excursion.

I'm only half guilty to announce that, complements of Paramount Pictures, I white-water rafted, body surfed on pristine beaches, and tramped through nameless jungles tracts, surrounded by 5,000-year-old trees.

Me as "Doctor Doom."

I often get hassled by fans about why I did that film. The thing that many folks don't understand is that an actor doesn't always do things for art. I would have *paid* to go to Costa Rica, and yet I had a chance to not only go there for free but get paid as well.

Escape from L.A. was familiar terrain and it was a chance to work with John Carpenter, whose film *Halloween* convinced us that the horror genre would be a viable choice for our first film.

In the two days that I worked on *Escape,* John only gave me one piece of direction. In a very friendly but direct way, he lowered his voice and said,

"Bruce, I want this dead straight." He must have been in collusion with Sam Raimi.

The real plus of playing the surgeon general of Beverly Hills was working with one of the best special-effects makeup guys in the business: Rick Baker. Because my role was that of a twisted freak, Rick patterned the look after the more celebrated plastic surgery mistakes in Hollywood.

The character wound up with a tight, ski-slope nose, an obvious face-lift, some collagen implants, Movie Star teeth, plucked eyebrows, and hair plugs, not unlike a Ken doll. The results were subtle, yet alarming—and took five hours to complete.

The other cool thing about working on big-budget films is that you go toe-to-toe with big-shot actors—Kurt Russell, in this case. I always had a lot of respect for Kurt—he had been around for a long time and I recalled seeing him in episodes of *Lost in Space* and even *Gilligan's Island* when I was a kid. It was nice to see him finally get his due as a big-buck, leading man.

I went to the set in preparation for my scene with Kurt and I spotted him chatting casually off in the corner. He was acting like he had just dropped by the set to see what was going on and happened to wind up in the film. When I introduced myself, he got a kick out of my makeup, but he was interested in something else.

<u>Kurt:</u> Hey, Bruce, say, "workshed."

<u>Bruce:</u> (incredulous) What?

<u>Kurt:</u> From *Evil Dead II.*

<u>Bruce:</u> Yeah, I know that, but how do you know that obscure line?

<u>Kurt:</u> My son is a big fan of that film. For some reason, he wanted me to have you say it.

Kurt was too polite to mention that "workshed" was an obvious overdub to

Ash: ventriloquist.

help audiences know where my character Ash was going next. If you watch the film, my mouth doesn't move at all during that line and it's a point of great ridicule on college campuses around the country.

Sometimes, an actor takes a role because he or she thinks it will advance their career. Other times, it will be to fulfill an artistic longing or to simply make a big payday. *McHale's Navy* would fall into the "none of the above" category. One day, I got a call from my manager, Robert Stein.

<u>Robert:</u> Bruce, something's come together that's really exciting.

<u>Bruce:</u> Cool, what is it?

<u>Robert:</u> It's a supporting role for Universal.

Bruce: Cool, what is it?

Robert: Bryan Spicer (who did the *Brisco* pilot) is going to direct it.

Bruce: Cool, but like I said . . . *what is it?*

Robert: *McHale's Navy.*

Bruce: The old TV show? They're gonna remake it?

Robert: Yes. There's a part Bryan wants you to play.

Bruce: Who?

Robert: His name is Virgil—one of the sailors. This part is really something you could have fun with. I'll send you the script.

When any script arrives, I always do a simple test to see how much dialogue my character has—I flip through the pages like I'm shuffling a deck of cards and try and spot the character's name in dialogue scenes. If it's easy to spot as I whiz along, it means that I have a lot of dialogue and often, it's a big role. When I finished the test for *McHale's Navy,* I was surprised to note that I never spotted the name Virgil.

Must have missed a few pages, I thought. *Better try this again.*

I leafed through the pages more slowly this time and caught a fleeting glimpse of Virgil early in the script, before the name disappeared from the radar screen entirely.

Finally, I sat down and read the full script. From an actor's point of view, the warning signs were everywhere:

McHale "and his men" scope out the joint.

McHale *"and his men"* search the area.

McHale *"and his crew"* go to Cuba.

McHale, *"and the others"* get off the boat.

The translation of that meant that I'd have many days with nothing *specific* to do. I recalled a brief conversation with Liam Neeson while he was looping *Darkman.*

Bruce: Hey, Liam, I caught the end of *The Bounty* the other day and I could have sworn that was you.

Liam: Yes, it was.

Bruce: Who were you?

Liam: I played the guy over Mel Gibson's left shoulder.

Bruce: What do you mean?

Liam: Well, I was one of the sailors. My big challenge each day was to see which of Mel's shoulders I could get behind. Usually, I wound up behind the left one.

With these omens, I called my manager in search of a logical reason why I should be in this film.

Bruce: Robert, I just read the script.

Robert: Funny, isn't it?

Bruce: Yeah, a *Laff Riot*, but there's only one problem.

Robert: Oh?

Bruce: My character doesn't do anything.

Robert: Well, they're going through a major rewrite right now, and Bryan has some big plans for beefing up all of the sailor parts.

Bruce: Do you really think anything's going to change?

Robert: Yes, I do. I think we should do this.

The reality of motion pictures is that the screenplay writer will concentrate their effort on the largest three or four characters, showering them with finely honed dialogue, endearing character traits and a full dramatic "arc." When you're lower on the "screen time" food chain, you get what falls from the table—*McHale's Navy* was all about table scraps.

I decided to at least do the basic actor prep stuff—find out what I can about this thing called the navy. I had my trusty assistant, Craig, drive a few hours south of LA to pick up a copy of *The Bluejackets' Manual*, the official training manual of the United States Navy—Anthony Hopkins, eat your method heart out.

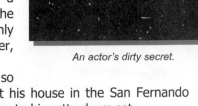

Upon delivery of this navy "Bible," I sat, with highlighter in hand, marking anything interesting, pertinent, or quirky. There were heaps of useless tidbits, but at first glance it appeared that there was no practical use for them in the film.

After rereading the script, I noticed a scene where McHale's crew stages a "telethon" to jam the radio signals of the bad guy, played by Tim Curry. The only thing the script actually specified, however, was that Virgil "jammed" on the drums.

An actor's dirty secret.

I had no idea how to play the drums, so I hastily arranged lessons with a man at his house in the San Fernando Valley. My sweaty, shirtless teacher led me to his ratty drum set.

"Okay, junior, let's see your stuff."

I showed him what I knew about playing drums, which didn't take long, and he walked me through a couple of basic drum exercises. After ten minutes, he rolled his eyes and grabbed my sticks.

"You will never be a drummer," he stated flatly. "Give me the check."

Despite the knowledge imparted by this gifted teacher, it was ultimately decided, on location, that there would be no band.

Instead, a talent show was devised for the climax of the film, but there wasn't any description beyond *Virgil and Happy* (played by French Stewart) *are on stage performing.* I knew I was on my own and I sure as hell didn't want to be caught improvising something at the last minute on set, so I dug up that navy manual and came upon a passable angle. Nautical terms like "Poop Deck," "Bull's Nose" and "Breast Line" seemed to cry out for some kind of vaudevillian bit.

I called up gagmeister pal Ron "One-liner" Zwang, and invited him over for a brainstorming session in my backyard. Together, we hashed out a seaworthy version of the classic Abbott and Costello routine, "Who's on First?" and renamed it, "Who's on Deck?"

On location in Mexico, before the talent show was filmed, I approached my fellow navy costar, French Stewart (of *Third Rock from the Sun).*

<u>Bruce:</u> Hey, French, I was thinkin' about this talent show . . .

<u>French:</u> Yeah, we're on stage together. What's up with that? What are we supposed to do?

<u>Bruce:</u> I have no idea. I'm afraid we're gonna have our thumbs up our asses.

<u>French:</u> No shit. Got any ideas?

I sold French on the new routine, and we pitched it to director Bryan Spicer to get him "on board." Brian appreciated our efforts, but we had to get it past star and coproducer Tom Arnold as well. French and I "ran it up his flagpole," and he gave us the nod.

Armed with the approval of the director and coproducer, I approached the costume designer and asked him to scare up an officer's uniform like the one worn by Captain Binghamton (played by veteran Dean Stockwell).

Operation Screen Time was complete—the only thing to do now was shoot the sucker. In the completed film, French and I wound up out of focus *over Tom's left shoulder* for the duration of our little act. Well, ya gotta try, right?

In case you're interested, here is the routine in its entirety:

NOTE: The setting is my character Virgil, imitating Captain Binghamton ("Bingy"), as he indoctrinates a young recruit (played by French).

"Hey, David, can I borrow a line?"

"WHO'S ON DECK?"

BINGY: Sailor let me see your Duty Roster. Did you clean the Mess Deck?
SAILOR: No, sir.
BINGY: Why not?
SAILOR: Well, say I spent twelve hours a day cleaning the Mess Deck from top to bottom. What would it be?

BINGY: The Mess Deck . . .

SAILOR: Right. So why bother?

BINGY: Where's your dingy, sailor?

SAILOR: Uh, where it always is, sir.

BINGY: Is it tied off to the Masthead?

SAILOR: That was just a one-time hazing prank, sir.

BINGY: Has your dingy been shellacked?

SAILOR: Uh . . . Don't ask don't tell?

BINGY: Did you hook up the Bending Shackle to her Breast Line?

SAILOR: I tried sir, believe me!

BINGY: And you had a good grip on your Jackstaff?

SAILOR: Like my life depended on it, sir.

BINGY: Where was your Chafing Gear?

SAILOR: Definitely broadside . . .

BINGY: I'm assuming you tightened up the Ram Tensioner . . .

SAILOR: Well, sure, a guy's gotta pace himself.

BINGY: What about the Ground Tackle?

SAILOR: I don't go in for that rough stuff, sir . . .

BINGY: Did you hold her forward, double up, and heave?

SAILOR: Well, we never got to heaving.

BINGY: I hope you took liberty . . .

SAILOR: Every chance I got!

BINGY: Are you prepared for launch?

French Stewart and I "over Tom's left shoulder."

SAILOR: Yes, sir, I had a light breakfast . . .

BINGY: You, sailor, are an idiot.

SAILOR: I'm not as big of an idiot as I used to be.

BINGY: How is that possible?

SAILOR: I lost weight . . .

McHale's Navy forced the sailors of Tom Arnold's crew to become method actors—each day, we had to concoct dialogue for ourselves. Some days it was easy, and other days it was like pulling teeth.

Brian Haley, a unique stand-up comic, was great at coming up with gags, but sometimes they were too elaborate for his own good. I first met him on the flight down to Mexico, and for some reason, we enjoyed tormenting each other immediately. Brian had been in the film *Baby's Day Out*—a bomb in the States, but a big hit in places like Mexico, where it was known as *Bebé Suarto.*

The airline stewardess recognized Haley and made a fuss about how famous he was. Brian, always at the ready, produced an eight-by-ten photo.

Brian: Hey, Bruce, you see that? She wants my autograph. I'm not so good at Spanish. What should I write on it?

Bruce: How about, *Best Wishes, Señor Cajones* (testicles).

Brian: What does that mean?

Bruce: It means you're a strong man.

Brian: That's perfect! Thanks, pal. . . .

Haley proudly scribbled it on the picture and handed it over to the stewardess, who immediately giggled and showed it to her coworkers.

Brian: Hey, they *like* it.

Bruce: Yeah, they seem to get a real kick out of it.

Haley wasn't so pleased when he found out what it really meant.

Brian: Goddammit, Campbell, I'm gonna kill you! I can't believe you let me write that on that lady's picture!

McHale's Morons.

Bruce: Get used to it, Haley, this is gonna be a long, hot summer—we're gonna need all the gags we can come up with down here.

The next gag was on me—at the Manzanillo customs office. The system in place was supposedly impartial. Each passenger pushed a button near the exit of customs and activated a light—if it was green, they could pass without question, but if the light was red, they were subject to having their bags searched.

As I approached the button, a customs officer waved a hand at me.

"Uno momento, por favor, señor."

Other passengers filed in front of me, and each time I attempted to push the impartial button, the customs officer gave me the same line until everyone had exited before me. Maybe it was the seven shipping cases that tipped off the customs officers, but it became very clear that I was not going to get a green light—under any circumstance.

Soon, the other actors became aware of what was unfolding and began to crowd around the exit. Haley led a chant:

"Red light, RED LIGHT, *RED LIGHT* . . ."

The customs officer finally gestured to me and I pushed the button. I don't think a single person in the building was surprised to see the light flash red and the actors erupted in a cheer.

"Yeah, laugh it up, assholes," I said, producing a stack of paperwork.

Fortunately for the payoff of the gag, I had heard tales of questionable Mexican customs and had taken every precaution to defend myself.

I tend to take my life with me on the road, so I had unusual travel items in my bags. To head off potential problems, I generated lists of everything I brought, complete with make, model and serial number. In addition, I got a letter from a "Hollywood" doctor, explaining why I needed particular food items like Turkey Jerky and dried mango, then translated everything into Spanish. It was a scam of major proportions, but I figured, *Why not fight fire with fire?*

Eventually, by the third case, the customs official threw up his hands and waved me through. The crowd of jeering actors parted as I stepped through.

"Who's laughing now, funny men?" I winked.

Gags were the only thing that got us through the three-month schedule. Haley would often come up with what we coined "the Haley button"—the final

"Papers, please."

gag in a scene. In many cases, it was a good "ender," like the protein powder choke, or the ventriloquist dummy made out of coconuts, but Haley was also prone to overachieving.

One scene required all the sailors to perform manual labor on the base. I was content to slowly paint a fence in the background, but Haley insisted on an elaborate gag.

Brian: Okay, get this: it looks like I'm wearing a white T-shirt, but it's really just painted on . . .

Bruce: Gee, Brian, that sounds like a pain in the ass to me . . .

Brian: No, it'll be great—that's what my character would do.

Bruce: Okay, but how will the audience know?

Brian: They won't, but it doesn't matter.

Bruce: Hey, knock yourself out. . . .

My favorite image of the day was Haley, slumped over at lunch, realizing that he had to be covered with latex paint all day in 100-degree weather.

IT'S THE ROLE, STUPID . . .

Actors make decisions all the time and some are abysmally bad. On many occasions, I've taken a part because it was the only thing available, and was grateful for the work, but after being in a string of stinkers, I decided that some discretion was advised. This has had uneven results career-wise, but for me it was all about peace of mind.

I put my new theory to the test when I got a script that could be described as *Die Hard* on a space station. Hardly original, but it intrigued me enough to consider the part of the Bruce Willis-type hero. As I thumbed through the script, it occurred to me that the hero had the worst part of all—his lines, never more than two at a time, were always in the vein of, "Get down! Wait here. C'mon! Let's go! Now!"

I did notice, however, that the bad guy in this script had eloquent speeches—he was witty, urbane and seemed to be having a lot of fun. Call me crazy, but I took that role instead.

"Relax, it'll be over in seventy minutes."

I also decided to take roles regardless of the budget, since having a lot of money is no guarantee of a good product. I did buddy Josh Becker's independent film, *Running Time,* which, at $120,000, was virtually unreleasable. I say this not because it was bad in any way, but because it violated the Hollywood "Three Strikes" law by being 16mm, black-and-white, and only seventy minutes long.

Every so often, projects fall into my lap and I simply can't say no.

I remember watching an obscure French film on TV late one night and the lead actor was Stuart Whitman. He played a hopeless romantic, painting pictures and staring out to sea. *What the hell was this?* I thought. *This guy does Westerns, doesn't he?*

I was working in New Zealand on a *Xena* episode and a script arrived, along with an offer to play an American actor in a French film. The script was so unusual, so non-Hollywood, it really caught my interest, but I didn't even know how to judge whether the part was good or not. There were plenty of references to my character, but he didn't have a lot of dialogue.

What the hell, I figured. *It would mean a trip to France—I'd be crazy not to follow through on it.*

Next thing I knew, I was puffing a cigar on the balcony of my groovy pad in the middle of Paris. How an actor, known primarily for slice-and-dice genre films would wind up in a French film was a puzzler, even to me, and I must admit that it was hard to mask my smirk for the first couple days.

The film was called *La Patinoire.* Translated, it means, *The Ice Rink,* and it was a film within a film. Jean Phillipe Toussaint was the *auteur*—he had a Woody Allen/Robert Altman sensibility and that seemed fine by me.

The next three weeks were spent in an ice rink in Franconville, a suburb of Paris. I was whisked there, at outrageously high speeds, courtesy of my appointed driver, Lionel. To get the feel of what that was like, run out and buy the soundtrack to *The Saint* and rent the film *Ronin.* Crank up the volume on the title track, cue *Ronin* to the big car chase, and you'll get a basic sense of the horror/ecstasy I endured every morning.

Because I wanted to be a gracious guest during my stay, each morning, as Lionel narrowly avoided pedestrians, he would help me translate a greeting into French. It became the "phrase of the day," usually something utterly absurd, and I would announce it to the crew upon arrival. A personal favorite was, "Last night, my good friend Jacques Chirac and I were drinking beer and watching soccer. He insulted me, so I was forced to kick his pimply ass."

Chilling on my balcony in Paris.

Because France was outside the jurisdiction of the Screen Actors Guild, rules like overtime, fringes, forced calls or dressing rooms had no bearing whatsoever. All the actors tossed their stuff in a small room and the only place to hang out was on set.

One day, between shots, I happened to ask producer Anne-Dominique how the hell they had even heard of me, let alone why the role was offered. She casually pointed to a production assistant, Raphael.

"He recommended you," she said, matter-of-fact. "He was a fan of your films."

MESSIN' WITH THE MYTH   46

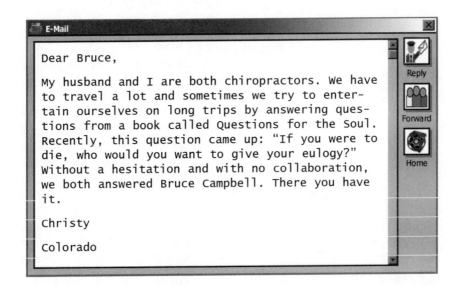

```
E-Mail                                              X

Dear Bruce,

My husband and I are both chiropractors. We have
to travel a lot and sometimes we try to enter-       Reply
tain ourselves on long trips by answering ques-
tions from a book called Questions for the Soul.     Forward
Recently, this question came up: "If you were to
die, who would you want to give your eulogy?"
Without a hesitation and with no collaboration,      Home
we both answered Bruce Campbell. There you have
it.

Christy

Colorado
```

Ask anyone where New Zealand is, and nine times out of ten, they'll say, "I don't even know where *Old* Zealand is..."

Situated in the Southern Hemisphere, in the shadow of Australia, New Zealand consists of two islands, running north and south, and boasts a population of three million people and sixty million sheep—with stats like that, where else would you shoot a TV show about *Hercules*?

Universal Studios brought the idea of a show, based on the mythical character, to the attention of Rob Tapert and Sam Raimi in 1993.

<u>Bruce:</u> So, these guys just came to you and said, "Do this"?

Rob: Yeah, they did. We had a production deal there, so it was only logical. Sam and I said, "Okay we will, but we'll make it our own way." And so, we took the formula for *Army of Darkness*—a funny hero who speaks kind of modern in ancient times.

The lead actor cast was Minnesotan, Kevin Sorbo. Ironically, Kevin had worked in New Zealand even before Sam and Rob—he was known locally as "the Jim Beam guy," for several liquor commercials he'd done there.

Rob: We said we needed big location value, so we sent our line-producer, Eric Gruendemann, to a few different places and one was New Zealand. We got the pictures and videos back and they had lava pits and deserts and oceans and woods and a—

Bruce:—And it was cheap.

Rob: Almost fifty cents on the dollar. Plus, they spoke English, so we said, "All right, we'll try it."

The original idea was to shoot five TV films and see how it went from there. Josh Becker was brought down early on, originally as second unit director.

Josh: I talked Rob into it during a fishing trip in northern Michigan. I wound up on the same flight going down as Kevin Sorbo.

Bruce: Did anyone think this would go as a series?

Josh: We had no idea. Most of us thought it would be the five TV films and out. After shooting some shots for the last one, I was walking with Kevin on location and I go, "I talked to Rob and he's getting really good responses and this thing might very well go to series." Kevin says, "You know, I've heard that so many times. I've been in about five pilots—I'm not holding my breath."

Before the TV films had wrapped shooting in mid-1994, *Hercules: The Legendary Journeys* TV show got the green light for thirteen episodes, and the Southern Hemisphere Saga began.

At first glance, Auckland, New Zealand, seems just like any other moderately-sized metropolis. Upon closer inspection, or in my case, upon repeated visits, the differences became apparent.

For starters, cars drive on the left side of the road—a remnant of the fading British Empire. After being corrected numerous times, I have since dropped the notion that they drive on the "wrong" side of the road, merely the "opposite" side. This funky concept was compounded by a steering wheel that is on the "opposite" or "wrong" side of the car, along with various controls. I can't tell you how many times I tried to make a turn and fired up the windshield wipers instead.

Money is interesting in New Zealand—each denomination is a different color and the bills are tear-proof, with a cute see-through window. Single dollar and two-dollar coins are very popular, but an extended stay can produce enough weight in coins to injure someone. The exchange rate tends to lessen the pain of such hardship—as of this printing, our dollar is worth twice as much.

The Kiwi dollar may be weak, but their power is a robust 220 volts compared to our 110—a burned-out Zip drive and CD player attest to my ignorance of this. I have enjoyed the obvious difference in super-heated water, insta-hot irons and kick-butt microwave ovens.

Kiwi foods and beverages are stronger as well—beer has almost twice the alcoholic content and the food is, to borrow a Kiwi phrase, "full on." Kiwi bacon could easily be mistaken for ham in the U.S., and the phrases "lite" and "fat free" are only now seeping into their mainstream marketing.

With regard to processing, food in New Zealand hovers around fifteen years behind the States, but I don't find that entirely undesirable—I'll take simple, hearty food over multiprocessed pseudo-food any day of the week. Interestingly, to the naked eye,

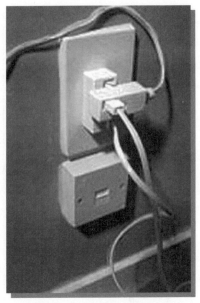

A wacky Kiwi phone jack.

* Good-bye—Cheers
* Ground Beef—Mince

- H -
* High School—Tertiary Education
* Horny—Randy
* Humorous Person—Dag

- J -
* Jacket—Jumper
* Jello—Jelly

- K -
* Ketchup/catsup—Tomato Sauce
* Kindergarten—Kindy
* Kitchen Counter—Bench

- L -
* Large American Automobile—Yank-tank
* Lawyer—Barrister
* Lemonade—Lemon Squash

- M -
* Man—Bloke
* Mechanical Pencil—Propelling Pencil
* Mile—Kilometer (sort of)

- N -
* Native American—Maori
* New Zealand—Godzone
* New Zealander—Kiwi

- O -
* Oatmeal—Porridge
* One Shot—One Off
* Overgrown Zucchini—Marrow

- P -
* Pedestrian Crossing—Zebra
  Crossing
* Popsicle—Ice Block
* Pound Sign—Hash Mark
* Prick—Wanker

- Q -
* Q-Tips—Cotton Buds

- R -
* Raining Hard—Pissing Down
* Rice Krispies—Rice Bubbles
* Rural Areas—Wops

- S -
* Sexual Intercourse—Bonk
* Soda Pop—Fizzy Drink
* Speed Bump—Judderbar

- T -
* Table Napkin—Serviette
* Testicles from Castrated Lambs—
  Mountain Oysters
* Toilet—Loo

- U -
* Umbrella—Brolley
* Underwear/panties—Knickers
* University Graduation Ceremony—
  Capping

- V -
* Vacation—Holiday
* Valedictorian—Dux
* Vegetables—Salads

- W -
* Walking—Shanks' Pony
* Wicked Personality—Hard Case
* Wrench—Spanner

- Y -
* Yarn—Wool
* Yield (sign)—Give Way

- Z -
* Z—Zed
* Zero—Nought
* Zucchini—Courgette

the Kiwis are generally a hearty, less obese group of people.

Make no mistake, however—culturally speaking, the Americans have landed. I found a charming example of this in an exchange with a crew member.

"Do you have KFC in the States?" he asked innocently.

"Uh, yes we do," I explained delicately. "See, it stands for *Kentucky* Fried Chicken."

Suiting Up 47

During the run of *Brisco,* and subsequent TV shows, I often found myself thinking, sometimes out loud, *I wouldn't have done it that way,* or *Man, nobody knows what's going on, why doesn't this director communicate?*

The cancellation of *Brisco,* in the spring of 1994, silenced my inner monologue. Suddenly, I was a free agent, so I decided to toss my hat into the uncharted waters of directing.

It wasn't a tough decision—I had been behind the scenes for fifteen years in various production capacities and knew my way around a film set. I can't say that I grew up with an overwhelming desire to emulate John Ford or Alfred Hitchcock—I was led toward directing so I could be the director I always wanted as an actor.

The job, as I have observed, requires a challenging blend of technological know-how and gut instinct—at least that's what I told Rob Tapert, now executive producer of *Hercules*: *The Legendary Journeys.*

"C'mon, Rob, how bad could it be? Send me down . . ."

The badgering was successful, and I made my way to the Southern Hemisphere to direct episode nine of the first season.

The word *director* conjures up all sorts of clichés—usually those of a hard-charging tyrant, clad in jodhpurs, barking orders to a subservient cast and crew. The director is indeed a captain . . . of sorts.

Running with the nautical analogy, he or she is looked upon by a large crew to steer the ship. However, regardless of what you have heard, this able seafarer is, by design, at the helm of *someone else's ship.*

This vessel is either seaworthy or a leaky tub. Initially, the design is in the hands of writers—if they are clever, a clear course is charted and the ship is hardy enough to weather the storms of inept directors and misguided producers. On the other hand, a weak hull punctures easily and

"Kevin, this is how I would do it . . ."

the ship will soon find itself beached, regardless of the skipper.

Producers finance the shipyard—if they're boat lovers, their ships will inevitably become the envy of the nautical world and any captain would be proud to take the wheel. Pound-foolish producers, on the other hand, crank out ships that only morons or greenhorns would command.

In the case of television, the director-of-the-week is often stepping into territory familiar to everyone *except* themselves. Sets, cast, crew and script are all decided well in advance. In this case, a director takes on the role of Enhancement Coordinator, Star-Coddler, Cheerleader, or Fall Guy.

A director under these circumstances must simply strive to get the best use out of the elements provided—to avoid rocking the boat, if you will, and return it safely to port for the next poor slob.

Josh Becker found the challenges of directing TV different from the independent world of filmmaking:

Josh: It's fun, but it's not the same thing as trying to actually exert your ability. The only real ability I'm getting to exert in TV is *how fast can you go?*

Bruce: Right, but I have to say, it's an excellent proving ground—a place where discipline rules the day. . . .

Josh: I agree—I'm glad to know I can do it, and I really believe that if you can do *Xena* or *Hercules* you can do anything.

On a TV schedule, there are only so many ways to get five to seven pages shot (otherwise known as "in the can") per day, particularly in a fixed shooting period. A keen eye for composition isn't necessarily going to bail you out when a prop doesn't work or the weather suddenly turns foul. I've been directed by plenty of "shooters" (an industry term for directors who have a distinct visual style) who didn't have the first idea about blocking, storytelling, or even how to talk to actors. At the same time, an "actor's director" isn't going to succeed if he shows up on set with a bag full of motivations but no idea how to commit it all to film.

The first hurdle of directing a *Hercules* episode was remaining awake after a twelve-and-one-half-hour red-eye flight from Los Angeles to Auckland. The only successful way to adjust to this new time zone (technically *tomorrow,* minus a few hours) was to stay awake until that evening—it was just as well, since my first meeting was 10:00 that same morning.

After stumbling through a blitz of meetings, each with a multitude of questions from every department, my next goal was to test the waters of the leading man, Kevin Sorbo—was he Demanding? Egotistical? An idiot?

The only way to find out was to sneak onto the set of the current episode shooting and watch from the shadows. You can learn a lot from the "vibe" of a set—a lot of shouting tells you that the crew is either behind, or they have bad leadership. A deathly quiet set is deceiving because it either means all is well, or there's a lot of tension.

As I entered the stage, affectionately called 911 (for its address), the set was very, very quiet. I tiptoed to a dark corner and watched Kevin squaring off with a centaur—half man, half horse. The take seemed to go well and the director printed it. Immediately, Kevin's face brightened and the set became a cheery buzz of activity.

Okay, I thought. *So far, so good.*

When I was introduced to Kevin, he was relaxed and gracious—another good sign. I figured Kevin wouldn't want to pussyfoot around, so I got right down to business.

<u>Bruce:</u> Hey, uh, Kevin, I wanted to get together with you at some point and go over the next episode.

<u>Kevin:</u> Good idea—do you golf?

<u>Bruce:</u> G-g-golf? You mean with clubs and everything?

<u>Kevin:</u> Yeah—they have a lot of good courses around here.

<u>Bruce:</u> Uh . . . sure . . . I golf . . .

<u>Kevin:</u> Cool—how's Saturday?

So, our first "meeting" was on the golf course. Thankfully, Kevin and I had a lot in common—having just come off a series myself as a single male lead, I could relate to his workload.

By the time we reached the second hole, I knew Kevin was going to be great to work with—I had lost my fourth ball and he was still in good spirits. Kevin is, in fact, an excellent golfer,

Watching a scene from "Video Village."

but it didn't affect my game plan one bit—for the good of the show, I let him win.

Following the first take of the first shot of the first episode I ever directed, I forgot to call *cut.* Sitting behind a portable monitor, concentrating on the scene at hand, I simply became lost in the act of watching television. George, my sarcastic assistant director looked over at me after the actors were done with their dialogue.

director: *n*. A bitter actor.

"So . . . that would be . . . *cut?*"

"*Right . . . cut! Cut!*" I yelled, as I leapt, mortally embarrassed, from my chair.

The challenges, aside from developing an attention span, are many for a director, and in New Zealand, they were somewhat unique.

With the two lead actors sporting long hair (Kevin Sorbo and Michael Hurst), I was encouraged to find locations that weren't overly windy—dramatic confrontations don't always work when you can't see the hero's face. The frustration, of course, is that visually speaking, higher elevation locations looked more dramatic and offered greater depth and scope.

On any given shooting day, Hercules and his sidekick Iolaus might stroll down a shady lane (known as a "walk and talk"), wake up in a campground, fight a monster and toss a pre-Hellenic football around. Technically, that's four locations, but the transportation department won't tolerate four company moves—therefore, it became a game of, *How close can the next location be?* In many cases, the answer was as simple as pointing the camera 180 degrees in the opposite direction.

Once you actually start filming, new challenges present themselves. Just when you had everything figured out, an actor would ask a question about motivation, a prop would break, or an hour-long downpour would commence—that's when the job of director gets truly creative.

But, let's not forget the delicate issue of deciding which shot to use in the final version. In one take, the actors might absolutely nail the dialogue, but the camera was out of focus in a specific part. In another take, the acting might only be serviceable, but the dolly move was dead on.

What to do?

In these cases, I tend to print both takes and work out the problems with the editor in postproduction. Editing is a beautiful and powerful thing—during that process, now wonderfully controlled by computers, you can edit around a jerky camera move, tighten an unwanted pause from an actor, or remove a useless shot.

In the hour-long format, commercials take up eighteen minutes (by the time you read this, it'll be longer), so the director must also allow enough time to get all those Budweiser and Chevy Truck spots in.

Aside from the obvious nightmares, there are many pleasures to be found in directing. Where else would you get a memo from the costume department that reads like this?

Bruce,

In the event that you would like to attend the following fittings:

Famine at 10:30
Pestilence at 11:15
War at 12:00
Death at 2:00

LEATHER AND MACE: 48
ACTING IN A PARALLEL UNIVERSE

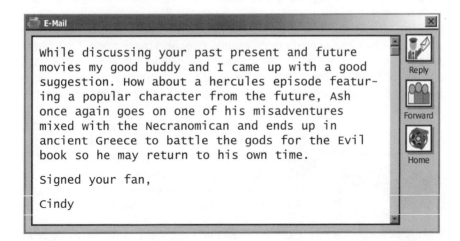

E-Mail ×

While discussing your past present and future movies my good buddy and I came up with a good suggestion. How about a hercules episode featuring a popular character from the future, Ash once again goes on one of his misadventures mixed with the Necranomican and ends up in ancient Greece to battle the gods for the Evil book so he may return to his own time.

Signed your fan,

Cindy

Reply

Forward

Home

Ironically, I began acting in New Zealand *after* I directed down there.

The role of Autolycus, AKA the King of Thieves, came about following a call from Rob Tapert. He felt that this character, a despicable rogue, was just right for me. I wasn't sure if Rob's endorsement was an insult or a complement, but upon reading the script, aptly titled "The King of Thieves," I wholeheartedly agreed.

As things evolve in the fluid world of TV, characters crop up that can be useful in subsequent episodes. Autolycus, I'm happy to say, fell into this category. From a series point of view, he could be a source of aggravation for Hercules, yet the "thief with a heart of gold" aspect made him slightly more useful.

As the seasons rolled along, "Auto" began to steal his way into more episodes. Nineteen ninety-eight proved to be a banner year for a number of reasons. Kevin Sorbo was confronted with a life-threatening physical condition and had to drastically pare back the amount of hours he could work per episode. I was asked to assist with the very large task of taking up the slack. Fortunately for the show, Michael Hurst as Iolaus, the trusty sidekick, was more than up to the job as well.

While I was delighted and relieved to see that Kevin has made an apparently full recovery, it did provide for some unique episodes in his absence. These are the times to pity the writing staff of a TV show—they had to produce a raft of new story ideas out of thin air and, I think, to a large degree, they succeeded.

My deal with the studio at that point was to be in eleven episodes between *Hercules* and its popular spawn, *Xena: Warrior Princess*. It was always a pleasure to see what the writers had dreamt up next. Usually the titles gave you a basic idea of what you were in for.

An episode called *Porcules* confirmed an actor's motto: never perform with animals or children. Hercules, by a cruel act of the gods, is transformed into a pig, complete with leather pants. Nothing beats the sight of a gyrating pig, racing across the countryside, desperately trying to shed the little costume velcroed to his body.

Pigs, in case you've never been around one, also make noise. On its best behavior, a pig utters an endless stream of grunts, since they're always looking for food. As their impatience grows, so does their decibel level. A disgruntled pig can launch a litany of squeals that could drown out even the loudest actor.

Autolycus: King of Thieves.

Pigus New Zealandus also have nasty, cloven little hoofs. I watched with great pity as Hercules' mother, Alcmene, attempted to share a tender moment with her "son." The cradled pig transformed into a bruise machine as it stampeded across the poor actress' legs.

It seemed like the writers spent most of their time concocting ways to extract revenge on the actors. "Men in Pink" was a textbook case of such abuse—it called for my character and his unlikely partner, Salmoneous (played by the irascible Robert Trebor), to cavort in drag.

What's the big deal? I thought. *Ya slap on a wig, a little extra makeup and bing, bang, boom—away you go.*

In addition to the basic humiliation of changing sexes, our "female" characters had to perform a strip tease—this meant that almost all manly body hair had to be removed. Here's a Kodak moment for you: Bruce standing buck ass naked in his Auckland bathroom, while a ghastly cream denudes him of precious hair.

After festering for some twenty minutes, the hair on my body decomposed into a seaweed-like substance that could be washed away in the shower.

Once that ghoulish task was completed, we were shoehorned into girdles, complete with fake breasts and fitted for "sexy" shoes. Why women wear high heels is an absolute puzzlement to me. With a four-inch spike, my size 10½ toes nose-dived into the triangular part of the shoe and remained bloodless until released. Dancing in them was an exercise in self-mutilation.

I've been thinking of forming an organization called A.S.P.C.A.— Association for the Prevention of Cruelty to Actors.

Once our bodies were denuded and "fitted," makeup was applied by the truckload. Between covering my thick beard growth, accenting cheekbones and "bringing out the eyes," I must have added another half a pound— weight that would shove my toes even deeper into the recesses of my high heels.

It was also vitally important to film this type of episode in the dead of a New Zealand summer—that's the best way to insure that sweat will eject itself from every pore in the body. This Herculean effort resulted in the ugliest woman ever committed to film. I e-mailed a digital picture of "Autolyca" to my wife, Ida.

"I had to delete it halfway through down-loading," she told me, without a hint of regret. "It was too hideous."

"Men in Pink" was a lesson in human endurance, but an episode called "One Fowl Day" snagged the abuse award.

Michael Hurst is a man bursting at the seams—the more responsibility he has, the more he relishes the opportunity. He's an exuberant actor and a very ambitious director. Combine these qualities with a difficult script and the results were positively over-the-top.

In this episode, Autolycus and Iolaus find themselves chained together, naked, and must make their way through a bizarre world, cleverly orchestrated by Ares, the god of war. Eventually, the hapless heroes find burlap sacks to wear (which itched like hell) and soon find themselves slogging through a swamp, only to become utterly encased in mud.

"Autolyca": A textbook case of abuse.

"I know mud is good for you, but this is ridiculous."

As the absurdity of it all crept up on us, Michael and I got to the point where we could not look at each other without laughing. That had never happened to me before as an actor, and it's a terrifying thing. Instead of having fun, I was freaked out by the loss of control. It's also not a good thing if you expect to make your shooting schedule. There is a scene in the finished episode where Michael and I are giggling the entire time. Thankfully, several layers of mud helped conceal our idiocy.

Because this couldn't be enough, Ares inflicts us with three-foot long shoes, fright wigs (with eyebrows) and horselike teeth. If you've ever attended clown school, you'd know how hard it is to perform simple tasks with extendo-shoes, like walking up stairs or crossing your legs, let along running from a giant chicken—but that's another story.

My favorite image of the shoot was Michael, stumbling over his own feet in the freakish outfit, while attempting to seriously communicate with the crew through a mouthful of fake teeth.

"Oh-hay, neth thettup ith oher hewe," he lisped. "We'wre yooking thith way widda tweddy-eight miyyimeeder yens . . ."

I could translate, but what fun would that be?

Because Michael was also playing a dual role of actor and director, he'd invariably dash back to the TV monitor after a take, forgetting that I was chained to him, and yank me into next week.

At the end of each filming day, the only way to loosen the caked mud on my body was to hurl myself into a nearby lake, and soak. I have to say, as much as I love to complain, it was the most fun I've ever had being miserable.

XENA: WARRIOR SPIN-OFF 49

Hercules gained a solid foothold in the land of syndication and eventually found a worldwide audience. I think the appeal of the show lay in the fact that the hero is a little old-fashioned. Kevin Sorbo portrayed a good guy who always did the right thing, and I'm sure that sat well with parents who were nervous about the lack of "morals" on TV.

This is a good chance to sound off about another aspect of *Hercules*. Syndicated shows, in the world of television, are bastard step-children and therefore little attention is paid to their production values.

Pound for pound, *Hercules* has more *true* design—in sets, costumes, and special effects—than *ER* and *Frasier* combined, yet you'll never hear the words "Emmy" and "Hercules" in the same sentence.

With the success of *Hercules,* a new show came into being. Lucy Lawless, a Kiwi actress, appeared in a three-episode arc and the Universal executives took notice. I'd say they got a woody for her, but that would be unprofessional.

Lucy, as *Xena: Warrior Princess,* was a female hero, and she wasn't afraid to kick ass and take names. It made her character more extreme and intense than Hercules and it inspired a loyal following outside the Herc fan base.

On the *Hercules* set, *Xena* was alternately referred to as "the girl show," or "the little show"—initially, it was even filmed in 16mm. Ironically, *Xena* soon became, by way of ratings, "the Big Show."

Lucy knew that *Xena* had punched into the consciousness of mainstream America when her character appeared on MTV's *Celebrity Dead Match.* She was pitted, in claymation action, against Calista Flockhart from Fox's *Ally McBeal.* I sat in Lucy's living room as we watched Calista ram her head up the warrior princess's butt and suffocate—thereby terminating the match.

"Oh, my God—I've made it . . ." Lucy shouted between peals of laughter. "I've really made it . . ."

By the time I appeared in a *Xena* episode, I had seen Lucy Lawless on camera only once before—as a tour guide on the travel video, which aired on the plane during my trips to New Zealand. To Lucy's credit, she quickly and gracefully made the transition from *Kiwi Actress* to *Big-Shot Female Role Model.*

Personally, I was glad to see that Lucy is nothing like her character on TV. Traveling back to the U.S. together, I watched with great amusement as she rummaged through a huge carry-on bag. She had dumped a little bit of everything in it, but couldn't find anything.

"That phone book was in here earlier," she mumbled as she fumbled.

The incident proved to me what a good actress Lucy is, because the character *Xena* couldn't be further from this unassuming Kiwi.

The dynamics of every TV show are different. *Hercules* was a guy show, through and through, and the character of Autolycus fit in easily. *Xena* presented a different challenge for the smarmy King of Thieves. Surrounded by women, and tough ones at that, he was forced into uncharted waters.

Acting with two very attractive women has many advantages—professionally, it gave my character much to do, but as a man it wasn't bad either. Lucy Lawless is a striking woman, on camera and off. It was always fun to flirt with her as Autolycus, because I really didn't have to work that hard to get motivated.

"Renee, I need to do that one more time..."

One scene called for Autolycus to kiss Renee O'Connor, Xena's sidekick Gabrielle, on the lips. As a perfectionist, I insisted that the scene be shot over and over—until we got it *just right.*

I had never directed myself as an actor before. The episode *King of Assassins* provided that first opportunity, and I was excited to work with Sam Raimi's younger brother Ted again.

I'd known Ted since he was nine and even took him to cello lessons—he still owes me five bucks for an impromptu stop at Dairy Queen. Ted was in many of our early Super-8 films and several of the features, but I never paid much attention to his overall game plan. Nothing made me happier than to see him wind up on *Xena* as the recurring character of Joxer—King of Idiots.

Directing Ted was great, because I didn't have to go into lengthy explanations about what I hoped to accomplish—I could use old Super-8 jargon and he was unfazed.

Ted and I Shemping on "King of Assassins."

Bruce: Okay, Ted, after Gabrielle leaves, keep Shemping like you did in "Uncivil Warbirds" until I call "*noise.*"

Ted: Right . . .

Bruce: When you react, do that Larry thing, like in *A Plumbing We Will Go.*

Ted: Yep . . .

Bruce: Then, I need you to vaso-glide left to reveal Xena behind you.

Ted: Gotcha.

During "King of Assassins," I realized that the Raimi Insanity Gene had successfully transferred through to Ted. He was an in-front-of-the-camera version of his brother Sam—always full of ideas and ready to share a heightened sense of absurdity with the world. Ted's greatest asset is the ability to make a complete ass of himself on camera.

Aside from the usual grief, torment and agony, there are times in the film business when you can't help but feel like you're cheating the system. While other folks labor in their thankless jobs, thespians get to play hooky all day long and get paid for it.

An interesting dynamic evolves from wearing the two hats of director and actor. Aside from severe sleep deprivation, an odd sense of freedom exists. Amid the delirium, I found myself wandering around the set thinking, *I can basically do anything I want.* . . . Of course, too much control has its own dark side, but I was happy to operate, albeit briefly, in a world with relaxed limitations.

FULL CIRCLE

50

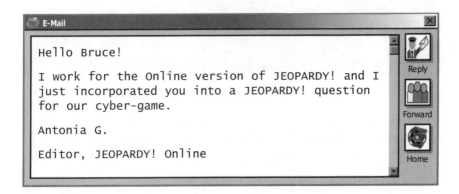

E-Mail   X

Hello Bruce!

I work for the Online version of JEOPARDY! and I
just incorporated you into a JEOPARDY! question
for our cyber-game.

Antonia G.

Editor, JEOPARDY! Online

Reply

Forward

Home

Season #7 of *Hercules* was upon us. It had been a long haul, even for a relative newcomer like myself—I had only worked on the show for five years. This was the longest I had ever worked on *anything,* other than raising a couple of groovy kids.

As could be eventually expected, the word came down from on high: *Herc* is dead—the big guy was to walk off into the mythical land of heroes forever. A lethal combination of fragmented market share, increasing production costs and a general sense of creative exhaustion spelled the death toll for this successful show. Sad, yes, but it happens eventually to every TV show ever produced, and 111 episodes in this age of nano-second attention spans is huge. It was a great run and I'm glad to have my name on a mere eighteen episodes in various capacities.

I was given what I consider the prestigious job of directing the series finale. It was my responsibility to assist in tying up all the loose ends in a satisfying package. I was eager to help and quite excited by the challenge, but as you might expect, it was an experience ripe with irony.

For starters, the "last" episode wasn't even filmed last. Because this one involved tons of special effects, not to mention titans, Zeus and Hera—plus all the brand-name players—it needed a longer postproduction period.

The last shot I filmed as a director was not even with the main crew—it was on a Saturday and Kevin Sorbo was nowhere in sight. The shot in question was an added angle of Atlas (you know, the guy with the world on his shoulders), crashing to the ground in slow motion. Afterward, there were no hugs or gifts—I was calling "Cut! Print it!" while sprinting out to a cab so I could catch my flight home.

Herc and pal Iolaus walking into the sunset.

The last shot of the episode (and series) involved Kevin Sorbo and Michael Hurst walking away across a vista of sand and sea. In our desire for attractive light, we waited until the sun was precariously close to dropping below the horizon. Between virgin sand and a setting sun, it gave us only one chance to get this semi-epic crane shot. We rolled camera, and as our heroes walked across the untrammeled landscape, Mother Nature came through with a delightful ripple of wind across the sand dunes, lending an intangible elegance and beauty to our rushed shot. Five minutes later, the light was gone.

Technically, this would have been the time to pop the champagne and give a teary-eyed speech, but in all the rush to wrap equipment, it hadn't dawned on any of us.

Riding back across the sand dunes in a truck full of crew members, I couldn't decide whether to be elated or depressed. This was so typical of the film business, because you never get that big, on-set finale. The magic always seems to take place in front of the camera, while behind-the-scenes, where it all really comes together, it's one anticlimax after another.

It's always been like that—*Brisco* ended with an obscure shot on the Warner Bros. back lot, and since there was no way of knowing whether the show would be canceled or not, most of the cast and crew never took the time to say good-bye. This was a good reminder of why I should just kick back and enjoy the process, because perfect endings only happen in the movies.

If you hang around a TV show long enough, you're bound to witness a milestone or two. Since I started directing back in 1994, I have introduced main characters, killed them off, brought them back to life, and sent them into the netherworld of series cancellation.

Finally, the last episode to be filmed arrived, and I was grateful to be included as Autolycus. "Hercules, Tramps and Thieves" presented a new "last" something, almost every day—the last read-through, the last scene with so-and-so, etc. As befits my theory of anticlimaxes, we were appropriately tormented by the New Zealand weather during our last day on location.

Fluffy clouds at sunrise transformed into a blanket of rain-spitting thunderheads at call time—by lunch, the rain was sideways. Let me just go on record here by saying that the weather in Auckland, with regard to filming, should be held in contempt. Because the city of sails is situated on a narrow spindle of land, weather patterns aren't affected at all. Josh Becker summed it up rather well.

"It's like being on a raft in the middle of the ocean."

Personally, I have no problem with rain—my Scottish heritage always kicks in during foul weather and I adopt an inexplicably positive attitude. Golfing with Kevin Sorbo during a nasty downpour one day, my game jumped up to a whole new level—a chronic slice disappeared and my ball went as straight as a Mormon father of twelve.

The last shot I appeared in coincided with the last shot ever to be filmed for *Hercules.* In a Karmic turn of the wheel, it was also on the stage where I first worked and where Kevin had done his Jim Beam commercials from 1993. As the shot was set up, producers and office staff filed into the studio, and I could feel the anticipation mounting.

"That's a wrap on the big guy!"

The frame consisted of a two-shot with Kevin and I bantering about the happy conclusion of the episode. At 6:55 P.M. exactly, July 22, 1999, Kevin spoke his last line: "Autolycus, I think you many have found your calling . . ."

What calling is that? I asked myself. *Unemployed actor?*

With that, Kevin walked out the doorway and director Charlie Siebert called, "Cut! Check the gate!"

While the camera assistant checked to make sure the film gate was free of dust, as they always do before a shot can be printed, a low buzz started in the room. Kevin hadn't come back through the doorway yet. I'm sure he was sharing some unknowable moment with himself off stage.

"The gate is *very* good," the assistant announced.

"Print it—that's a wrap on *Hercules*!" Charlie yelled.

With that, the studio erupted in a sustained cheer. Rob Tapert and Eric Gruendemann gave fine, off-the-cuff summations about what we all had accomplished. Kevin emerged from backstage and shared, or rather *tried* to share some touching words of gratitude for all the hard work everyone had put in on the show.

I don't think Kevin would mind if I told you that he couldn't connect more than two sentences without choking up. He had been through a war of attrition and did the best he could to express complicated emotions. There is something beautiful about watching a 6'4", manly man cry like a new bride.

The company threw a big wrap party and, at least this time, I had a chance to say my good-byes properly—albeit quickly. I brought my luggage to the party because I had to catch a cab to the airport in twenty minutes.

Still, it gave us a chance to voice why we liked working on the show. For me, it was the most creative atmosphere I have ever worked in. The directors, writing staff, and the actors all shared a genuine desire to make a good show, and the producers, much to their credit, gave us the support and the leeway to do it.

My agent and manager always hated when I went down to New Zealand. To them, I was wasting my time working on a syndicated "guilty pleasure"—out of touch, out of sight and most certainly out of the mind of Hollywood.

Frankly, I can never be far enough from Hollywood. What my representatives failed to understand, being infested with deadly spores, was that New Zealand represented a place where we could be free from studio interference, politics, parties, and misguided ambition.

Hard as I tried, I could never fully explain that I had grown weary of chasing that elusive Fame Train and was far more interested in revisiting those childhood summers of Super-8 films, when it wasn't about money or status. I wasn't working on *Herc* and *Xena* to advance my career—I was doing it to have fun.

Hercules: The Legendary Journeys Fun Facts

- 7 Seasons
- Aired in over 60 countries
- Over 1,000 featured roles cast
- 17,000 extras engaged
- 7 million feet of 35mm film stock exposed
- More than $150,000,000 (NZ) spent locally shooting the series

WHAT YOU DON'T SEE IS WHAT YOU GET   **51**

To one way of thinking, actors have a charmed life—we are artists, free to express childlike emotions and we are pampered beyond reason. When working, we travel first class, stay in fancy hotels, are driven to and from work, have a comfortable place to hang out during the day and get free lunches.

As a fringe benefit to this public life, actors are recognized, applauded, awarded, revered. Then, of course, there is the issue of money—a well-paid actor can get more for a single job, not counting residuals, than a teamster and his extended family would ever hope to earn in an *entire lifetime.*

To another way of thinking, actors are a miserable lot—they are insecure, vain and temperamental, clawing about in a world more competitive than almost any other profession. How many rocket scientists would line up around the block, in the rain, lobbying to work for just one day?

Actors face rejection weekly and are willing to tolerate years of subhuman living conditions, all in the hopes of being "somebody." Still, ninety-seven percent of them will fail—on average, Daddy's sperm has a better chance of fertilizing Mommy's egg than an actor has of succeeding.

As actors age, the pressures to remain eternally young are almost unbearable. A plumber will never hear the phrase: "I'll hire you, but you need to lose twenty pounds."

Well-known actors are hounded by the media and approached by complete strangers. I feel fairly confident that Joe Bob factory worker never has his garbage searched by tabloid reporters and almost never gets undergarments in the mail.

Actors may enjoy fame, but they also face public ridicule when they cannot live up to their on-screen personas. Subjective notions of success and failure are shoved in the faces of people whose shelf life is about as long as cottage cheese on a July afternoon.

Once you look past the hype, actors are nothing more than fugitives from reality who specialize in contradiction: we are both children and hardened adults—wide-eyed pupils and jaded working stiffs.

I've enjoyed being an ad-hoc member of the film business and I'm grateful for a unique, fly-on-the-wall perspective—hovering around the white-hot center of the big H, but never quite close enough (or is it high enough?) to crash and burn.

I've had the opportunity to meet fascinating people and see places I normally would never have ventured. I've delighted in learning new tricks, refining others and discarding enough bad ones to make a decent living in a very hard profession. If that isn't glamour, I don't know what is. . . .

Be careful of the "small print."

ACKNOWLEDGMENTS

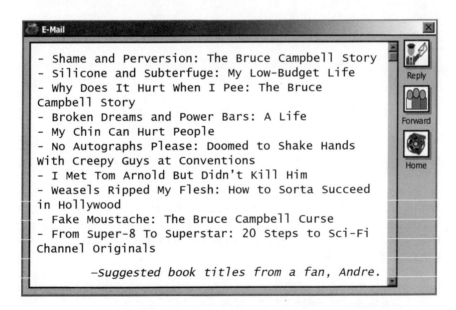

A hundred years ago, a guy named John Hodgeman contacted me by e-mail.

"Ever thought about writing a book?" he wrote.

John, it turned out, was a literary agent in New York.

"Yeah, right," I answered. "Another actor writes a lame-ass book. Snoresville, baby."

John refused to back off, based on a series of rants and anecdotes I had posted on my website. He was convinced that if I could put together a "demo" book, a publisher would step up to the plate.

From here, we cut to Cannes, France, about a month later. I was walking through the lobby of the hoity-toity Carleton Hotel, searching for a business associate, when a Dutch fellow collared me.

"Mr. Campbell, I have an excellent screenplay for you to star in."

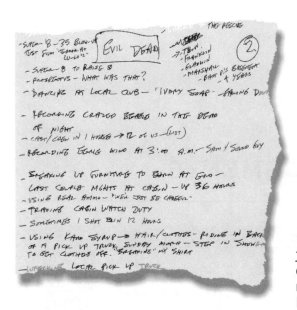

Crappy script/great scratch paper.

I was in Cannes for the film festival, so hawking projects like this happens about five times every nano-second.

"Uhhh, sure pal . . ." I responded with a smile and accepted his manuscript.

Later, while sipping a nine-dollar 7-Up, I thumbed through the incomprehensible manuscript. It would make a terrible film, but the backside of this permanently bound document would be perfect to use to jot down a jumble of my memories, incidents and anecdotes. I hope I run into that Dutch guy again because I'll tell him, with all sincerity, that I got a lot out of his script.

However, I realized that if a book was going to be made of all this, I had to clear out the cobwebs, get organized, and break open the proverbial cookie jar. . . .

In my attic, I rummaged through high school era diaries, old business logs and photographs. A more complete picture began to form, but it wasn't until I paid a visit to buddy Scott Spiegel's apartment that it all came into sharp focus. Scott, for as long as I've known him, has never thrown out a script, a letter, a ticket stub—nothing.

Sifting through these artifacts whipped my mental pot into a frenzy and fresh stories sprung to life. With a combination of excitement and trepidation, I proceeded to write a Cliff Notes version of this book.

To jazz up the look of it, I enlisted my trustworthy assistant, Craig Sanborn. He's one of those infuriatingly computer-literate guys who can master a new software program in minutes. This ability, combined with a good sense of art direction, made Craig an integral part of this book.

We let technology assist us in this new medium. Multiple software and hardware purchases later, we kicked out a ninety-page proposal that was distributed to about a dozen publishers in New York.

As expected, fifty percent of the prospective buyers fell away immediately. Writing a book about the "unglamorous" side of Hollywood was about as exciting to some publishers as a mom-and-pop soda shop would be to a Fortune 500 company.

Still, a few curious publishers dangled in uncertainty and a meet-the-press trip to the Big Apple followed. Fifty percent of the fifty percent fell away upon meeting in person (must have been my aftershave), and we were left with but a brave few.

St. Martin's Press, in their wisdom/foolishness decided to give me a shot on this tale of Hollywood's unrecognized lower middle class.

Once a contract was signed, and the celebrations tapered off, I was left with the realization that *I actually had to write the damn thing.* A year was provided to piece it all together and the first six months flew by without a blink.

The cover for the "Kifs Notes" version.

Hey, I'm a busy actor, I told myself. *I'll get to it . . .*

Eventually, a deadline loomed and I had to get my doughy butt in gear. In compiling this book, I relied upon the good graces of many folks—in particular, my old pals from the Michigan "daze." In order to jolt our collective memories, I interviewed most of them, much like a cub reporter. It was great to rehash the stories and challenges of the past, and I owe a great deal of thanks to Jan Holbrook for wading through the eighteen tapes, transcribing hours of nonsequiturs, inside jokes and unexplained laughter.

Because my day job as an actor kept me very busy during this time, I wrote this book in my "spare" time. During film shoots, it meant knuckling down after 7:00 in the evening or on weekends. Airplanes also provided a fine opportunity to get writing done. As a captive passenger, there was often no better way to pass those one-, three-, five-, or twelve-hour flights than to crack open my Dell Laptop and peck away until its double battery was drained.

In case it's of any interest at all, this book was concocted in two hemispheres and on three continents. Hand-written musings were hammered into a structure from a groovy bachelor pad in Paris and at my former home in Los Angeles, California. The lion's share of the real work was assembled in countless hotels, apartments and townhouses in and around Auckland, New Zealand—not to mention my trailer on set.

I can't tell you how often I shouted to an assistant director, "Okay, okay—I'll be right there," as I typed the last few thoughts before dashing out to torment Hercules or Xena.

Chapters were refined in enough cities to choke a Rand McNally guide, including Detroit, Minneapolis, Ontario, Cherry Hill, Tulsa, Austin, Dallas, Medford, New York City, Wilmington, as well as the countries of Mexico, Costa Rica, Canada, Australia and Africa.

The purpose of this list is not to name-drop on a global scale, but rather to illustrate how this book came to be in my near-gypsy existence. As much as I would have enjoyed writing in some idyllic locale, undisturbed for months on end, it simply wasn't in the cards.

I also want to thank my editor, Barry Neville, for forcing this book down the throat of Thomas Dunne Books. I wasn't privy to the back-room arm-twisting, but I'm sure it cost Barry dearly.

Because this book took four years to compile, I wasn't really surprised when Barry called to tell me he was moving away from publishing.

<u>Bruce:</u> Hey, I just hope it wasn't because of this book . . .

<u>Barry:</u> Well, I have suffered the tortures of the damned for you, but I've got some other opportunities I want to explore.

Fortunately for me, Barry's superior, Pete Wolverton, took the reigns as my new editor/boss and I hardly got lectured at all.

I'd be remiss if I left out a nod to Mike Ditz, chronicler of my childhood. Without his ever-present camera lens, much of the pictures you see would not exist—an official thanks is *long* overdue.

As always, I owe a great debt to my wife Ida and my two kids, Rebecca and Andy—they have been *extremely* patient with me since I've known them. Their support remains underappreciated and any attempt to make up for it now would be unsatisfactory. Fortunately, they know how cool they are.

PHOTO CREDITS

Page xii: Bruce Campbell; p. xiii: Bruce Campbell; p. 2: Charles Campbell; p. 3: Charles Campbell; p. 4: Bruce Campbell; p. 11: Bruce Campbell; p. 12: Charles Campbell; p. 13: Bruce Campbell; pp. 14–16: Unknown; p. 17: Bruce Campbell; p. 18: Unknown; p. 19: Bruce Campbell; p. 20: Charles Campbell; p. 21: Bruce Campbell; p. 23: Mike Ditz; p. 24: Mike Ditz; p. 25: Mike Ditz; p. 26: Mike Ditz; p. 27: Mike Ditz; p. 28: Mike Ditz; pp. 29–31: Bruce Campbell; p. 32: Bruce Campbell; p. 36: Unknown; p. 37: Mike Ditz; p. 38: Mike Ditz; p. 42: Mike Ditz; p. 43: Mike Ditz; p. 46: Unknown; p. 48: Sheri Morrison; p. 49: Unknown; p. 51: Bruce Campbell; p. 53: Bruce Campbell; p. 60: Mike Kallio; p. 63: Bruce Campbell; p. 64: Mike Ditz; p. 66: Sheri Morrison; p. 70: Mike Ditz; p. 71: Mike Ditz; p. 75: Craig Sanborn; p. 78: Mike Ditz; p. 84: Mike Ditz; p. 86: Mike Ditz; p. 87: Mike Ditz; p. 88: Joe Masefield; p. 92: Sheri Morrison; p. 93: Sheri Morrison; p. 94: Mike Ditz; p. 95: Mike Ditz; p. 97: Unknown; p. 98: Unknown; p. 101: Unknown; p. 102: Mike Ditz; p. 107: Sheri Morrison; p. 109: Unknown; p. 110: Unknown; p. 111: Sheri Morrison; p. 112: Sheri Morrison; p. 114: Unknown; p. 115: Mike Ditz; p. 116: Mike Ditz; p. 119: Unknown; p. 120: Bruce Campbell; p. 122: Bruce Campbell; p. 128: Sheri Morrison; p. 129: Joe Masefield; p. 130: Joe Masefield; p. 131: Joe Masefield; p. 132: Sheri Morrison; p. 136: Mike Ditz; p. 138: Unknown; p. 139: Mike Ditz; p. 140: Mike Ditz; p. 141: Kurt Rauf; p. 143: Kurt Rauf; p. 144: Kurt Rauf; p. 145: Bruce Campbell; p. 146: Bruce Campbell; p. 151: Unknown; p. 154: Craig

Sanborn; p. 156: Mike Ditz; p. 157: Bruce Campbell; p. 158: Sheri Morrison; p. 159: Sheri Morrison; p. 162: Sheri Morrison; p. 163: Sheri Morrison; p. 164: Sheri Morrison; p. 165: Sheri Morrison; p. 166: Unknown; p. 167: Bruce Campbell; p. 168: Bruce Campbell; p. 172: Unknown; p. 173: Unknown; p. 176: Unknown; p. 180: Bruce Campbell; p. 181: Sheri Morrison; p. 185: Sheri Morrison; p. 186: Ida Gearon; p. 191: Sheri Morrison; p. 192: Bruce Campbell; p. 194: John Cameron; p. 195: Unknown; p. 199: Bruce Campbell; p. 200: Sheri Morrison; p. 202: Unknown; p. 204: Sheri Morrison; p. 208: Sheri Morrison; p. 209: Sheri Morrison; p. 211: Universal Studios; p. 213: Sheri Morrison; p. 214: Universal Studios; p. 215: Sheri Morrison; p. 220: Sheri Morrison; p. 221: Sheri Morrison; p. 222: Bruce Campbell; p. 225: Craig Sanborn; p. 227: Unknown; p. 228: Sheri Morrison; p. 229: Unknown; p. 234: Sony; p. 235: Sony; p. 236: Sheri Morrison; p. 238: Bruce Campbell; p. 239: Unknown; p. 240: Sheri Morrison; p. 241: Universal Studios; p. 242: Unknown; p. 243: Sheri Morrison; p. 248: Bruce Campbell; p. 252: Sheri Morrison; p. 253: Sheri Morrison; p. 254: Sheri Morrison; p. 258: Sheri Morrison; p. 261: Sheri Morrison; p. 262: Sheri Morrison; p. 264: Sheri Morrison; p. 265: Sheri Morrison; p. 266: Sheri Morrison; p. 267: U.S. Government; p. 268: Sheri Morrison; p. 269: Sheri Morrison; p. 270: Sheri Morrison; p. 271: Sheri Morrison; p. 272: Sheri Morrison; p. 273: Bruce Campbell; p. 277: Bruce Campbell; p. 280: Zo Hartley; p. 281: Zo Hartley; p. 282: Zo Hartley; p. 286: Zo Hartley; p. 287: Craig Sanborn; p. 288: Zo Hartley; p. 290: Sheri Morrison; p. 291: Sheri Morrison; p. 294: Sheri Morrison; p. 295: Sheri Morrison; p. 296: Sheri Morrison; p. 298: Unknown